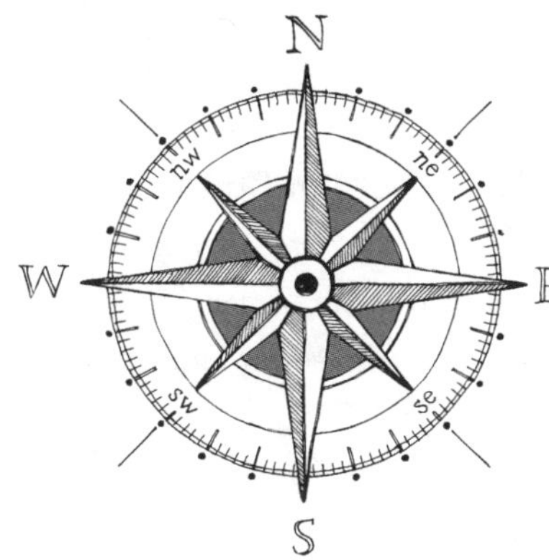

Praise for *The Life and Times of Jim Bridger*

When the tall, genial Virginian Jim Bridger ventured West as a "green" teenager in the early years of the fur trade, no one predicted that he would become the legendary "old man of the mountains." Packing his life with enough adventure for at least ten mountain men, Bridger led beaver-trapping brigades, hunted buffalo, fought hostile Blackfeet, married a Shoshone woman, mapped trackless wilderness, guided the U.S. Army during Red Cloud's War, and more. Although illiterate, he spoke several European—and Indian—languages. Did Bridger really leave the grizzly-mauled Hugh Glass to die alone? Markley delves deep into his subject's extraordinary life. Wonderfully illustrated with period maps and artwork, this book is for all who love true tales of the raucous fur trading era of the early nineteenth century.

Bridger once said, "Sir, the grace of God won't carry a man through these prairies! It takes powder and ball." And how.

—**Nancy Plain,** four-time Spur Award winner,
past president of Western Writers of America

Bill Markley has done it again with The Life and Times of Jim Bridger. *The mythic mountain man comes to life in Markley's biography and by the end you will be ready to go West and discover for yourself the West of Jim Bridger.*

—**Stuart Rosebrook,** editor-at-large, *True West* magazine

Bill Markley has established an enviable reputation as a western biographer. His excellent new biography of Jim Bridger will only augment his status. Crisply written and carefully researched, this biography of the greatest of the mountain men will both captivate and inform readers for years to come.

—**Paul Hutton,** author of *The Undiscovered Country*

Bill Markley's The Life and Times of Jim Bridger *vividly captures the adventures of a legendary mountain man whose courage, ingenuity, and deep connection to the American West shaped a nation's frontier. From fur trapping to guiding emigrants, Bridger's story is a testament to resilience and cultural fluency, brought to life with meticulous research and engaging prose.*

—**Jon Nelson,** Board Director for the Museum of the Fur Trade, Chadron, Nebraska; co-author of *Crossing the Plains with Custer,* co-author of *Tools and Utensils of the Fur Trade;* and editor of *Gun Accessories & Hand Weapons of the Fur Trade and Ornaments & Art Supplies of the Fur Trade.*

The Life and Times of Jim Bridger *is the colorful saga of this bigger-than-life historic figure, placing the man within the larger context of the fur trade era, early exploration, westward migration, and the ensuing period of conflict with Native Americans. Bridger seemed to be everywhere at once, traveling this vast unexplored region, present at many key historic events. As his contemporaries wrote: "Everything Bridger has seen, he recollects with entire precision, and in his wild life . . . he has traveled the whole country in many directions." A notable feature of the book is a brief history of each tribe or historical figure as they are introduced. The author also probes enduring historical controversies, for example, was Jim Bridger the young man present when Hugh Glass was mauled by a grizzly bear and left for dead?*

Among Bridger's most noted accomplishments were blazing the Bridger Trail, a safer route used by emigrants bound for the Montana gold fields, and pioneering the Overland Trail, the primary overland stage route from 1862 to 1869.

As Jim Bridger aged, he bore witness to the settlement and "taming" of the West. As early as 1857, Captain John Phelps observed Bridger standing alone on a high point of land observing the countryside. "He was a perfect monarch of all he surveyed," Phelps wrote, "and never dreamed that his kingdom would ever be disturbed by emigration in his day—so remote was it from the United States."

Bridger died in 1881 at the age of 77 at his home in Westport, Missouri, far from his beloved West. In 1904, General Grenville Dodge had Bridger's remains reburied in Kansas City's Mount Washington Cemetery with a seven-foot monument. Dodge declared, "So remarkable a man should not be lost to history and the country, and his work allowed to be forgotten." With this fresh view, Bill Markley has brought Jim Bridger back to life in the pages of The Life and Times of Jim Bridger.

—**Robert Rosenberg,** Rosenberg Historical Consultants, Cheyenne, Wyoming

The Life and Times of Jim Bridger

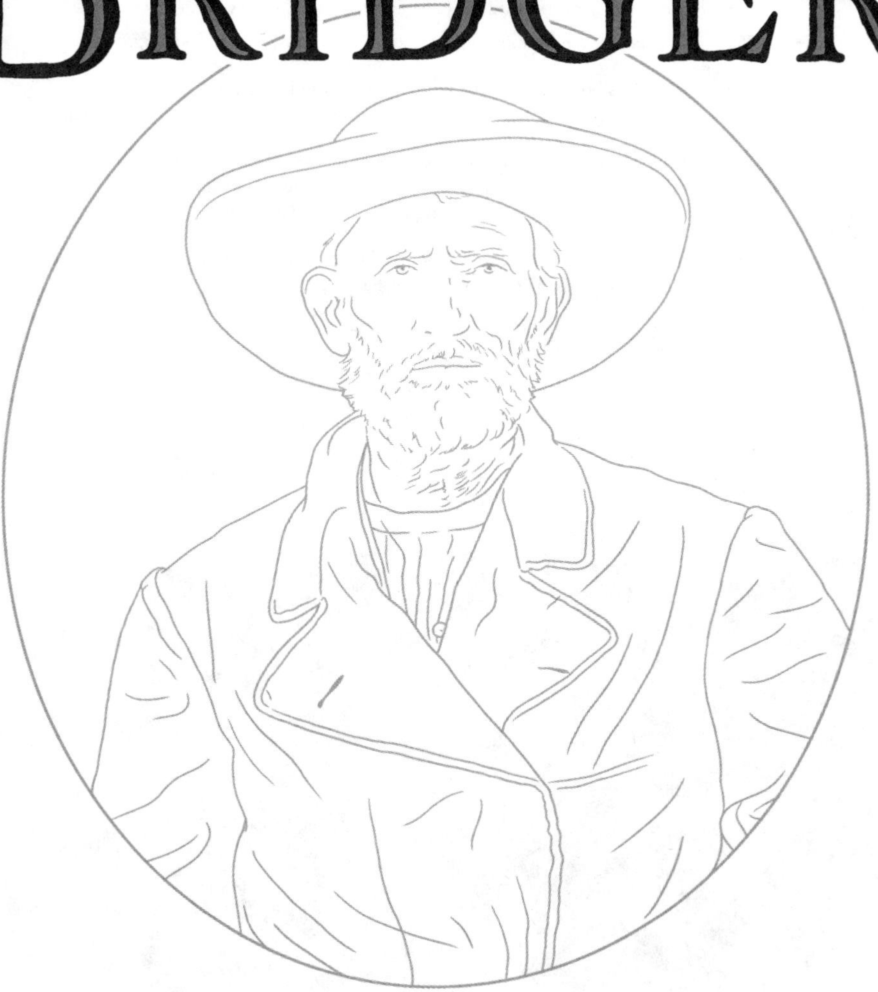

Bill Markley

ISBN: 978-1-56037-840-2

Design by Steph Lehmann

Front cover: Jim Bridger. 1866 PHOTOGRAPH COURTESY OF THE KANSAS STATE HISTORICAL SOCIETY.

Front and back cover: Fur trade rendezvous. PAINTING BY ALFRED JACOB MILLER, COURTESY OF THE WALTERS ART MUSEUM, 37.1940.159.

This page: Beartooth mountains. PHOTOGRAPH © B NORRIS/SHUTTERSTOCK.

For more information about our books, write Farcountry Press, P.O. Box 5630, Helena, MT 59604; call (800) 821-3874; or visit www.farcountrypress.com.

Library of Congress Control Number: 2025941727

Produced and printed in the United States of America.

30 29 28 27 26 25 1 2 3 4 5 6

Dedicated to my parents,
Bill and Gloria,
who showed my brother Doug and me the West.

I wish I was back there among the mountains again—
you can see so much farther in that country.

—Jim Bridger

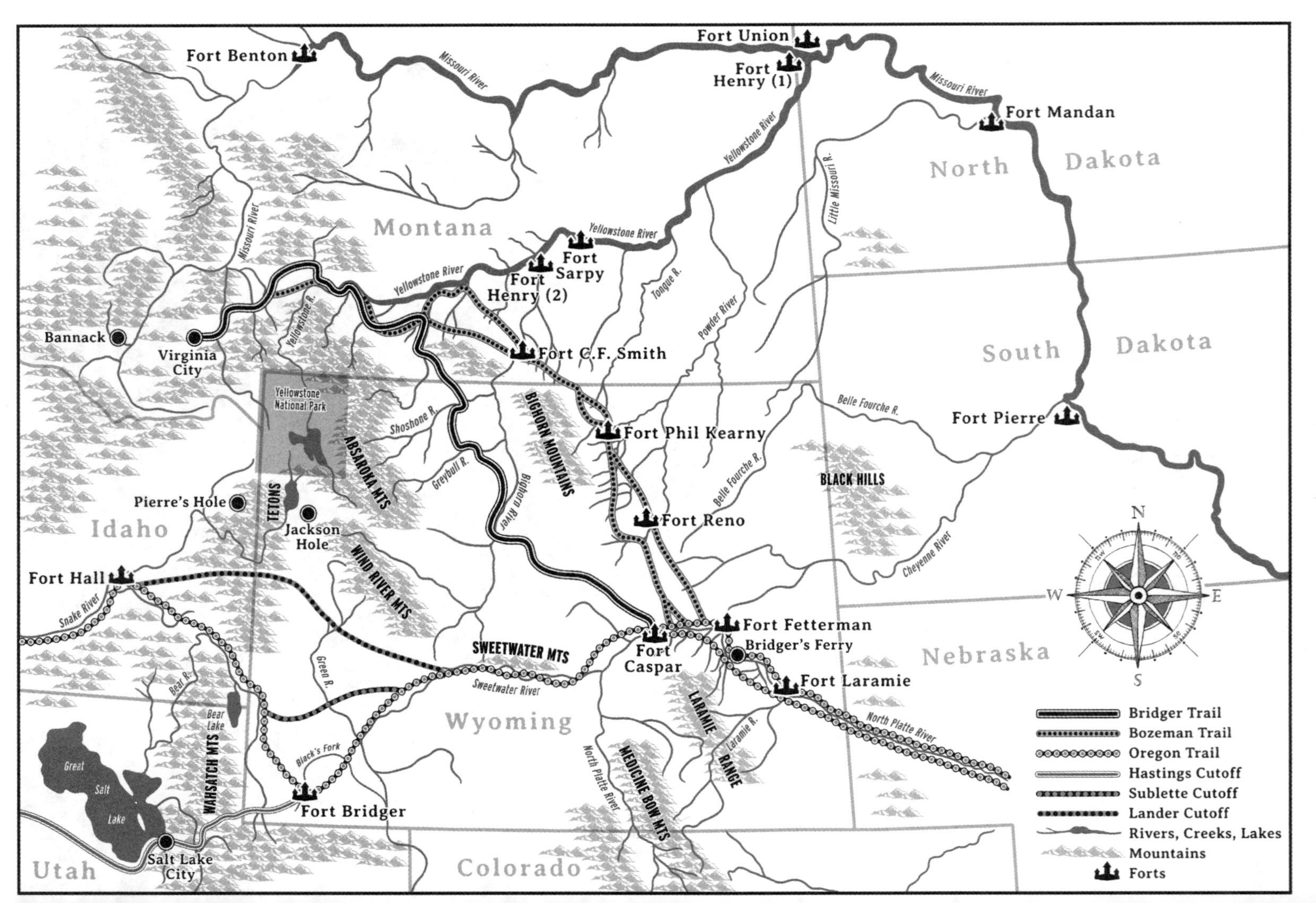
Fort Benton
Missouri River
Fort Union
Fort Henry (1)
Missouri River
Fort Mandan
Yellowstone River
North Dakota
Little Missouri R.
Montana
Yellowstone River
Fort Sarpy
Fort Henry (2)
Yellowstone River
Missouri River
Yellowstone R.
Tongue R.
Powder River
Bannack
Virginia City
Fort C.F. Smith
South Dakota
Yellowstone National Park
Shoshone R.
BIGHORN MOUNTAINS
Belle Fourche R.
Fort Pierre
Fort Phil Kearny
ABSAROKA MTS
Greybull R.
Bighorn River
Belle Fourche R.
BLACK HILLS
Pierre's Hole
TETONS
Jackson Hole
Fort Reno
Idaho
WIND RIVER MTS
Cheyenne River
N
W
E
S
Fort Hall
Snake River
Fort Fetterman
SWEETWATER MTS
Fort Caspar
Bridger's Ferry
Nebraska
Fort Laramie
Green R.
Sweetwater River
Bear R.
Bear Lake
LARAMIE RANGE
Wyoming
Laramie R.
North Platte River
Great Salt Lake
WAHSATCH MTS
Black's Fork
North Platte River
MEDICINE BOW MTS
Fort Bridger
Salt Lake City
Utah
Colorado
Bridger Trail
Bozeman Trail
Oregon Trail
Hastings Cutoff
Sublette Cutoff
Lander Cutoff
Rivers, Creeks, Lakes
Mountains
Forts

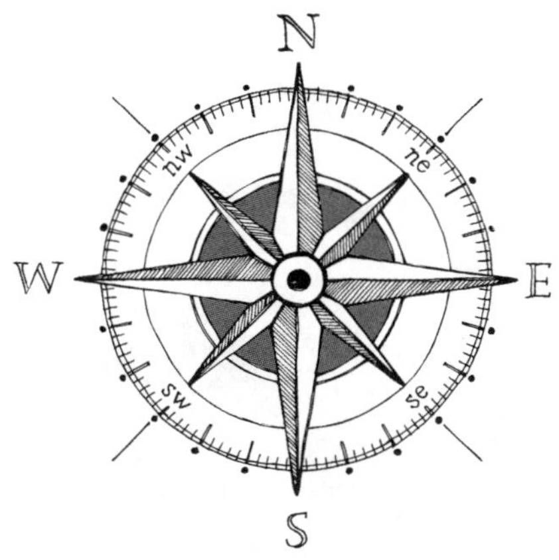

Contents

This sketch by Frederic Remington shows an older Jim Bridger, the "veteran mountaineer." PHOTOGRAPH COURTESY OF THE LIBRARY OF CONGRESS, LC-USZ62-2623

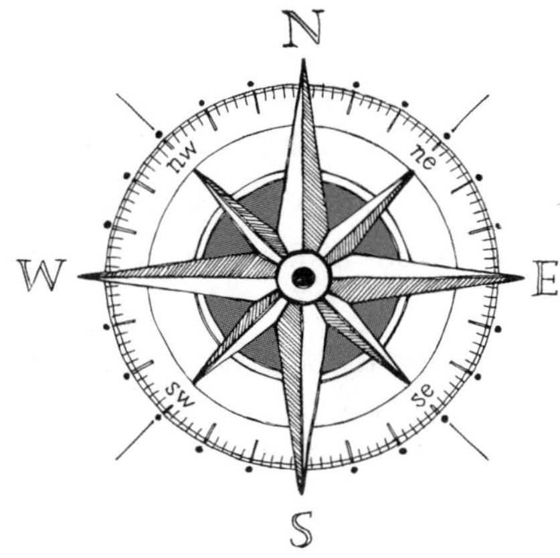

A Man Made for the Frontier

The nineteenth-century American frontier was ever-changing as it advanced westward. Jim Bridger played a role on that frontier for roughly seventy years. Born in Virginia in 1804, he grew up on the frontier in western Illinois and headed up the Missouri River with a fur trapping and trading expedition to the Rocky Mountains in 1822. He did not return to the States until 1839 for a brief visit to St. Louis.

Bridger thrived in the Rocky Mountains, becoming friends with Indian tribes and adopting their ways. Even though he could not read or write, he spoke fluent English, French, and Spanish, as well as several Indian languages. He was so well versed in sign language he could tell humorous stories, making his viewers laugh.

When the fur trade dwindled, he switched to providing goods, livestock, and blacksmithing services to emigrants on the Oregon Trail. He guided expeditions and emigrants over safe trails. He tried to avoid conflict, but, when necessary, he was in the forefront of any confrontation. He was kind and generous; most people who met him liked him.

Since Jim Bridger did not write, others recorded information about him. Despite the paucity of details about his life, we can infer much about the man from the better documented lives of his companions, business partners, and military associates. Many fur trapping and trading stories were written years after the fact, so some of them may have been misremembered, embellished, numbers exaggerated, and time frames confused. When referring to Indian tribes, I use the most common names for them. For the people misnamed Sioux, where possible I use Dakota, Lakota, or Nakota. If I could not identify the proper name, I use Sioux.

Jim Bridger loved the West, its landscapes, its wildlife, its peoples, and most of all its freedom. Are you ready? Let's enter the frontier world of Jim Bridger.

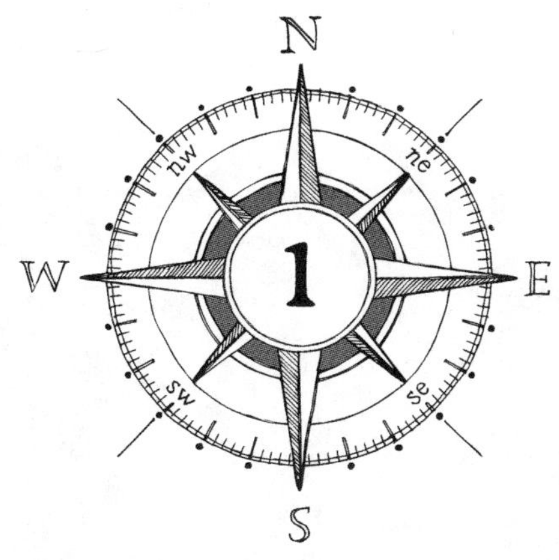

Frontier Beginnings
1804–1822

Jim Bridger had no formal education, no wealth, and no influential friends to get his start in this world. If he was going to make it, he would need to be a self-made man.

James was born on March 17, 1804, to James and Chloe Bridger.[1] Little Jim's father was a surveyor and, with Jim's mother, farmed and kept a hotel at Richmond, Virginia. In 1812, James and Chloe gathered their three children, livestock, and belongings and headed west. They probably traveled into Kentucky through the Cumberland Gap, following the Wilderness Road. Reaching the Ohio River, the Bridger family would have traveled downriver by flatboat until they reached the Mississippi River (near today's Cairo, Illinois) and then headed north.[2]

The Bridgers settled across the Mississippi River from St. Louis, Missouri Territory, at Six Mile Prairie in southern Illinois Territory's fertile American Bottom. This was the frontier, and times were dangerous. The region's tribes were angered by settlers invading their lands. When the United States declared war on Great Britain on June 18, 1812, many tribes allied with the British.[3]

Nevertheless, the Bridgers established a farm and James continued working as a surveyor. The family needed to stay on constant alert for attack. Eight-year-old Jim would have done chores around the farm, learned to use a firearm for small game hunting, and likely assisted his father with surveying.[4]

When the Bridger family moved to the frontier, they left behind a more settled, comfortable life in Richmond. ENGRAVING BY WILLIAM. J. BENNETT FROM A PAINTING BY GEORGE COOKE, CIRCA 1834, COURTESY OF THE LIBRARY OF CONGRESS, LC-DIG-PGA-03119

In 1816, Jim's mother became ill and died while his father was away from home. The children's aunt, James' sister, arrived to manage the farm and care for the children. Jim's brother died that same year, and in 1817 his father died. Now Jim and his younger sister were orphans. Barely an adolescent, Jim bought a flatboat and earned money for the family by providing ferry service across the Mississippi River.[5]

At age thirteen, Jim became an apprentice to Philip Creamer, an Illinois gunsmith whose guns were considered the best throughout the countryside. Jim's apprenticeship lasted five years. His duties included cleaning the shop,

Philip Creamer was renowned for his fine gunsmithing, such as seen on this rifle he made for William Clark. PHOTOGRAPH COURTESY OF THE MISSOURI HISTORICAL SOCIETY, 1939-026-0004 maintaining tools, polishing parts, keeping the forge fires burning, and pumping the bellows. As time went on, Creamer gave him more advanced duties.[6]

The Potawatomi tribe had allied itself with the British during the War of 1812, but as the war dragged on, the Potawatomi stopped fighting, and on July 18, 1815, they signed a peace treaty with the United States.[7]

The federal government established an Indian agency at Peoria, Illinois. The Potawatomi had blacksmithing needs, including firearms repair, so Indian agent Richard Graham hired Creamer to handle those tasks. In April 1817, Graham, Creamer, and thirteen-year-old Jim Bridger traveled 150 miles north to Peoria, where young Jim came into contact with the Potawatomi people. He observed their customs, learned sign language, and came to see them as peaceful neighbors, not as enemies.[8]

Jim could not read or write, and there is no record he attended school or church. By age eighteen, the brown-haired, hazel-eyed boy had grown into a six-foot-tall, muscular youth, and by 1822, his gunsmithing apprenticeship ended.[9] Coincidentally, a year earlier, the southeastern portion of Missouri Territory had been admitted to the Union as the State of Missouri, the remaining land (north to Canada and west to the Rockies) reverting to "unorganized territory." Fur trappers and traders were intent on "organizing" it for their own purposes.

Jim was free to do as he pleased and go where he wanted. The West beckoned.

---

1 Hiram Martin Chittenden, *The American Fur Trade of the Far West,* Vol. 1 (Stanford, CA: Academic Reprints, 1954), 257. Grenville Dodge, *Biographical Sketch of James Bridger, Mountaineer, Trapper, and Guide* (New York, NY: Unz and Company, 1905), 5. Bridger may not have been sure of his age. The 1850 census listed him at 41 years which means he was born in 1801, source Ancestry.com, accessed January 28, 2023, Ancestry.com—1850 United States Federal Census; the 1860 census listed him at 55 years which means he was born in 1805, source Ancestry.com accessed January 28, 2023, Ancestry.com—1860 United States Federal Census; the 1870 census listed him at 69 years which means he was born in 1801, source Ancestry.com accessed January 28, 2023, Ancestry.com—1870 United States Federal Census; and the 1880 census listed him at 76 years old, which means he was born in 1804, source Ancestry.com accessed January 28, 2023, Ancestry.com—1880 United States Federal Census.

2 Jerry Enzler, *Jim Bridger: Trailblazer of the American West* (Norman, OK: University of Oklahoma Press, 2021), 1.

3 Ray Allen Billington, *Westward Expansion: A History of the American Frontier* (New York, NY: The MacMillan Company, 1949), 275, 279, 282. Dodge, *Bridger,* 5.

4 Stanley Vestal, *Jim Bridger, Mountain Man* (Lincoln, NE: University of Nebraska Press, 1946), 2.

5 Dodge, *Bridger,* 5–6.

6 James McLaird, *Hugh Glass: Grizzly Survivor* (Pierre, SD: South Dakota Historical Society Press, 2016), 35. Enzler, *Bridger,* 5. Vestal, *Bridger,* 7. Chittenden, *Fur Trade,* Vol. 1, 257.

7 R. David Edmunds, "The Illinois River Potawatomi in the War of 1812" *Journal of the Illinois State Historical Society* (1908–1984) Vol. 62, No. 4 (Champaign, IL: University of Illinois Press, Winter, 1969), page 362. Accessed January 28, 2023, https://www.jstor.org/stable/40190888?read-now=1&seq=22#page_scan_tab_contents

8 Enzler, *Bridger,* 5–6.

9 1880 Census, Ancestry.com. Enzler, *Bridger,* 1, 105.

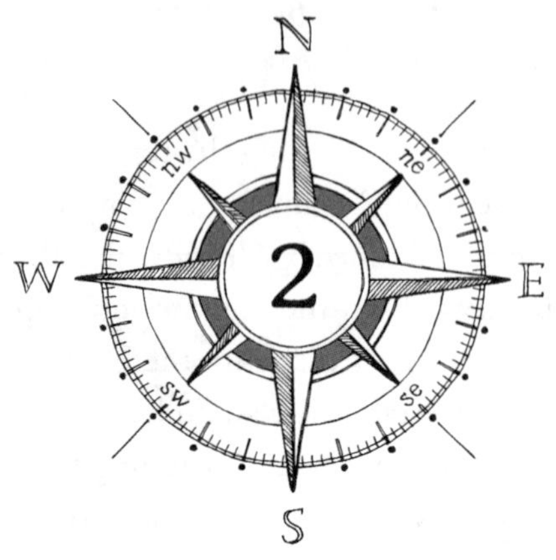

Up the Missouri
1822–1823

St. Louis was bustling in 1822. It had been established as a fur trading post in 1764 by French fur trader Pierre Laclède Liguest and his stepson, Auguste Chouteau. Located along the Mississippi River's west bank twenty-three miles downriver from its confluence with the Missouri River, St. Louis grew into one of the most important cities in the West, and the Chouteau family remained leaders in the fur trade.[1]

Even before Meriwether Lewis and William Clark's Corps of Discovery headed up the Missouri River in 1804, fur traders traveled the river's lower reaches. Along with the Chouteau family, Manuel Lisa, owner of the Missouri Fur Company, was a major player. But in August 1820, Lisa died, and by 1822, Joshua Pilcher managed the business from Fort Lisa, about six miles south of Lewis and Clark's "Council Bluff."[2] (Not to be confused with today's Council Bluffs, Iowa, on the east side of the Missouri River, the landmark named Council Bluff by Lewis and Clark is west of the Missouri River on the outskirts of today's town of Fort Calhoun, Nebraska.)

The first steamboat arrived at St. Louis on August 2, 1817. With the establishment of steamboat service, the city became the western hub of the fur trade. There had always been a demand for furs in China, Europe, and the eastern United States, and by 1822 fashion and durability increased the demand for beaver pelts to make hats. The Missouri and its tributaries held thriving beaver

St. Louis, portrayed here by George Catlin as it appeared in 1832, quickly grew as a hub of the steamboat trade. LITHOGRAPH BY GEORGE CATLIN, COURTESY OF THE LIBRARY OF CONGRESS, LC-DIG-PGA-08971.

populations, and whoever brought their pelts to market would make money. That year, John Jacob Astor's American Fur Company and others were elated that the federal government was ending the so-called factory system in which tribes traded furs and hides directly with the federal government for manufactured goods. Tribes deemed these goods inferior to those they obtained from British traders from Canada.[3]

The British fur trade was formidable. The British government had forced its two major competing Canadian fur companies, the Hudson's Bay Company and the North West Company, to merge. On March 26, 1821, the companies combined into a new Hudson's Bay Company, a strong competitor to any American company.[4]

The best route for American fur traders and trappers to reach the beaver-rich Upper Missouri tributaries was to travel from St. Louis up the river.

With its headwaters in the Rocky Mountains of present-day Montana, the Missouri River flows east into the Great Plains, then bends south (see map on page iv), eventually merging with the Mississippi River at St. Louis. From the Missouri's headwaters to its mouth, it runs 2,341 miles, draining a watershed of more than 500,000 square miles. Historically, the Missouri's major discharge occurred during spring runoff and was divided into two events. The first, called "the April rise," was snowmelt from the prairies, and the second was "the June rise" from Rocky Mountain snowmelt. Flows after that could be extremely low, so travelers heading upriver needed to catch the spring flows.[5]

Yet spring discharges were hazardous. The river's course changed rapidly, creating sandbars where channels once existed and sweeping away islands. The raging river tore at its banks, carrying away tons of soil as well as trees that either floated exposed on the surface or, more dangerously, submerged below. Snags were trees with trunks and branches pointed upriver, and sawyers were trees with trunks and branches pointed downriver.[6]

In addition to river hazards, the weather changed constantly, with unpredictable and violent storms, blistering heat, and frigid temperatures. Swarms of mosquitoes feasted on people and livestock alike, and farther upriver huge grizzly bears showed little fear of humans. The Missouri River traveler also needed to be aware of the many tribes and deduce, despite ever-changing alliances, which ones were friendly, cautiously neutral, or outright hostile.

The keelboat was the most reliable mode of transportation on the Missouri. A keelboat had a shallow draft and was usually seventy feet long with a steering oar mounted on the stern. Along the boat's sides were walkways where the crew, up to twenty men, walked to pole it forward. Seats were affixed for rowing. A mast was mounted for sailing where a rope could be attached to haul the boat forward, if necessary. Writer T. B. Thorpe, who lived in Baton Rouge, Louisiana, for sixteen years, wrote that keelboat men were hearty and powerful. "Their professional pride was in ascending 'rapids.' This effort of human strength to overcome natural obstacles was considered by them worthy of their steel."[7]

On February 13, 1822, after months of planning, General William Ashley and Major Andrew Henry stepped onto the scene as key players in the fur trade, announcing in St. Louis' *Missouri Gazette:*

Keelboats were most often propelled by men with poles, while an aft oar enabled steering. ILLUSTRATIONS COURTESY OF THE NATIONAL PARK SERVICE.

TO
Enterprising Young Men.

> The subscriber wishes to engage ONE HUNDRED MEN, to ascend the river Missouri to its source, there to be employed for one, two, or three years.—For particulars enquire of Major Andrew Henry, near the Lead Mines, in the County of Washington, (who will ascend with, and command, the party) or with the subscriber at St. Louis.
> Wm. H. Ashley.[8]

Longtime friends, fellow army officers, and mining partners, Ashley and Henry partnered to establish a trading post at Three Forks (in today's Montana) where the Gallatin, Madison, and Jefferson Rivers join to form the Missouri River. Henry had spent three years in the Upper Missouri region from 1809 to 1811 as a partner with Manuel Lisa in the Missouri Fur Company. While Ashley found investors, he and Henry also obtained federal permits to trade with the tribes. They planned to supplement their fur trade by having their men trap beaver. They obtained trade goods, supplies, and traps to transport upriver on two keelboats and bought fifty horses for their men to ride and herd along the riverbank. Ashley and Henry continued to advertise in St. Louis newspapers, while news of the expedition spread by word of mouth.[9]

Since young Jim Bridger could not read, someone would have informed him about the advertisement. Ashley and Henry must have considered him an asset, given that Bridger had worked on a flatboat and was a gunsmith. Bridger would have signed on with an X, and he planned to give his earnings to his sister.[10]

Ashley and Henry would pay their trappers for half the furs they obtained. They furnished them with gunpowder, lead, and other necessities, and the men agreed to build and defend the company's fort. The partners divided their expedition into two parties. Henry would lead the expedition, traveling with the first party, while Ashley remained in St. Louis. Jim Bridger was a member of the first party, which numbered over 100 men. He was part of the crew manning the keelboat, while the larger party of men rode and herded the horses along the riverbank. The expedition left St. Louis on April 3, 1822.[11] The *St. Louis Enquirer* noted in its April 13, 1822, issue:

> They will direct their course to the three forks of the Missouri, a region it is said, which contains a wealth in *Furs,* not surpassed by the mines of Peru. The party is composed entirely of young men, many of whom have relinquished the most respectable employments and circles of society, for this arduous but truly meritorious undertaking. They will be gone three years, during which time it is contemplated to visit the heads of the different rivers under the Mountains, and perhaps to go as far on the other side as the mouth of the Columbia.[12]

Henry's men reached Council Bluff on May 1, where they would have stopped at Fort Atkinson on the Missouri's west bank, nine miles north of present-day Omaha, Nebraska. This was the U.S. Army's farthest western outpost, and all upriver traffic would stop there for supplies and news before venturing farther upriver.[13]

On May 8, 1822, the second party, commanded by Daniel Moore, left St. Louis on the second keelboat, *Enterprise*. By June 1, they were 300 miles from St. Louis when the *Enterprise* was lost. Jedediah Smith, a member of the party, wrote:

> [O]n a windy day and turning a point full of sawyers the boat by an unexpected turn brought the top of her mast against a tree that hung over the water and wheeling with the side to the powerful current was swept under in a moment. The boat and its valuable cargo worth ($10,000) Dollars was lost with the exception of a few articles. . . .

Fortunately, no one drowned. Moore left his men and returned to St. Louis, reporting to Ashley the disastrous news. Undeterred, Ashley acquired another keelboat, stocking it with supplies, and hired an additional forty-six men. He decided to lead the party himself, and by June 24, they left St. Louis. Reaching the *Enterprise's* men, Ashley picked them up and proceeded upriver.[14]

Meanwhile, Henry's party had reached the Missouri Fur Company's Cedar Fort 500 miles upriver from Council Bluff. Also known as Fort Recovery, it was located along the Missouri's west bank above the White River in present-day South Dakota. Henry's men were low on provisions, game was scarce, and they were hungry.[15]

Henry's party continued upriver. Most likely they stopped above the mouth of the Bad River on the Missouri's west bank where the Columbia Fur Company was constructing its trading post, Fort Tecumseh.[16]

Days later and farther upriver, Henry's men might have stopped at two Arikara villages above the Grand River on the Missouri's west bank. The villages consisted of circular earthen lodges, up to sixty feet in diameter. Each village was surrounded by a ditch, an earthen embankment, and a wood palisade. The Arikara grew corn and vegetables and hunted buffalo. Their villages were major trading centers. The tribe acquired horses from the south and firearms from the east then traded them to northern tribes. Lewis and Clark had sent one of the Arikara leaders, Too Né, to Washington, D.C.[17] He died on his return trip in April 1806, and the Arikara blamed the Americans. There had been times of conflict and times of peace between Americans and Arikara ever since. Fortunately for Henry, the Arikara allowed his party to proceed in peace.[18]

Life bustles around the domed lodges in an Arikara village, 1832. PAINTING BY GEORGE CATLIN, COURTESY OF THE SMITHSONIAN AMERICAN ART MUSEUM, 1985.66.386.

In this scene by Karl Bodmer, Mandan women cross the Missouri River in bull boats below their village on the bluff. PAINTING BY KARL BODMER, COURTESY OF THE LIBRARY OF CONGRESS, LC-DIG-PGA-04448.

Next, they came to the villages of the Mandan and Hidatsa near the Knife River on the Missouri's west bank in present-day North Dakota. Like the Arikara, these tribes lived in fortified villages with large, domed earthen lodges. They grew corn and other crops, hunted buffalo, and their villages were trade centers. The Mandan and Hidatsa had been dealing with traders from Canada since the mid-1700s, and later, St. Louis traders. They were friendly to Whites, and there were no confrontations with Henry's men.[19]

In August, they continued upriver. One day, the keelboat and the shore party herding the horses became separated by a long distance. A band of Assiniboine making signs of friendship approached the shore party.[20]

The nomadic Assiniboine followed the buffalo herds, so increasing the size of their horse herds was vital to the tribe's welfare. Horse stealing was part of proving an individual's manhood and gaining respect.[21] Henry's herd of horses would have presented a powerful temptation.

While Henry conferred with the leaders, mounted Assiniboine approached the men guarding the horse herd. The Assiniboine fired their muskets in the air in salute, and the guards fired their guns in response. The warriors charged the herd, running off twenty-five horses with saddles, tack, and equipment. Henry sent men in pursuit, but they couldn't catch the Assiniboine.[22]

Ashley and Henry had planned to build a fort farther upriver at Three Forks. The loss of half their horses made Henry reconsider. In September, with the prospect of a long, cold winter just around the corner, Henry stopped at the confluence of the Missouri and Yellowstone Rivers and built a fort on the Missouri's south bank 400 yards upriver from the confluence, a few miles east of the present-day North Dakota and Montana border. They named it Fort Henry, and Henry immediately sent out trappers to hunt beaver.[23]

On September 8, 1822, Ashley's party reached the Arikara villages where he bought horses and split the party in two. Ashley led the mounted men upriver, leaving the keelboat to proceed at a slower pace. On October 1, Ashley arrived at Fort Henry; the keelboat arrived a few weeks later. Ashley didn't stay long; he and a few men left for St. Louis, paddling and sailing a pirogue laden with packs of beaver pelts.[24]

Henry divided his men into three groups, leading one trapper brigade up the Missouri to the Musselshell River where they built cabins. Leaving his trappers there, he returned to Fort Henry. A former Danish sea captain named John Weber led the second brigade, taking his men up the Yellowstone to the Powder River where they spent the winter. The third group remained at Fort Henry, trapping and trading with Indians. Forty-three Missouri Fur Company employees led by Michael Immell and Robert Jones stopped at Fort Henry heading to the Powder River where they planned to trap.[25]

It's not certain which of Henry's groups Jim Bridger was with, but he would have been trapping beaver, hunting game, and repairing weapons. During the winter, Jedediah Smith, at the Musselshell River camp, wrote, "we were as happy as we could be made by leisure and opportunity for unlimited indulgence in the pleasure of the Buffalo hunt." Daniel Potts, also at the Musselshell, wrote, "the River froze to the emmense [*sic*] thickness of four feet and did not brake [*sic*] up until the fourth of April."[26]

The men looked for beaver sign along streams: stripped bark, felled trees, slides along the streambanks, domed lodges, and dams. They trapped until the waterways froze.

Trapping beaver was cold, physical work, portrayed in this Alfred Jacob Miller painting. COURTESY OF THE WALTERS ART MUSEUM, 37.1940.111.

Trappers used five-pound steel traps with attached chains. As the trapper spread the trap's two connected semicircular jaws, two elbow-shaped bands became compressed under pressure, held in place by a rod connected to a flat pan. When a beaver stepped on the pan, the rod released, and the jaws snapped together on the beaver's leg.[27]

The trapper didn't want to leave human scent to warn the beaver, so he entered the icy cold water downstream then waded upstream to where he wanted to set the trap. He found a spot out from the bank in about four inches of water. The trapper fastened the chain to a stick driven into the stream bottom, and he pushed a long twig down into the bottom alongside and overhanging the trap. On the twig, he smeared castoreum, what trappers called their "medicine." Mature beavers secrete castoreum to mark their territory. Other beavers are drawn to it, and when they get close to sniff the twig, they step on the trap's pan, springing the jaws on a leg. The beaver's instinct was to swim to deep water, but the trap's chain allowed it to swim only so far. The trap dragged the beaver to the bottom where it drowned. Sometimes the beaver pulled out the anchor stick, but then it usually floated on the water's surface, allowing the trapper to recover both beaver and trap. After removing the dead beaver from the trap, the trapper reset it, carried the beaver downstream, and left where he first entered. He skinned the carcass, saved the tail (considered a delicacy), and removed the castoreum glands. A trapper ran a line of about six traps, checking them in the morning and again in the evening. After trapping most of the beavers in an area, the trapper moved to a new location.[28]

The trapper tied the green, or uncured, beaver pelt to a willow hoop to stretch it. After the trapper cleaned, dressed, cured, and marked the pelt, he placed it with other pelts in a pack. Then he wrapped the pack to protect it from the elements. Each pack contained about eighty pelts, the best placed in the middle. Weighing roughly 100 pounds, a pack could be worth $500 (about $17,000 today). Men would kill for a pack, so trappers closely guarded them.[29]

Trappers acquired the best beaver furs in the spring and the second best in the fall. Not much trapping took place in winter when watercourses froze. During the summer, beaver fur was too thin to be worth anything.[30]

In the spring of 1823, Henry's men were again on the hunt for beaver. They were not the only ones hunting. Blackfeet war parties were active.

The Blackfeet lived in teepees and followed the buffalo herds. Acquiring guns and horses, they became a powerful tribe in what is now northern Montana and central Alberta. The Blackfeet comprised three nations: Blackfoot (Siksika), Blood (Kainai), and Peigan, the last of which was itself split into Piikani and Aamskapi Pikuni. Allied with them were the Sarcee and the Gros Ventre. The Blackfeet traveled to British posts on the North Saskatchewan River to exchange furs and hides for manufactured goods. They saw American trappers as competitors.[31]

One of Henry's brigades was trapping the Smith River above the Missouri's Great Falls. On May 4, 1823, Blackfeet attacked, killing four trappers. The seven survivors abandoned 30 set traps, buried 172 more, and fled to Fort Henry.[32]

After wintering on the Powder River, Michael Immell and Robert Jones' Missouri Fur Company trappers worked the watercourses above Three Forks. By mid-May, they had acquired fifty-two packs of beaver pelts and were returning down the Yellowstone River. On May 31, a Blackfeet war party ambushed them, killing Immell, Jones, and five trappers and wounding four others. The Blackfeet stole thirty-five packs, along with horses, traps, and other equipment.

Like most Plains tribes, the Blackfeet relied on horses—and eventually rifles—to hunt buffalo. PAINTING BY KARL BODMER, 1840, COURTESY OF THE BEINECKE RARE BOOK AND MANUSCRIPT LIBRARY, YALE UNIVERSITY, ZZC20 839WIG.

Many in the fur trade believed British traders instigated the Blackfeet attack. It convinced Missouri Fur Company manager Joshua Pilcher to abandon the Upper Missouri.[33]

Henry was short on horses. Some had died, others wandered off, and Blackfeet raiders had stolen some. Horses were necessary for the men in their hunt for beaver. They rode horses along streams too narrow or shallow for watercraft. Horses packed in supplies and traps and packed out beaver pelts. Henry knew Ashley would be returning to Fort Henry with more men and supplies. He sent Jedediah Smith downriver with a message for Ashley to buy horses from the river tribes.[34]

Unknown to the men at Fort Henry, an incident hundreds of miles downriver at the Missouri Fur Company's Cedar Fort would impact Ashley and Henry's enterprise. The Arikara had captured several Sioux women. One of

Four Arikara "night" men perform a medicine ceremony. PHOTOGRAPH BY EDWARD S. CURTIS, COURTESY OF THE LIBRARY OF CONGRESS, LC-USZ62-101185.

them escaped and fled toward Cedar Fort pursued by Arikara warriors. Running within sight of the fort, she was close to being overtaken by the Arikara. Men from the fort rushed out to save her, killing two pursuers, one of whom was the son of Grey Eyes, an Arikara leader. The Arikara considered this an act of war.[35]

Meanwhile, William Ashley had returned to St. Louis. There, during the winter of 1822 to 1823, he outfitted a second expedition to Fort Henry. He hired 100 men, including Tom Fitzpatrick, Bill Sublette, James Clyman, and Hugh Glass; and loaded supplies onto two keelboats, the *Rocky Mountain* and the *Yellow Stone Packet*. Ashley led the expedition, leaving St. Louis on March 10, 1823. They proceeded upriver past Cedar Fort, and in late May, Jedediah Smith reached Ashley downriver of the two Arikara villages and gave him Henry's message to buy horses. Ashley decided to trade with the Arikara for horses as he had the previous year.[36]

The keelboats reached the villages on May 30. Even though the Arikara had been friendly the previous year, Ashley did not want to take any chances.

He was aware of the Cedar Fort incident and knew the Arikara would be angry. He had the keelboats anchor in the middle of the river near the lower village, then using a skiff, he went ashore to meet with Arikara leaders. He explained he wanted to buy forty to fifty horses, and after he gave them presents of gunpowder and musket balls, they appeared friendly and willing to trade. Forebodingly, the only items they accepted in exchange for horses were gunpowder and musket balls. By the evening of June 1, Ashley had bought the horses he needed. His plan was to lead an overland party to Fort Henry while the keelboats continued up the Missouri.[37]

The Bear, a principal chief, invited Ashley to visit his lodge, which he did accompanied by his interpreter, Edward Rose. The Bear and other leaders acted friendly, but Rose worried it was a trick and warned Ashley to move the boats away from the villages to the opposite riverbank. Ashley didn't believe it was necessary. He had his forty-man overland party stay with the horses and camp on shore near the villages. The two boats with the rest of the men aboard were forty yards from the shore camp. Ashley returned to the keelboats planning to set off on his journey the next morning.[38]

Later, Rose and several men entered the village without permission. Around midnight, Rose ran into camp saying the Arikara had killed Aaron Stephens and declared war. The rest of the night, the men in camp and on the boats waited for an attack. At daybreak, the Arikara began firing their muskets into the shore party. The attack was intense, lasting fifteen minutes. Several of Ashley's men were killed, as were most of the horses. What was left of Ashley's shore party paddled the skiffs or swam to the keelboats. Thirteen men were killed and twelve wounded, two of whom later died.[39]

Ashley regrouped downriver and made plans to proceed past the Arikara, but most of the men refused until they had reinforcements from Henry or troops from Fort Atkinson. Ashley had no choice but to comply. Jedediah Smith and a French-Canadian volunteered to go to Fort Henry to bring Henry and his men. They left on foot, traveling westward along the Grand River then turning north toward the fort.[40]

Ashley retreated downriver to the mouth of the Cheyenne River. Only thirty-one men agreed to remain. Supplies were transferred from the *Yellow Stone Packet* to the *Rocky Mountain,* and with forty-three men, five of whom were wounded, the *Yellow Stone Packet* headed downriver. When the keelboat reached Fort Atkinson on June 18, the men gave Ashley's report about the attack to the commander, Colonel Henry Leavenworth, who began assembling a force, naming it the Missouri Legion.[41]

After experiencing a few close calls, Jedediah Smith and his companion reached Fort Henry. Andrew Henry immediately prepared to assist Ashley. Leaving twenty men at the fort, he and his men, including Smith and Jim Bridger, headed downriver in pirogues loaded with beaver packs.[42]

No one shot at them as they passed the Arikara villages during the night. Henry reached Ashley at the Cheyenne River on July 2. Together, they had eighty men. Leaving some men to guard their supplies, Ashley and Henry proceeded downriver to the Bad River to buy horses. The Columbia Fur Company's Fort Tecumseh located there was becoming a major fur trading center for the Sioux, especially the Tetonwan Lakota, Yankton Nakota, and Yanktonai Nakota.[43]

The name Sioux was a misnomer for three allied linguistic groups: the Dakota, Lakota, and Nakota, each of which were divided into tribes and further into bands. They were nomadic, pursuing the buffalo. Given the opportunity, they looked forward to acquiring horses.

Leaving most of the men at the Bad River, Ashley descended the Missouri to Fort Kiowa to buy additional horses. The fur trading outfit Berthold, Chouteau, & Pratte had built the post in the fall of 1822 on the Missouri River's west bank twenty-five miles north of the White River. There, Ashley learned that Colonel Henry Leavenworth, leading the Missouri Legion, was headed upriver to punish the Arikara. Ashley returned to the Bad River where he and Henry awaited the arrival of the Missouri Legion and prepared their men for the anticipated fight.[44]

Leavenworth led 230 men of the Sixth Infantry. Three keelboats mounted with swivel guns, loaded with supplies, and transporting two six-pounder cannons followed the men marching along the river. Joshua Pilcher, manager of the Missouri Fur Company, joined the Missouri Legion with sixty men in two keelboats and brought along a 5½-inch howitzer from Fort Atkinson. Benjamin O'Fallon, Indian agent at Council Bluff, appointed Pilcher a subagent to the Sioux during the expedition. Pilcher sent messages to Lakota and Nakota bands inviting them to join them. As the legion proceeded upriver, warriors began arriving. The Missouri Legion reached Ashley and Henry at the Bad River near the end of July, their ranks swelled by 700 Lakota and Nakota warriors.[45]

The combined forces arrived at the Arikara villages on August 9. Mounted Sioux warriors spotted Arikara in their cornfields and raced ahead to attack. The troops and civilians advanced at a slower pace. Ashley's men, including Jim Bridger, were formed into two companies and were on the extreme right with the Missouri to their right. As the Sioux and Arikara fought, Leavenworth hesitated to send in his troops and civilians. He did not want his men to shoot and hit Sioux allies and wanted to wait for the artillery to arrive. When the Arikara saw the troops, they retreated into their fortified villages. The keelboats with the artillery didn't arrive until sundown, so Leavenworth decided to attack the next day.[46]

The following morning, Leavenworth's troops surrounded the two villages, and artillery began firing shells into the villages. Chief Grey Eyes was killed, but for the most part, the shelling had little effect. Ashley and Henry's men held the same position as the day before. Leavenworth asked Ashley to test the firepower of the lower village. Ashley found a ravine his men could use for protection as they fired at the village. Leavenworth wrote that Ashley's men "maintained a spirited action."[47]

Other than surrounding and shelling the villages, Leavenworth did not order his troops to attack, and by 3 P.M., he ordered all troops to cease firing and return to camp. The Sioux, who had been eager to raid the Arikara villages, were disgusted and left, taking Arikara corn as well as six army mules and seven of Ashley's horses.[48]

Late that afternoon and into the next day, Leavenworth met with Arikara leaders. He believed they negotiated in good faith; Pilcher did not trust them. Leavenworth drafted a treaty, but Pilcher would not be a party to it. Leavenworth wanted the Arikara to restore to Ashley the number of horses he had bought and to return the firearms and supplies they had taken from Ashley's shore party. The Arikara said most of their horses had been stolen by the Sioux or killed during the attack, but they would restore what property was still there. Leavenworth insisted they must agree to be peaceful with American traders in the future.[49]

Six officers, Ashley, and eleven Arikara leaders signed the treaty; Pilcher would not. The items the Arikara returned were underwhelming: three rifles, one horse, and fifteen buffalo robes. This was unacceptable. The army officers, Henry, and Pilcher were all in agreement to continue the attack. Leavenworth hesitated then said he would resume the attack the following morning. Rose entered the villages and persuaded the Arikara to give up a few more buffalo robes. He returned to camp and reported the Arikara were packing to leave. Leavenworth made no attempt to prevent that possibility. By the morning of August 12, the villages were empty except for the mother of Grey Eyes. Leavenworth believed he had "completely humbled" the Arikara, and they would not attack American traders in the future. Pilcher disagreed and believed Leavenworth had botched the attack, giving allied tribes as well as hostile tribes a poor opinion of American power.[50]

On August 15, Leavenworth withdrew his troops and began the return to Fort Atkinson. He ordered that the villages were not to be harmed, but after the troops left, two of Pilcher's men set them on fire.[51]

Ashley and Henry followed Leavenworth's troops to Fort Kiowa. They decided traveling up the Missouri to Fort Henry was too dangerous and modified their plans. While Ashley returned to St. Louis to prepare for next year's trapping and trading activities, Jedediah Smith would lead eleven trappers westward, cross-country to the Green River in the Rocky Mountains of present-day Wyoming. Henry would lead the rest of the men overland to Fort Henry. With Missouri River traffic restricted by hostile Arikara, Ashley and Henry realized they needed an alternative overland route to transport supplies and trade goods and bring back beaver packs.[52]

No one recorded Henry's brigade's journey to Fort Henry. The number of men varies. James Clyman wrote that Henry led thirteen men. Daniel Potts said the number was thirty. Whatever the party's size, Jim Bridger was included, as was Hugh Glass. Henry's brigade left Fort Kiowa mid-August, on foot, acquiring enough horses to haul supplies. They followed the Missouri upriver to the Grand River then walked westward along that watercourse. On the night of August 20, Mandan and Gros Ventre warriors attacked, killing two men, wounding two others, and stealing two horses. At least one attacker was killed. Henry's party turned north, eventually reaching Fort Henry.[53] Along the way, another horrific incident occurred along the Grand River in which Jim Bridger may or may not have played a part.

---

[1] Bill Markley, "Fur, Defeat, and Pluck." *True West Magazine,* April 2005.

[2] Landon Jones, *William Clark and the Shaping of the West* (New York, NY: Farrar, Status, and Giroux, 2004), 256, 263. R. G. Robertson, *Competitive Struggle: America's Western Fur Trading Posts, 1764–1865* (Boise, ID: Tamarack Books, Inc., 1999), 150.

[3] J. A. Dacus and James A. Buel, *St. Louis or the Inside Life of a Great City* (St. Louis, MO: Western Publishing Company, 1878), 14, 23. Eric Jay Donlin, *Fur, Fortune, and Empire* (New York, NY: W. W. Norton & Company, 2010), 212. Jones, *Clark,* 245, 263–266.

[4] Peter Newman, *Company of Adventurers: Caesars of the Wilderness,* Vol. 2. (Ontario, Canada: Viking, 1987), 206–207.

[5] "Missouri River," *Wikipedia,* accessed April 3, 2023. https://en.wikipedia.org/wiki/Missouri_River.

[6] T. B. Thorpe, "Remembrances of the Mississippi," *Harper's New Monthly Magazine,* No. LXVII, Vol. XII (New York, NY: Harper & Brothers, Publishers, December 1855), 28. Jones, *Clark,* 273.

[7] Paul O'Neil, *The Rivermen* (Alexandria, VA: Time-Life Books, Inc., 1975), 22–23. Thorpe, "Remembrances," 29–30.

[8] "TO Enterprising Young Men," *Missouri Gazette and Public Advertiser* (St. Louis, MO, February 13, 1822), 2, Newspapers.com, March 31, 2023, https://www.newspapers.com/image/249517987/.

[9] Donald McKay Frost, "Notes on General Ashley, the Overland Trail, and South Pass," *The Proceedings of the American Antiquarian Society – 1944,* Vol. 54, Part 2 (Worcester, MA: American Antiquarian Society 1944), 169–170, 177, 226. Robertson, *Struggle,* 126, 211, 213. Donlin, *Fur,* 223–224. Chittenden, *Fur Trade,* Vol. 1, 251, 263.

[10] Dodge, *Bridger,* 6.

[11] Aaron Woodard, *Soft Fur and Iron Men* (Montgomery, AL: E-Book Time, LCC, 2006), 96–97. Donlin, *Fur,* 224. Enzler, *Bridger,* 11–12. Robertson, *Struggle,* 129. Frost, "Ashley," 177.

[12] "Franklin," *Columbia Herald-Statesman* (Columbia, MO, April 30, 1822), 3. Newspapers.com, April 14, 2023, https://www.newspapers.com/image/338261977/. Frost, "Ashley," 178.

[13] "Franklin," 3. Chittenden, *Fur Trade,* 263. Robertson, *Struggle,* 61, 187. Jones, *Clark,* 258.

[14] Frost, "Ashley," 179–180. Chittenden, *Fur Trade,* 263. Woodard, *Fur,* 99.

[15] Frost, "Ashley," 178–179, 217. Robertson, *Struggle,* 215.

[16] Barton Barbour, *Fort Union and the Upper Missouri Fur Trade* (Norman, OK: University of Oklahoma Press, 2001), 11. Harold Schuler, *Fort Pierre Chouteau* (Vermillion, SD: University of South Dakota Press, 1990), 8–9, 11–12. Robertson, *Struggle,* xvii.

[17] *Too Né,'s* name can be confusing. His name has also been recorded as *Arketarnashar, Piaheto,* and Eagle/Eagle's Feather. Brad Tennant, Historian/Humanities Scholar, personal communication.

[18] Linda Hasselstrom, *Roadside History of South Dakota* (Missoula, MT: Mountain Press Publishing Company, 1994), 186. J. Leonard Jeannewein and Jane Boorman, editors, *Dakota Panorama* (Freeman, SD: Brevet Press, 1973), 3–5. Herbert Schell, *History of South Dakota* (Lincoln, NE: University of Nebraska Press, 1968), 52–53. Raymond DeMallie, volume editor, *Plains, Handbook of North American Indians,* Vol. 13, Part 1, (Washington, D.C.: Smithsonian Institution, 2001), 368–369, 370–371. Jones, *Clark,* 152, 161.

[19] DeMallie, editor, *Plains,* Vol. 13, Part 1, 329, 332, 350, 352, 355. Robertson, *Struggle,* 157–158.

[20] Chittenden, *Fur Trade,* 263.

[21] DeMallie, editor, *Plains,* Vol. 13, Part 1, 579.

[22] Enzler, *Bridger,* 18.

[23] "Franklin," 3. Chittenden, *Fur Trade,* Vol. 1, 263. Robertson, *Struggle,* 129. McLaird, *Glass,* 55–56.

[24] McLaird, *Glass,* 55. Robertson, *Struggle,* 129. Frost, "Ashley," 180, 217.

[25] Dale Morgan, *Jedediah Smith and the Opening of the West* (Lincoln, NE: University of Nebraska Press, 1953), 42. McLaird, *Glass,* 56. Robertson, *Struggle,* 129.

[26] McLaird, *Glass,* 57.

[27] Donlin, *Fur,* 181.

[28] Winfred Blevins, *Give Your Heart to the Hawks* (New York, NY: Avon Books, 1973), 46. Chittenden, *Fur Trade,* Vol. 2, 820–821.

[29] Chittenden, *Fur Trade,* Vols. 1 and 2, 40, 821.

[30] Blevins, *Hawks,* 46.

[31] DeMallie, editor, *Plains,* Vol. 13, Part 1, 604, 608. Chittenden, *Fur Trade,* Vol. 2, 854.

[32] Robert Utley, *A Life Wild and Perilous: Mountain Men and the Paths to the Pacific* (New York, NY: Henry Holt and Company, 1997), 47.

[33] Chittenden, *Fur Trade,* Vol. 1, 151, 153, 155.

[34] Robertson, *Struggle,* 129.

[35] Linda Hasselstrom, ed., *Journal of a Mountain Man, James Clyman* (Missoula, MT: Mountain Press Publishing Company, 1998), 11. McLaird, *Glass,* 62. Chittenden, *Fur Trade,* Vol. 1, 264–265.

[36] John Sunder, *Bill Sublette: Mountain Man* (Norman, OK: University of Oklahoma Press, 1959), 34, 36. Dale Morgan, ed., *The West of William H. Ashley* (Denver, CO: F. S. Rosenstock, Old West Publishing, 1964), 22. Frost, "Ashley," 229–230, 232. Chittenden, *Fur Trade,* 264. Robertson, *Struggle,* 129–130. Hasselstrom, ed., *Clyman,* 9–10.
[37] Chittenden, *Fur Trade,* 264–265. McLaird, *Glass,* 63. Frost, "Ashley," 233, 237. Hasselstrom, ed., *Clyman,* 11.
[38] Chittenden, *Fur Trade,* 267. Frost, "Ashley," 237.
[39] Hasselstrom, ed., *Clyman,* 11. Frost, "Ashley," 233–235. Robertson, *Struggle,* 130–131.
[40] Chittenden, *Fur Trade,* 268–269. Robertson, *Struggle,* 132.
[41] McLaird, *Glass,* 67, 68. Robertson, *Struggle,* 131.
[42] Robertson, *Struggle,* 131. Chittenden, *Fur Trade,* 269. Dodge, *Bridger,* 6.
[43] Robertson, *Struggle,* 131. Chittenden, *Fur Trade,* 269–270, 589. Schuler, *Fort Pierre,* 11–12. Hasselstrom, ed., *Clyman,* 16. Brad Tennant, Historian/Humanities Scholar, personal communication.
[44] Robertson, *Struggle,* 138. Sunder, *Sublette,* 42.
[45] Chittenden, *Fur Trade,* 588–589, 601. McLaird, *Glass,* 70, 72. Jones, *Clark,* 270. Robertson, *Struggle,* 132.
[46] Chittenden, *Fur Trade,* 592–593. McLaird, *Glass,* 72. Robertson, *Struggle,* 132.
[47] McLaird, *Glass,* 73. Jones, *Clark,* 270.
[48] Chittenden, *Fur Trade,* 595–597. Frost, "Ashley," 266.
[49] Chittenden, *Fur Trade,* 596.
[50] Ibid, 598–600, 602–603.
[51] Chittenden, *Fur Trade,* 600. McLaird, *Glass,* 78.
[52] McLaird, *Glass,* 87. Frost, "Ashley," 190.
[53] McLaird, *Glass,* 87–88. Frost, "Ashley," 285–286.

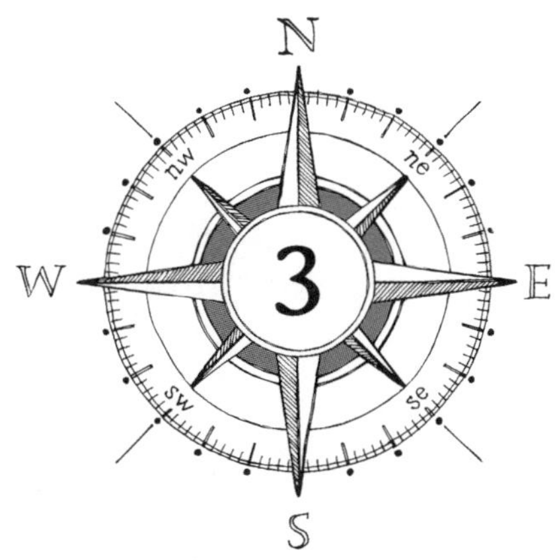

Hugh Glass, the Man and His Myth

Many people believe Jim Bridger is part of Hugh Glass' story. Little would've been written about Glass if he had not survived a grizzly bear mauling. His story has several variations. A number of chroniclers added details despite a lack of collaborating evidence, and some writers created entirely fictional accounts. In 1915, John Neihardt wrote his epic poem, *The Song of Hugh Glass,* and in 1954, Frederick Manfred wrote his novel, *Lord Grizzly.* Movies portrayed the event. Richard Harris played Glass in *Man in the Wilderness* (1971), and Leonardo DiCaprio played him in *The Revenant* (2015), based on a novel by Michael Punke.

It's not certain when and where Hugh Glass was born. He may have been a runaway apprentice gunsmith from Pittsburgh, Pennsylvania. He may have been a sailor kidnapped by pirates. As that tale goes, after escaping the pirates along the Texas coast, Glass headed north only to be captured by a band of Pawnee. Escaping again, he traveled to St. Louis where in 1823 he joined William Ashley's second Missouri expedition. Ashley listed him as being wounded during the Arikara attack.[1]

After the battle at the Arikara villages, Glass continued as a member of Andrew Henry's party on its overland march to Fort Henry. Several days after Mandan and Gros Ventre warriors attacked them along the Grand River, Glass was out away from the main party. He encountered a grizzly bear; some stories say it was a female with cubs. The bear attacked Glass, and as it mauled him, either he or some of his companions killed it. When Henry and the main party

Native to the plains, grizzly bears attained near mythic status among early Euro-American explorers and trappers. ETCHING BY LUCAS WEBER FROM A PAINTING, CIRCA 1840, BY KARL BODMER, COURTESY OF THE LIBRARY OF CONGRESS, LC-DIG-PGA-044405.

reached Glass, they saw he was so mangled, they feared he would die if moved. Henry left two volunteers with Glass until he recovered or died. One volunteer was John Fitzgerald, and the other an unnamed seventeen-year-old boy. Some speculate the boy was Jim Bridger. After several days, Glass was not improving, so they left him to die, taking his gun and possessions. Rejoining Henry's party, they reported Glass had died.

Glass, however, was not dead. Somehow, he survived and regained enough strength to extricate himself from his predicament. He made his way down the Grand River, then followed the Missouri down to a trading post. After he recovered, the traders outfitted him with a gun and supplies. Surviving several adventures while traveling back into trapping territory, Glass eventually found

Henry's brigade, which had headed up the Yellowstone River and built a fort at the mouth of the Bighorn River. Before Glass' arrival, Fitzgerald (with Glass' gun), had left, heading downriver. But the boy was still there. After realizing the boy had repented, Glass forgave him. In February 1824, Glass joined a group taking dispatches to Fort Atkinson.[2]

On April 19, 1824, Fitzgerald enlisted in Company I of the 6th Regiment at Fort Atkinson. When Glass reached the fort, he learned Fitzgerald was in the army and thus protected from vengeance. He told everyone Fitzgerald had deserted him, taking his gun. The commanding officer ordered Fitzgerald to return Glass' gun, which appeased him. Glass later joined a Santa Fe trading party. By 1828, he had returned to the northern Rocky Mountains. During the winter of 1832 to 1833, Glass' luck finally ran out. A band of Arikara killed Glass, Edward Rose, and a man named Menard along the Yellowstone River.[3]

Glass's life may have ended there, but the argument over the identity of the young man with John Fitzgerald when they abandoned Glass was just getting started. Was it Jim Bridger? It's important to start with the fact there were no first-hand accounts of the bear attack and desertion. The best we have are second-hand accounts from Daniel Potts and James Clyman, both Ashley and Henry employees.

Potts, stationed at Fort Henry during the attack on the Arikara villages, heard of Glass' mauling when Henry's brigade arrived at the fort, and was present at the Bighorn post when Glass returned from the dead. On July 7, 1824, Potts wrote to a Pennsylvania friend, "one man was also tore nearly all to peases [*sic*] by a White Bear [grizzly bear] and was left by the way without any gun who afterwards recovered."[4]

James Clyman and Hugh Glass were members of Ashley's 1823 party. When Ashley sent Jedediah Smith west, Clyman was part of Smith's brigade; he later learned of Glass' mauling. Clyman lived in Napa, California, when on April 17, 1871, he wrote about the Hugh Glass incident. Unfortunately, he made no mention of the volunteers left with him.[5]

In March 1825, Glass's story received national attention when James Hall published "The Missouri Trapper" in the Philadelphia-based magazine *Port Folio.* Hall did not identify the men who deserted Glass, but he wrote that, of the two men, Glass wanted to confront only the one, and he headed to Fort Atkinson to find him.[6]

Lieutenant Phillip St. George Cooke wrote about Glass in the December 2 and 9, 1830, issues of the *St. Louis Beacon.* In "Some Incidents in the Life of Hugh Glass, a Hunter of the Missouri," Cooke wrote that the men left with Glass were "Fitzgerald, and a youth of seventeen." Reaching Henry's fort, Glass learned Fitzgerald had departed. In this account, after confronting the youth and seeing he was repentant, Glass forgave him.[7]

Edmund Flagg wrote "Adventures at the Headwaters of the Missouri," published initially in the *Louisville Literary News Letter* on September 7, 1839, and later republished in other newspapers. Flagg claimed he took his material from rough notes written by a "very intelligent" man who claimed he was present when Glass was mauled. Flagg said the two men were named "Fitzpatrick" and "Bridges." Flagg's article contains several errors besides the misnaming of Fitzgerald, so the identity of "Bridges" remains blurry at best.[8]

George Yount met Glass years after the mauling. Writing his memoirs in 1855, he recounted the bear attack story, identifying the deserters as a man and a boy. When Glass reached Henry's post, the man was gone; Glass forgave the boy and got his rifle back.[9]

In 1837, William Stewart hired artist Alfred Miller to travel with him to the rendezvous on the Green River. Miller recorded the Hugh Glass tale told around the campfire. He wrote that, after the mauling, Glass appeared dead, so his companions took his gun and other items, and left. Miller continued:

> Months elapsed;—the company was returning to the Fort;—they saw a man slowly approaching by the banks of the river, as he came nearer their eyes rested on a cadaverous figure with a head so disfigured as to be unknown. The astonishment of the party may be conceived when they heard a well-known voice call out, "Hallo! Bill! you thought I was 'gone under,' didn't you? hand over my horse and 'fixens.' I ain't dead yet by a cussed sight." It was the veritable Glass whom they left with the bear.[10]

Was the seventeen-year-old deserter's name Bill?

In 1896, seventy-three years after Glass' mauling, historian Hiram Chittenden interviewed Joseph LaBarge, a Missouri riverboat pilot. Chittenden wrote in *A History of the Fur Trade in the Far West:*

> Who the young man was is not known, but the late Captain LaBarge, who remembers the tradition well, says that it was Jim Bridger. Bridger is supposed to have been born in 1804 and this would indicate 1821 or 1822 as the year of the occurrence. The discrepancy is not great enough to preclude the possibility of its being Bridger, but there is no other proof of it than this intangible tradition.[11]

If Bridger was born in 1804, he was nineteen when the bear mauled Glass in 1823, not 1821 or 1822. Jim Bridger biographer Jerry Enzler wrote, ". . . it is possible LaBarge's remembered tradition was of the Flagg article rather than an independent, confirming source." There is nothing to collaborate LaBarge's statement.[12]

The theory Jim Bridger was the un-named boy is based on the last name "Bridges" mentioned in a newspaper story sixteen years after the event, and LaBarge remembering a tradition that the boy was Jim Bridger, seventy-three years later.

James Stevenson (1840–1888), a scientist with the U.S. Geological Survey, spent several years in the field with Bridger and knew him well. In 1886, Stevenson was asked if Jim Bridger was one of Glass' deserters. He responded, "Bridger told me the story of your Glass; but there was no desertion."[13]

---

1 McLaird, *Glass,* 34, 41. Frost, "Ashley," 235.

2 McLaird, *Glass,* 91.

3 Ibid, 89, 94, 98, 102.

4 Clay Landry, "Chronology of Publication of the Hugh Glass Story," Museum of the Mountain Man, Sublette County Historical Society, accessed May 11, 2023, http://hughglass.org/sources/. McLaird, Glass, 7.

5 Hassselstrom, *Clyman,* 18–19.

6 James Hall, "The Missouri Trapper," *Port Folio* Vol. XIX (Philadelphia, PA: Harrison Hall, 1825), 218. Museum of the Mountain Man, Sublette County Historical Society, accessed May 12, 2023, http://hughglass.org/wp-content/uploads/2015/09/1825-Hugh-Glass-article.pdf. McLaird, *Glass,* 9, 12.

7 Landry, "Chronology," accessed May 12, 2023. Phillip St. George Cooke, "Scenes and Adventures in the Army," *The Southern Literary Messenger* (Richmond, VA: Thos. W. White Publisher and Proprietor, 1842), 585, 588–589, http://hughglass.org/wp-content/uploads/2015/09/Glass-story-by-Crook.pdf.

8 Edmund Flagg, "Adventures at the Headwaters of the Missouri," *Louisville Literary News Letter* (Louisville, KY: September 7, 1839). Museum of the Mountain Man, Sublette County Historical Society, accessed May 12, 2023. http://hughglass.org/wp-content/uploads/2015/12/FLagg.pdf. McLaird, Glass, 23–24, 27.

9 McLaird, *Glass,* 25, 31–32.

10 Alfred Miller, Marvin Ross, ed., *The West of Alfred Jacob Miller* (Norman, OK: University of Oklahoma Press, 1999), 125.

11 Chittenden, *Fur Trade,* 704–705.

12 Jerry Enzler, "Jim Bridger" excerpt from "Tracking Jim Bridger" published in *Rocky Mountain Fur Trade Journal* (Vol. 5) 2011. Museum of the Mountain Man, Sublette County Historical Society, accessed May 12, 2023, http://hughglass.org/jim-bridger/. Chittenden, *Fur Trade,* 348.

13 Enzler, *Bridger,* 30.

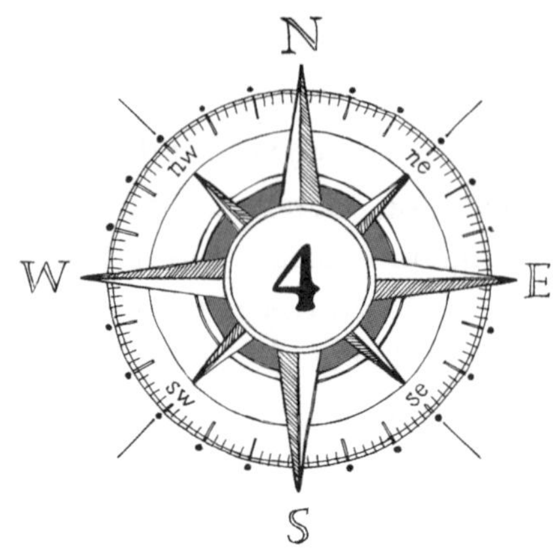

In Search of Beaver

1823–1825

Andrew Henry's party arrived at Fort Henry in late September 1823 after losing two men to an Indian attack and another, apparently, to a grizzly bear. The men at the fort told Henry that raiders had stolen twenty-three horses. Raiders soon ran off seven more.[1]

He decided to abandon the fort and head up the Yellowstone River. The men loaded a boat with supplies, equipment, and trade goods, then traveled west upriver. Near the Powder River, they came upon rapids over which they could not take the boat. There they met a band of Crow from whom they bought forty-seven horses. The Crow told Henry the Blackfeet were determined to hunt down and kill trappers whenever possible.[2]

The Crow were nomadic, following the buffalo herds. Horses were so important they developed their culture around them. The more horses a man possessed, the wealthier he was and the higher his status. It was important for a man to have horses to marry a wife. As they increased their herds, the Crow expanded their territory to present-day eastern Montana and northern Wyoming.[3]

Henry sent a brigade southwest to the Green River and planned to send a second brigade to follow. He knew the Green River area well, having explored it in 1810. He led his remaining men up the Yellowstone to the Bighorn River. There, in Crow country, they constructed a second Fort Henry.[4]

The two brigade leaders' identities are obscure, though that hasn't stopped historians from conjecturing. Dale Morgan wrote, "It has to be supposed that the party was led by the moody Captain [John] Weber." Hiram Chittenden wrote, "[Henry] then organized a party which he probably placed under the charge of Etienne Provost. . . ." Grenville Dodge wrote, "[Henry] then divided his party, placing one part under Etienne Prevost [*sic*]. . . . With this party was Bridger."

Etienne Provost was an experienced fur trader based out of Taos, New Mexico. In 1823, he returned east and was at Fort Atkinson on August 1. Provost could have joined the attack on the Arikara villages, then traveled with Henry to Fort Henry. If he led one of Henry's brigades, he must have seen the possibility of a bountiful beaver harvest, left Henry's men that fall or early winter, returned to Taos where he outfitted his own brigade, and returned to the Green River to trap in the spring of 1824. John Weber was most likely a brigade leader since he had led a brigade the year before.[5]

Daniel Potts later wrote of the first brigade's travels in a July 16, 1826, letter. They followed the Powder River to the eastern slopes of the Bighorn Mountains, which they crossed to the Bighorn River valley, then crossed the Owl Creek Mountains during frigid conditions. Potts' feet froze, losing two toes. The brigade descended into the Wind River valley where they spent the 1823 to 1824 winter with the Crow. A chief took Potts into his lodge and personally cared for his damaged feet.[6]

Henry's second brigade would have joined Potts' brigade, but Potts did not mention them in his letter. Jedediah Smith's brigade also reached the Wind River and stayed with the Crow. They were joined by a Missouri Fur Company brigade that had followed Henry's two brigades.[7]

During that winter, Jim Bridger would have strengthened friendships with fellow trappers and immersed himself in Crow culture. Smith's brigade would have told Henry's brigades of the hardships they had experienced during their travels. Jedediah Smith had been attacked by a grizzly bear, and Jim Clyman had stitched together his ripped face and head and sewed an ear back into place.[8]

The trappers joined the Crow in buffalo hunts. The entire encampment was involved—men on horseback driving and killing the buffalo, while women and children followed behind, butchering the carcasses.[9]

South Pass offered by far the most gradual transit over the Continental Divide. PHOTOGRAPH COURTESY OF THE NATIONAL PARK SERVICE.

In February 1824, Smith's eleven-man brigade left the Crow, heading west to cross the Wind River Range, but they had to turn back due to deep snow. The Crow told Smith if they traveled to the southeast, they could get around the mountain barrier. This route would become known as South Pass. Smith's brigade set out, but wind, cold, and snow bogged them down. By mid-March they made it across the broad, open, treeless summit of South Pass. Following the Big Sandy River, they arrived at the beaver-rich Green River on March 19.[10]

Jedediah Smith and his men are credited with discovering South Pass, through which thousands of emigrants would pass in the future. It might be better to say Smith and his men made Americans aware of South Pass. Indians had been using it for ages.

Smith and Weber's brigades maintained communication between each other and with Fort Henry. Andrew Henry knew Smith's party had crossed the mountains and the Continental Divide. That spring, he sent five men to Council Bluff. The Monday, June 7, 1824, edition of the *St. Louis Enquirer* reported:

> Mr. Vasques [*sic*], just from the Upper Missouri, states that five men of Major Henry's party in descending the Platte, were attacked by a party of Aurickaree [*sic*] Indians—and that three, More, Chapman and Glass, were killed [Hugh Glass escaped]; that the others, Dutton and Marsh, made their escape, and arrived at the Council Bluffs [*sic*]. They state that Major Henry, has built a Fort at the mouth of the Big Horn—that a Mr. Wheeler was killed by a white bear. Captain Smith, with some of the party, had crossed the Mountains.[11]

John Weber, leading more than twenty-five men, including Jim Bridger, followed Smith's route through South Pass to the Green River. They must have trapped along the way, either caching their beaver packs or sending them back to Fort Henry. They arrived at the Green River in mid-July 1824.[12]

That summer, Andrew Henry abandoned Fort Henry and returned down the Missouri with a company of his men and many beaver packs. Reaching St. Louis in August 1824, he and William Ashley terminated their partnership. Henry provided information about South Pass that made national news. The November 16, 1824, issue of *The Arkansas Gazette* reprinted an article from the *St. Louis Enquirer:*

> By the arrival of Major Henry from the Rocky Mountains, we learn that his party have discovered a passage by which loaded waggons can at this time reach the navigable waters of the Columbia River. This route lies South of the one explored by Lewis and Clarke, and is inhabited by Indians friendly to us.[13]

By June 1824, Jedediah Smith's brigade had finished its Green River beaver hunt. Smith planned to explore westward, while Tom Fitzpatrick and two men took the beaver packs to St. Louis. Before they split up, the brigade built a bull boat for the three men to float the packs down the Sweetwater River to the Platte River. But Jim Clyman failed to return from a scout. Not finding Clyman and discovering evidence Indians had been trailing him, they believed the worst and ended the search. Fitzpatrick and his two companions reached the North Platte, but in attempting to pass through rapids they swamped their bull boat.

They saved the beaver packs, which they dried and cached, hoping to return and recover them. After a difficult journey, they reached Fort Atkinson in late August 1824. To their surprise, Clyman was there, very much alive. Weak and starving, he had arrived ten days earlier. He had escaped his pursuers who were between him and the brigade, so he began his journey to Fort Atkinson. Along the way, he was nearly killed, then robbed, and later cared for by a Pawnee band.[14]

Fitzpatrick sent William Ashley a letter updating him on Smith's brigade, the plentiful beaver population, and South Pass's accessibility for wagons. Lucien Fontenelle, in charge of the Missouri Fur Company's Fort Bellevue nearby, agreed to provide horses and resupply Fitzpatrick and his men in exchange for their cached beaver packs. They rode to the cache site, retrieved the packs, and were back at Fort Bellevue by late October.[15]

After learning from Andrew Henry about the Green River and the accessible South Pass, Ashley had begun preparing to resupply his men and bring back their beaver pelts. Fitzpatrick's letter confirmed Henry's report. Ashley desired to reach the Green River as soon as possible even though it was late in the year. Reaching Fort Atkinson on October 21, he made final preparations to lead his party to the Rocky Mountains. Picking up Fitzpatrick and Clyman, Ashley left on November 3, leading twenty-five men with fifty pack horses, a wagon, and draft animals loaded with supplies and trade goods. It would be a difficult trip. They would not arrive at the Green River until April 19, 1825.[16]

In early July 1824, Jedediah Smith, leading six men including Bill Sublette, headed west, looking for more beaver. John Weber and his brigade, including Jim Bridger, Dan Potts, and twenty trappers, remained on the Green River, scouting beaver locations.[17]

Beaver were prized for their lustrous, water-repellent fur. PHOTOGRAPH COURTESY OF THE NATIONAL PARK SERVICE.

This was Eastern Shoshone country, and even though the tribe appeared friendly and were interested in trade with the Americans, Weber's men needed to be cautious. The Eastern Shoshone numbered around 3,000 people. Their territory was the western third of present-day Wyoming. They were divided into the Buffalo Eaters, located around the Green and Wind Rivers, and the Mountain Sheep Eaters in the Yellowstone headwaters. The Shoshone lived in small bands; individuals and family groups could leave one band and join another.

A chief, aided by two warrior societies, led each band. The Shoshone developed a horse culture and lived in buffalo-hide teepees. They were always ready to fight to defend their territory from their enemies, the Blackfeet, Arapaho, and Sioux. They had been acquiring guns and other goods from the Hudson's Bay Company but were willing to trade with Weber's men. If an opportunity arose, they would think nothing of stealing traps, horses, guns, or anything else, perhaps killing a lone trapper for his possessions. In fact, thirteen trappers[18] would be killed and many traps and weapons stolen over the next months.[19]

In September, the Green River valley became more crowded as Etienne Provost, leading his own independent brigade of eighty trappers, established a camp on the river. Provost sent his men trapping in all directions. He led ten men to the west across the Wasatch Range. Near Bear Lake, they met a band of friendly-acting Shoshone. Unknown to Provost, a Shoshone chief had been killed by Hudson's Bay men, and the Shoshone were out for revenge. As they prepared for the pipe-smoking ceremony, the Shoshone attacked. Only Provost and one other man escaped.[20]

As the days grew cooler and the beavers' fur thickened, Weber's men began trapping. In their explorations to the west, they came upon the Bear River. They followed its course as it headed north, made a bend to the west, and then flowed southward. Debating where it flowed, the trappers made bets and selected twenty-year-old Jim Bridger to explore its course. Self-confident and alone, Bridger rode his horse along the riverbank, passing through the two-mile-long Bear River Canyon. The river flowed out of the mountains through a wide-open valley and into an immense body of water. As he rode toward the watery expanse, he observed animal skeletons littering the valley floor; a white substance rimmed the shoreline. Dismounting at the water's edge, he tasted it—it was salty.[21]

Bridger returned to Weber's winter encampment in Cache Valley on the modern-day Utah-Idaho border. There he told the others what he had found.

Some believed he had reached the Gulf of California, while others thought it must be the Pacific Ocean. It wasn't until 1826 that other explorers followed the shoreline and discovered it was a lake with no outlet. Jim Bridger had discovered the Great Salt Lake, the largest saltwater lake in the Western Hemisphere.[22]

William Ashley and his men reached the Green River on April 19, 1825. The previous fall, winter conditions had set in as they followed the Platte River, traversing the plains and eventually reaching the Rocky Mountains after Pawnee warriors had robbed them. The leaders of those same warriors welcomed them to their village, returning most of their stolen goods. Ashley's party entered modern-day central Wyoming's Laramie Plains, skirted the Medicine Bow Range, and crossed the Continental Divide along the edge of the Great Divide Basin. Before they could reach the Green River, Crow raiders stole seventeen horses. Ashley's men gave chase but recovered only two horses. Four nights later, thieves stole two more horses.[23]

On April 22, 1825, Ashley sent out three parties while he led the fourth. Ashley and seven men took most of the goods down the Green River in bull boats. At the same time, Zachariah Ham led a seven-man brigade west into the Wasatch Mountains, Tom Fitzpatrick led six men southwest to the Uinta Mountains, and Jim Clyman took six men up the Green River. Ashley told them to look for Smith and Weber's brigades, which he assumed were beyond the mountains to the west. He told his men he would cache the goods and supplies downriver and mark it "as a place of General Rendezvous" where they were to assemble on or before July 10.[24]

Americans were not the only trappers in the region. Great Britain and the United States both claimed the vast northwest Oregon Country extending from the border of Mexico's northern California to the southern border of Russia's Alaska and eastward into present-day Montana. The Convention of 1818 between Great Britain and the United States resolved that for the next ten years the two nations would jointly control Oregon, and it would be open to both countries' citizens. As of 1825, only the British maintained a presence in Oregon Country. Hudson's Bay Company Governor George Simpson declared the company's policy was to eliminate all beaver from the Snake River basin, more than 100,000 square miles, creating a fur desert, leaving nothing for American trappers. One of Hudson's Bay Company's eastern forts in Oregon

Country was Flathead Post, located on the Clark Fork River near present-day Thompson Falls in northwestern Montana.[25]

Back in July 1824, Jedediah Smith and six men had headed west, hunting beaver. In mid-September, they ran into a Hudson's Bay trapping party on the Snake River. They were independent Iroquois trappers led by "Old Pierre" Tevanitagon. Shoshone had robbed them of most of their beaver pelts. They asked Smith for protection on their return to the main Hudson's Bay brigade, the Snake Expedition. Smith agreed to do so for 105 beaver pelts. In late October, they caught up with the Snake Expedition commanded by Alexander Ross. Smith believed their best chance for winter survival was to stay with the Hudson's Bay men. Ross reluctantly allowed the Americans to tag along to Flathead Post, arriving there on November 26, 1824.[26]

Ross learned that Hudson's Bay Company Governor George Simpson had replaced him with Peter Ogden, who was to take the Snake Expedition into the field during the winter to acquire more beaver pelts. Ogden's brigade, consisting of fifty-nine men, thirty Indian wives, and thirty-five children, left Flathead Post on December 20, 1824. The expedition was made up of gentlemen leaders (Ogden and William Kittson), eleven engagés or employees, and forty-six Freemen. Freemen were independent, mixed-race trappers who sold their furs to Hudson's Bay. Simpson called them "the very scum of the country and generally outcasts from the Service for misconduct . . . the most unruly and troublesome gang to deal with in this or perhaps any other part of the World."[27]

A few days after Ogden's brigade left, Jedediah Smith's party followed, catching up with them on December 29. Heading eastward and south, the two brigades traversed mountain passes and valleys, traveling together at times for protection. On January 31, 1825, Blackfeet raiders stole twenty-four horses from the Freemen, who recovered nine. In March, Bloods killed Antoine Benoit, a Freeman, while he was checking his traps. Smith and Ogden competed to get ahead of each other to be the first to trap beaver. On April 23, the Blackfeet ran off twenty horses belonging to Old Pierre and two others. One horse was recovered.[28]

Both brigades reached Cache Valley in late April, where they separated.[29] By mid-May, Jedediah Smith and John Weber had found each other. The Americans exchanged information on what had happened to each brigade while apart.

MAP
of the
UNITED STATES
TERRITORY OF OREGON
West of the Rocky Mountains,
Exhibiting the various Trading Depots or Forts occupied by the British Hudson Bay Company, connected with the Western and northwestern Fur Trade.
Compiled in the Bureau of Topographical Engineers, from the latest authorities, under the direction of Col. J.J. Abert, by
Wash: Hood.
1838.
M.H. Stansbury del.
The prolongation of the 49th parallel of latitude from the Rocky Mountains to the Pacific has been assumed as the Northern Boundary of the U.States possessions on the N.W. coast, in consequence of the following extract from the Hon. H. Clay's letter to Mr Gallatin dated June 19th 1826. (see Doc 199. 20th Cong 1 sess Ho: of R.) "You are then authorised to propose the annulment of the third article of the Convention of 1818, and the extension of the line on the parallel of 49, from the eastern side of the Stony Mountains, where it now terminates, to the Pacific Ocean as the permanent boundary between the territories of the two powers in that quarter. This is our ultimatum and so you may announce it"
The Posts of the British Hudson's Bay Company are marked thus. ○
PACIFIC OCEAN
NEW CALEDONIA
BRITISH TERRITORY
TERRITORY OF OREGON
NEW GEORGIA
NEW ALBION
NEW HANOVER
NEW CORNWALL
CALIFORNIA
MEXICO
Southern Boundary 1819
Longitude West from Greenwich
125°
120°
115°
50°
45°
40°
Ft. Simpson
Ft. St. James
Frasers Ft.
Babine Ft.
Ft. George
Ft. Alexandria
Ft. Mc Laughlin
Ft. Langley
Thompsons Ft.
Ft. Okanagan
Ft. Colville
Ft. Nasqually
Ft. Nezperces
Ft. Vancouver
Ft. Astoria or Clatsop
Columbia R.
Ft. Umqua
Lesser Slave Fort
Ft. Assineboins
Dixons Entrance
Str. of Juan de Fuca
Puget Sd.
Quadra & Vancouvers I.
Nootka Sd.
Rocky Mountains
Mt. Hood
Mt. St. Helens
Mt. Shasty
Mt. Mc Laughlin
Saptin or Lewis or Gt. Snake R.
Thompsons Rapids
Bellingham B.
Johnstone Str.
Wakash Nation
Clamet L.
New Years Lake
Swamp Lakes and Islands. Tide said to rise high in this Swamp Water Fresh.
Pt. Reyes
Ross (Russian Estab.)
Pt. St. Francisco
S. Carlos de Monterey

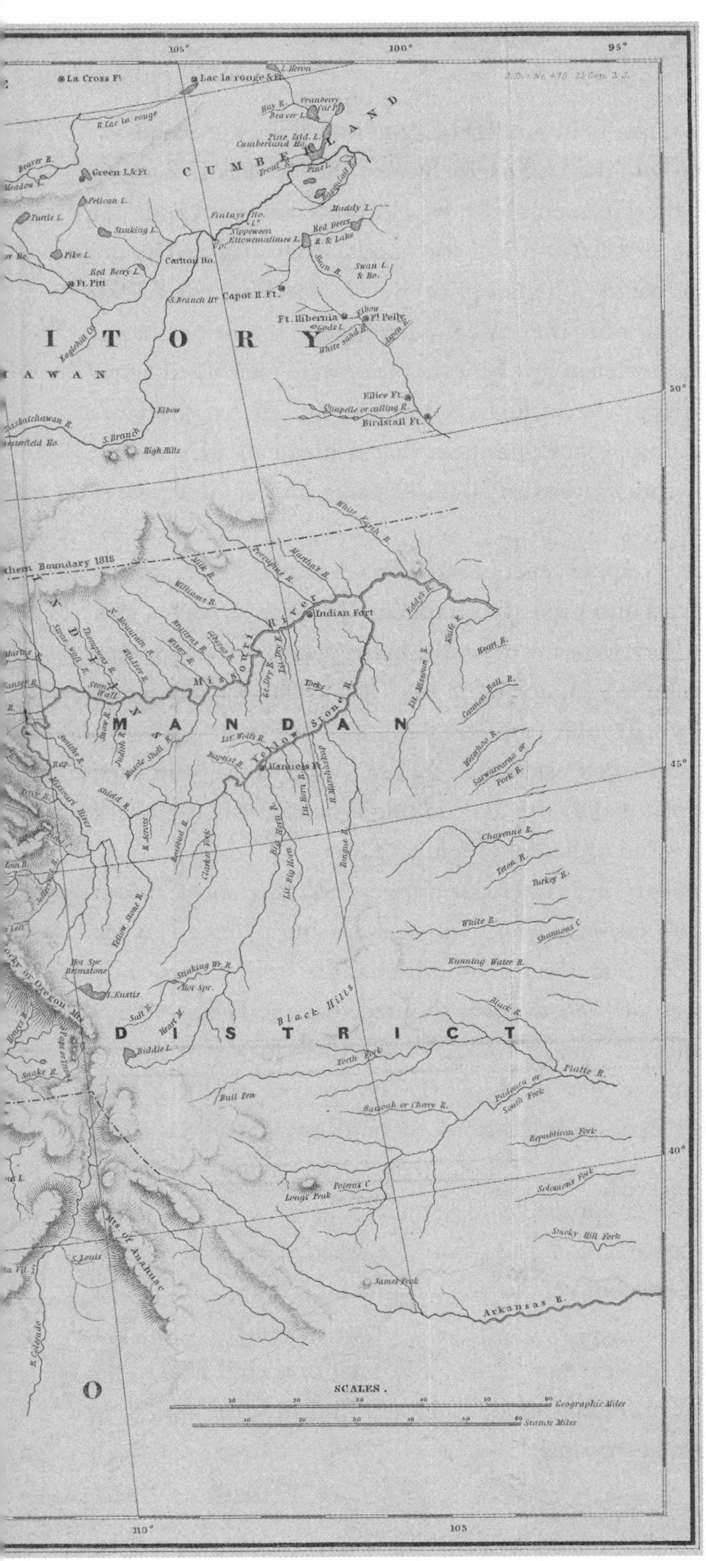

This 1838 map of Oregon Territory and British Territory, by Washington Hood for the U.S. Bureau of Topographical Engineers, shows Hudson's Bay Company's forts and trading posts scattered from Saskatchewan and the Yellowstone River to the Pacific Coast. MAP BY WASHINGTON HOOD, U.S. TOPOGRAPHICAL ENGINEERS, COURTESY OF THE BEINECKE RARE BOOK AND MANUSCRIPT LIBRARY, YALE UNIVERSITY, 80 1838B.

Smith, Sublette, and other trappers in Smith's brigade told Weber's men about Flathead Post and their time with the Snake Expedition. They spoke of Hudson's Bay's shabby treatment of the Freemen and how Hudson's Bay paid little for beaver pelts while charging expensive prices for goods. They believed if the Freemen learned Ashley was paying a higher price, they would leave the British and come over to the American side. They said Ogden hoisted the British flag at each camp. This made Weber's men angry, believing they were on United States soil. Weber's men planned to pay the Snake Expedition a visit. Zachariah Ham's brigade arrived at Weber's camp. Ham told them that Ashley had arrived with provisions and planned to rendezvous with all his brigades on the Green River around July 10.[30]

Two of Etienne Provost's trappers encountered Snake Expedition trappers, and on May 23, 1825, Provost and his fifteen trappers paid Peter Ogden a visit at his Weber River camp. They were not friendly, believing the Hudson's Bay men had provoked the Shoshone to attack them the previous fall. Ogden wrote that Provost and his men "would most willingly shoot us if they dared."[31]

After leaving Ogden's camp, Provost located Weber's camp where he learned of Ashley's rendezvous. He planned to attend, thinking it would be better to sell his beaver pelts to Ashley instead of hauling them to Taos.[32]

Later that same day, twenty-five American trappers carrying an American flag and fourteen of Ogden's trappers who had gone missing marched to the Snake Expedition camp. Stopping about a hundred yards from camp, their leader, Johnson Gardner, one of Weber's men, shouted that the Hudson's Bay men were on American soil and they were free to sell their furs to them for $3.50 a pound, which was more than Hudson's Bay was paying, and that they could buy goods far cheaper than from Hudson's Bay, and anyone who wanted to join them was welcome.[33]

The next morning, Gardner approached Ogden's lodge to meet with him. "Do you know in whose country you are?" Gardner asked. Ogden answered he did not know because it had not yet been determined. Gardner said he was wrong, that it belonged to the United States and Ogden needed to leave at once. Ogden said he would not leave until his government ordered him to do so. "Remain at your peril!" Gardner responded and left. In reality, the land they were on belonged to Mexico at the time.[34]

Twenty-nine Iroquois and other Freemen left Ogden and joined the Americans, bringing their families, horses, and beaver pelts. Ogden led what was left of his brigade back to Snake River country.[35]

During these events, Jim Bridger was with Gardner's party. Years later he remembered how the trappers "drove the Hudson Bay Company from American soil."[36]

By the end of June 1825, Ashley's brigades, Provost's trappers, and the Freemen with their families gathered at the spot Ashley had marked on the Green River near Henry's Fork. Jim Bridger was one of roughly 120 men who amused themselves by hunting, fishing, competing in target shooting, and racing.[37]

They moved to a better site twenty miles up Henry's Fork to a broad valley where, on July 1, Ashley began buying furs and selling trade goods. He bought beaver pelts ranging from $2 to $5 per pound depending on their quality. By the end of the day, he had acquired 8,829 pounds of beaver pelts. He sold gunpowder, lead, knives, blankets, coffee, sugar, tobacco, and other goods. One item he did not have that the trappers wanted was alcohol. Ashley would be taking the beaver packs down the Missouri River to St. Louis and then return overland the next year to resupply the trappers. He believed this was a good way to do business, and many of the trappers, including Provost and the Freemen, agreed. The Freemen gave Ashley orders for goods. Old Pierre Tevanitagon asked for ribbons, bells, beads, needles, combs, and other items for the women.[38]

Since Andrew Henry had retired from the partnership, Ashley needed a new, trustworthy partner who could transport the trade goods to the mountains, buy the beaver pelts, then bring them back to St. Louis. He selected Jedediah Smith.[39]

Ashley wasted no time preparing to return to St. Louis. He planned to follow the Bighorn River to the Yellowstone, then to the Missouri, and on to St. Louis. Ashley set out on July 2 with fifty men, including Jim Bridger. Twenty-five men were to accompany him with the packs down the waterways and the other twenty-five would remain trapping and trading. Thirty men headed directly toward the Bighorn River with beaver packs from the rendezvous, while Ashley took twenty men to dig up a cache of forty-five packs a few miles east of the direct route to the Bighorn. It's not known which party Jim Bridger was with.[40]

After recovering the packs, Ashley and his men began their ride to rejoin the advance party. They could not catch up and made camp for the night. At daybreak, sixty Blackfeet raiders attacked, wounding one man and running off all but two of Ashley's horses. They now had no means to transport their packs. Ashley sent an express rider to the advance party informing them of his predicament and to send back horses. Members of the advance party arrived with horses two days later. Ashley and his men proceeded ten miles before making camp for the night. Around midnight, they were attacked by a Crow raiding party. Ashley's men repelled the attack, killing one raider and wounding another. The next day, they caught up with the advance party.[41]

Ashley's recombined party proceeded north, following the Bighorn River parallel to and west of the Bighorn Mountains. When they reached Bighorn Canyon, Ashley wanted to know if they could float their beaver packs down the river instead of taking the difficult trail over the rugged terrain. The Crow said a spirit lived in the canyon ready to devour anyone who approached. Jim Bridger volunteered to learn if the river was passable. The men built him a raft and he shoved off down the river through the canyon. Steep walls rose over 1,000 feet on both sides as his raft was swept into turbulent rapids and whirlpools. After traveling downriver roughly forty miles, he walked back to Ashley, reporting the river was not suitable to float the packs. Years later, in 1859, Bridger described his descent of the Bighorn Canyon to Captain William F. Raynolds, who wrote, "[Bridger's] description of the grandeur of the scenery along its banks are glowing and remarkable."[42]

The men crossed over what would be named Bad Pass to the west of the canyon. Once downriver of the canyon, they built bull boats and floated down to the Yellowstone River. At some point after building the bull boats, Ashley parted from those of his men who remained to continue the hunt for beaver. They were led by Bill Sublette, and Jim Bridger was one of the twenty-five men remaining behind.[43]

Jedediah Smith accompanied Ashley to St. Louis where they would acquire more goods, and Smith would bring them west overland to the mountains. John Weber finished leading trapping brigades and returned. Ashley's party left August 7, 1825. They made good time on the Yellowstone, reaching the confluence with the Missouri on August 19. There, they made contact with a military

Bull boats were made of hide stretched over a stick frame and bound with sinew. Their primary advantage was that they could be assembled from immediately available materials. PHOTOGRAPH COURTESY OF THE BEINECKE RARE BOOK AND MANUSCRIPT LIBRARY, YALE UNIVERSITY, WA PHOTOS 49.

expedition from Fort Atkinson led by General Henry Atkinson and Indian agent Major Benjamin O'Fallon, who had traveled to the Upper Missouri making treaties with tribes. Atkinson offered to transport Ashley, his men, and his 100 beaver packs by boat to Council Bluff, which he accepted. Ashley had a boat at Council Bluff, and after transferring men and packs, they headed down the Missouri, arriving at St. Louis on October 4, 1825. The St. Louis newspapers estimated Ashley's beaver packs were worth up to $50,000. Ashley and Smith immediately began planning Smith's overland return to the mountains with merchandise for the 1826 rendezvous. On October 30, Jedediah Smith left St. Louis, leading seventy men with 160 mules and horses, hauling $20,000 of goods destined for the Rocky Mountains. It would be a long, hard winter before Smith and his men reached their destination.[44]

---

[1] Robertson, *Struggle,* 134. Frost, "Ashley," 286.

[2] Frost, "Ashley," 286.

[3] DeMallie, ed., *Plains,* Vol. 13, Part 2, 695–696.

[4] Frost, "Ashley," 170, 194, 286. Robertson, *Struggle,* 134. Chittenden, *Fur Trade,* 271. Morgan, *Smith,* 101.

[5] Leroy Hafen, "Etienne Provost, Mountain Man and Utah Pioneer," *Utah Historical Quarterly,* Vol. 36, Number 2, 1968, 100–101, https://issuu.com/utah10/docs/uhq_volume36_1968_number2. Chittenden, *Fur Trade,* Vol. 1, 271. Morgan, *Smith,* 87, 145–146. Dodge, *Bridger,* 6–7. Utley, *Life,* 69–70, 72. Frost, "Ashley," 247.

[6] Frost, "Ashley," 194–195, 219.

[7] Utley, *Life,* 58–59.

[8] Morgan, *Smith,* 19–23.

[9] Ibid, 24–25.

[10] Frost, "Ashley," 197. Utley, *Life,* 59, 60–61, Chittenden, *Fur Trade,* Vol. 2, 475. Morgan, *Smith,* 92–93.

[11] Frost, "Ashley," 290.

[12] Ibid, 199–200, 220.

[13] Robertson, *Struggle,* 134–135. Frost, "Ashley," 292.

[14] Utley, *Life,* 61–62. Frost, "Ashley," 204. Hassselstrom, *Clyman,* 31–35, 38–39.

[15] Utley, *Life,* 62. Robertson, *Struggle,* 63.

[16] "Letter From William H. Ashley to Gen. Henry Atkinson," William H. Ashley's 1825 Rocky Mountain Papers, Library of Western Fur Trade Historical Source Documents. Accessed June 11, 2023. https://user.xmission.com/~drudy/mtman/html/ashnar.html. Utley, *Life,* 62, 329 n16. Hassselstrom, *Clyman,* 43. Frost, "Ashley," 200, 203.

[17] Enzler, *Bridger,* 33.

[18] This number includes eight of Provost's trappers mentioned in the next paragraph.

[19] Warren D'Azevedo, ed., *Handbook of North American Indians: Great Basin,* Vol. 11 (Washington, D.C.: Smithsonian Institution, 1986), 308–309, 319, 321. Enzler, *Bridger,* 33. Morgan, ed., *Ashley,* 146.

[20] Utley, *Life,* 72, 331 n7.

[21] J. Cecil Alter, *Jim Bridger* (Norman, OK: University of Oklahoma Press, 1950), 59–60. Enzler, *Bridger,* 35.

[22] LeRoy Hafen, ed., *Mountain Men and Fur Traders of the Far West* (Lincoln, NE: University of Nebraska Press, 1965), 254. Enzler, *Bridger,* 35. Utley, *Life,* 73, 131 n10. Provost could have been the first white man to see the Great Salt Lake from a distance. Utley, *Life,* 72.

[23] Morgan, ed., *Ashley,* 101, 105–106. Hafen, ed., *Mountain Men,* 84. Utley, *Life,* 78.

[24] Morgan, ed., *Ashley,* 106–107, 269. Utley, *Life,* 78–79.

[25] Newman, *Company,* 276, 278. Utley, *Life,* 35. Robertson, *Struggle,* 108.

[26] Morgan, *Smith,* 128–130. Utley, *Life,* 66. Robertson, *Struggle,* 109–110.

[27] Morgan, *Smith,* 134. Newman, *Company,* Vol. 2, 275.

[28] Morgan, *Smith,* 131, 134, 136, 140. Robertson, *Struggle,* 110–111.

[29] Originally named Willow Valley.

[30] Robertson, *Struggle,* 112. Utley, *Life,* 75, 77–79.

[31] Utley, *Life,* 73, 75. Morgan, *Smith,* 148.

[32] Utley, *Life,* 79.

[33] Utley, *Life,* 76. Morgan, *Smith,* 148–149.

[34] Utley, *Life,* 76. Morgan, *Smith,* 149. Newman, *Company,* Vol. 2, 282.

[35] Morgan, *Smith,* 150. Hafen, ed., *Mountain Men,* 86.
[36] Enzler, *Bridger,* 37.
[37] Utley, *Life,* 80–81. Morgan, *Smith,* 170.
[38] Hafen, ed., *Mountain Men,* 85–86, 97. Utley, *Life,* 81–82. Morgan, *Smith,* 172.
[39] Morgan, *Smith,* 173.
[40] Morgan, ed., *Ashley,* 129.
[41] Ibid, 129–130.
[42] Morgan, ed., *Ashley,* 296 n247, 296–297 n248. Enzler, *Bridger,* 42–43.
[43] Morgan, ed., *Ashley,* 130. Enzler, *Bridger,* 43.
[44] Morgan, ed., *Ashley,* 130–131, 136–139, 298 n260. Enzler, *Bridger,* 43. Utley, *Life,* 83.

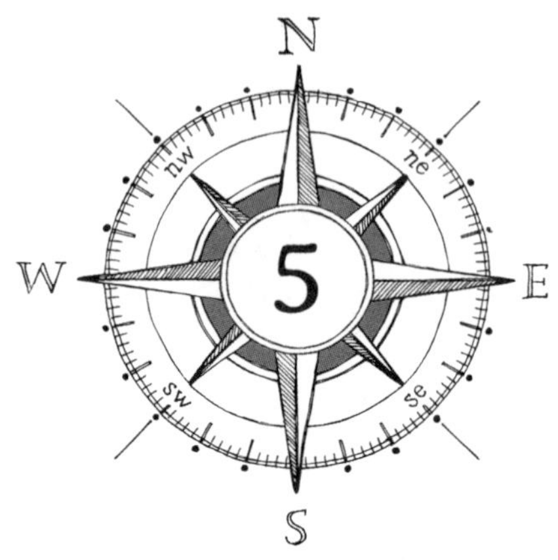

Trapper
1825–1830

When William Ashley and half his men paddled down the Bighorn River, on August 7, 1825, they left standing on the riverbank twenty-five men who would continue to trap and trade for beaver in the mountains. These men were called mountaineers, and twenty-one-year-old Jim Bridger had become one of the best.

Bridger stood straight. At six feet tall, he was muscular without an ounce of fat. His complexion was light olive and his hair brown. He had high cheekbones and a hooked nose. His eyes were hazel, and he had a mild, thoughtful look about him.[1]

He loved the waterways, mountains, and valleys of the West, and he enjoyed exploring them. He studied all aspects of the topography, the streams, rivers, lakes, and ponds. He knew how they changed with the seasons and how to negotiate them with those changes, what mountain passes could be crossed and when, where streams could be forded best and at what times. Bridger studied the animals and their habits. He observed the diverse forms of vegetation and where they grew. He admired and learned from the many tribes, respecting and adopting aspects of their cultures while perfecting his sign language skills and learning to speak their languages.[2]

He was self-reliant with a strong character. He was supportive of others and kind, especially to women and children, and he was welcoming and generous.

He liked to talk and was a master of tall tales. He told of a mountain of glass and of "peetrified" trees in which sat "peetrified" birds singing "peetrified" songs. David Brown would later write about Bridger, ". . . his bravery was unquestionable, his horsemanship equally so, and as to his skill with a rifle, it will scarcely be doubted. . . ." Bridger would have continued his gunsmithing skills, repairing the guns, traps, and other equipment of fellow mountaineers and Indians. Jedediah Smith nicknamed Bridger "Old Gabriel," shortened to "Old Gabe" or "Gabe," because he spoke with authority as the angel Gabriel spoke with God's authority in the Bible.[3]

Bridger would have carried a black powder muzzle-loading rifle, a powder horn and bullet pouch slung across his chest, and a butcher knife and pistol in his belt. He carried what mountaineers called a "possibles" sack containing flint and steel for fire-making, a pipe and tobacco, and other small paraphernalia. After two and a half years away from civilization, Bridger's clothes would have worn out, and he would be wearing Indian-made buckskin shirt, pants, and moccasins. His coat would have been made from a blanket or buffalo robe. If his original slouch hat was gone, his headgear would have been of fur or a wool cap.[4]

A horse was a necessity for Bridger and for each man in the brigade. Care and protection of the horses were of the highest importance. Each horse would be bridled and saddled and had one or two apishamores, or saddle blankets. Fastened to the saddle was a sack holding up to six beaver traps, a castoreum container, a hatchet slung from the pommel, and other accoutrements.[5]

Leaving the Bighorn River, Bill Sublette led the brigade westward for the 1825 fall beaver hunt. Riding toward the Bear River, the brigade separated into smaller trapping parties, then reunited in Cache Valley as they had the previous year. Jim Beckwourth, the son of a White Missouri planter and a Black slave, and two companions arrived with dispatches for Sublette from William Ashley. Mid-December, icy winds and heavy snowfall forced the brigade to move south to the Great Salt Lake where the weather was more moderate and large buffalo herds grazed. They established a camp at the mouth of the Weber River and another at the mouth of the Bear River. Freemen with their families joined them. Beckwourth related that, one stormy night, a Bannock raiding party ran off eighty horses.[7]

The Bannock lived in lodges made of buffalo hides, which they also used for robes and blankets. WOOD ENGRAVING FROM A PHOTOGRAPH BY WILLIAM HENRY JACKSON, COURTESY OF THE LIBRARY OF CONGRESS, LC-USZ62-106050.

The Bannock occupied the southern half of modern-day Idaho. They allied with the Northern Shoshone and banded together in common villages. Some bands acquired horses. Buffalo were a major source of food for these bands, and they used the hides to cover their teepees. The Bannock fished for salmon and gathered roots. Hunters wearing pronghorn skins would creep close to pronghorn to shoot them with arrows. Each band was small and membership fluid. Individuals and families would come and go as they saw fit. A band's chief was selected on merit, and a council advised him.[8]

Horses were a great advantage to anyone—Indian or White—who lived in the Rocky Mountain West. They provided transportation for people and supplies and were a major asset in hunting and in battle. As important as horses were for the Bannock, they were equally essential to the mountaineers for all aspects of their lives: discovering new areas to trap beaver; transporting supplies, trade goods, and beaver pelts; hunting buffalo and other game; and aiding in defense. The mountaineers had to recover their stolen horses from the Bannock.

Tom Fitzpatrick and Jim Bridger led forty men on foot following the stolen horses' hoofprints in the snow. After five days, they caught up with the raiders. They could see their horses mingled in with the Bannock's horse herd. Beckwourth, known to exaggerate, said there were more than 300 Bannock in camp. Fitzpatrick and Bridger divided the men into two groups. Fitzpatrick and his men would charge the camp, while Bridger's men would stampede the horses. The plan worked. They ran off more than 200 head of horses and killed six Bannock, and the Bannock injured no mountaineers. The Bannock reacted swiftly, recapturing many of their horses. The mountaineers recovered all their horses in addition to forty head of Bannock horses. When they returned to camp, the women and the men left behind greeted them "with the liveliest demonstrations."[9]

The returning mountaineers were surprised to find many Shoshone lodges surrounding their encampment. This was the Shoshone's preferred winter location. They were friendly, frequently inviting the mountaineers to a very large communal lodge where they performed religious ceremonies and gave speeches.[10] Over the winter, Jim Bridger would have continued to form friendships with the Shoshone and learn from them.

With the arrival of spring, the mountaineers returned to Cache Valley to hunt beaver. The Freemen with their families and many Shoshone joined them. By now, several mountaineers had married Indian women for companionship and to help process their furs.[11]

The brigade had acquired seventy-five beaver packs and dug caches to hide them. One cache collapsed, killing two Canadians. The Shoshone insisted on caring for the bodies in their traditional way. They were wrapped in blankets, secured by thongs, hoisted off the ground, and suspended in trees.[12]

One mountaineer shot at a pronghorn. When he reached what he thought was the dead animal, it turned out to be a Shoshone hunter in disguise meant to lure pronghorn close enough to kill. When Fitzpatrick told the chief what had happened, the chief said the man was a fool to use the disguise so close to camp, knowing that mountaineers shot at everything they saw. The chief asked for red cloth to wrap the body. The mountaineers gave him a scarlet blanket, and that was the end of the incident.[13]

Bill Sublette and David Jackson left Cache Valley leading a brigade that included Jim Bridger. Their goal was to hunt beaver in the arid region northwest of the Great Salt Lake. Jackson, whom the men called Davey, was thirty-eight years old, older than most mountaineers. He was quiet but strong in his convictions. It was said he had discovered the large valley on the east side of the Grand Tetons (Jackson Hole). Jedediah Smith later drew a map of the area the brigade explored based on information provided by Sublette and Jackson. One watercourse he named Bridger's Fork with a note: "This country is extremely rocky & rough, the river running through cleft rocks." The map showed Bridger's Fork flowing northwest toward the Owyhee River in present-day Idaho.[14]

One of William Ashley's goals for his mountaineers was to find the elusive Rio San Buenaventura, a great river said to flow westward from the Rocky Mountains all the way to San Francisco Bay. He believed it would provide an easy wagon route to California. He also believed the great water body Bridger had found could be the Buenaventura's source. Sublette sent four men in a bull boat to attempt to find the lake's outlet. After twenty-four days of paddling, they did not find one. Ashley did not give up on the idea that the river must be there.[15]

Sublette and Jackson's brigade was still out on its beaver hunt, while other mountaineers and Indian friends waited for the trade caravan to reach Cache Valley. In early May, Jedediah Smith, accompanied by Moses "Black" Harris, rode into the rendezvous site and informed the attendees that William Ashley's caravan would soon arrive. Up to seventy-five mountaineers rode out to escort it to the encampment.[16]

As related in the previous chapter, Jedediah Smith had left St. Louis on October 30, 1825, leading seventy men with 160 mules and horses, hauling $20,000 of goods. Their progress was slow, and they spent the winter with the Pawnee on the Republican Fork of the Kansas River. One third of their mules died; Smith sent word to Ashley that he needed more animals. Ashley gathered livestock and supplies, then decided to lead the twenty-five-member relief party, leaving St. Louis on March 8, 1826. He caught up with Smith at Grand Island on the Platte River in April. From there he sent Smith and Harris ahead to ensure the mountaineers would rendezvous at Cache Valley. Ashley followed the North Platte to the Sweetwater, then crossed South Pass, reaching Cache Valley on May 25.[17]

Ashley and Smith's caravan stayed in Cache Valley a few weeks, exchanging goods for the mountaineers' and Indians' beaver pelts. There were plenty of pelts. Bill Sublette and David Jackson's brigade was still away on their beaver hunt.[18]

Jim Beckwourth described the rendezvous festivities:

> the arrival of such a vast amount of luxuries from the East did not pass off without a general celebration. Mirth, songs, dancing, shouting, trading, running, jumping, singing, racing, target shooting, yarns, frolic, with all sorts of extravagances that white men or Indians could invent, were freely indulged in. The unpacking of the medicine water [whiskey] contributed not a little to the heightening of our festivities.[19]

Dan Potts wrote, "We celebrated the Fourth of July, by firing three rounds of small arms, and partook of a most excellent dinner, after which a number of political toasts were drank."[20]

At the rendezvous' end, Ashley told his men he was leaving the fur trade business. He thanked them for their efforts, their friendship, and their willingness to stand with him during difficult times. They were always welcome to stop by his St. Louis home.[21]

Ashley and Smith led their party west and found Sublette and Jackson's brigade on the Bear River. Ashley wanted to be finished with direct involvement in procuring beaver pelts. He sold his interest in the company to Jedediah Smith, Bill Sublette, and David Jackson. As part of the deal, the three took over the contracts with forty-two "hunters" hired by Ashley & Smith. After Ashley paid Smith $5,000 for his share of the partnership, the three men still owed Ashley $11,000 for the merchandise he was leaving them. They agreed to pay him in beaver fur at $3 per pound.[22]

The new company would be known as Smith, Jackson & Sublette. Many shortened the name to SJS. Ashley would still provide goods to the new firm. On July 18, 1826, he signed an agreement with the new partners to be their supplier, promising not to furnish merchandise to any other firm in the mountains "other than those who may be in his immediate service." The agreement stated that Ashley's men would bring the merchandise and rendezvous at Bear Lake on July 1, 1827.[23]

A Smith, Jackson, & Sublette supply caravan leaves St. Louis in 1830, headed for the rendezvous in the Rockies. ILLUSTRATION COURTESY OF THE NATIONAL PARK SERVICE.

Ashley left the mountains on July 19, traveling overland with fifty men and 100 horses and mules transporting 125 beaver packs. In late September, they arrived in St. Louis where the fur was valued at $60,000.[24]

With Ashley's departure, it was time for Jim Bridger and the mountaineers to get back to work. Smith, Sublette, and Jackson divided the men into two brigades. On August 15, 1826, Jedediah Smith led sixteen men to the southwest, looking for beaver and the Rio San Buenaventura they hoped would lead them to California.[25]

Bill Sublette and David Jackson led their brigade north into Blackfeet territory. It comprised twenty-six SJS men, including Jim Bridger, and Freemen for a total of roughly 100 trappers, not including wives and children.[26] At twenty-two years old, with four years of experience in the mountains and the fur trade, Bridger had risen to become one of the lieutenants capable of leading a brigade as well as an accomplished scout.[27]

The brigade traded with Shoshone, Crow, Sioux, and Flathead bands while trapping their own beaver. Once they entered Blackfeet territory, the Blackfeet harassed them daily. Following Henry's Fork upstream to the northeast, they turned east, entering Pierre's Hole (in present-day Idaho), named after Old Pierre Tevanitagon. They traversed the Teton Range from west to east into Jackson Hole in present-day Wyoming. The brigade followed the Snake River north, upriver, exploring and trapping.[28]

As Jim Bridger was out exploring for beaver sign, he followed a stream toward its headwaters in what is today the Bridger-Teton National Forest. He came to where the stream divided in two forming a "Y." Here, one branch of the Y flowed toward the Pacific Ocean, and the other branch flowed toward the Atlantic. Bridger claimed that a trout could swim across the Continental Divide from the Pacific side to the Atlantic and back. Many did not believe him. What Bridger had found was indeed such a phenomenon, today known as the Parting of the Waters at Two Ocean Creek atop Two Ocean Pass.[29]

The brigade entered a high, forested plateau in what is today Yellowstone National Park. There they came upon a large lake they named Sublette Lake, later renamed Yellowstone Lake. They encountered many thermal wonders: geysers; colorful, hot, mud paint pots; and boiling springs.[30]

The headwaters plateau of the Snake and Yellowstone Rivers held a wonderland of hot springs, fumaroles, and geysers, such as Castle Geyser shown in this 1871 image. PHOTOGRAPH BY WILLIAM HENRY JACKSON, COURTESY OF THE LIBRARY OF CONGRESS, LC-DIG-PPMSCA-68712.

Jim Bridger most likely discovered Bridger Lake in the headwaters of the Yellowstone River. Captain John Gunnison later wrote of Bridger's description of the Yellowstone geothermal area:

> A picture most romantic and enticing. . . . A lake sixty miles long, cold and pellucid. . . . The river issues from the lake, and for fifteen miles roars through the perpendicular canyons. . . . Waterfalls are sparkling, leaping and thundering down the precipices, and collect in the pools below. . . .
>
> On the west side . . . the ground resounds to the tread of the horses. Geysers spout up seventy feet, with a terrible hissing noise, at regular intervals. In this section are the great springs, so hot that meat is readily cooked in them; and as they descend on the successive terraces, afford at length delightful baths.[31]

The brigade followed the Yellowstone River northward from its outlet at Yellowstone Lake, continuing to acquire beaver pelts. One day, Bridger was out ahead, following bear tracks, when he saw smoke in the distance. Reporting it to Sublette, the two of them and Robert Campbell raced their horses toward the smoke to see if it was coming from a Blackfeet camp. When they reached the source of the smoke, they found it was a smoldering fire at a camp abandoned weeks before. The mountaineers jokingly called it "the battle of the burned logs."[32]

Winter approached as Sublette led the brigade northwest from the Yellowstone then arced south to Cache Valley and onto the Weber River where they encamped with the Shoshone for the winter.[33]

Jim Beckwourth later claimed that, as the brigade headed toward its winter encampment, Bannock warriors killed a Shoshone and wounded two trappers. Sublette selected Jim Bridger to lead a revenge attack where Beckwourth said the trappers killed 488 Bannock.[34] Other than Beckwourth's account, there's no record of this incident. Given the alleged scope of Bannock losses, it's unlikely that Sublette or others would have neglected to mention it. Then again, Beckwourth was known to exaggerate numbers and stretch the truth.

According to SJS's agreement with Ashley, they needed to send a supply and merchandise order to Ashley in St. Louis by March 1, 1827, or the agreement

The size and grandeur of this high-elevation lake amazed the trappers, who called it Sublette Lake. We know it today as Yellowstone Lake. 1871 PHOTOGRAPH BY WILLIAM HENRY JACKSON, COURTESY OF THE U.S. GEOGRAPHICAL SURVEY, WH0104C.

was void. Sublette would take the order himself, accompanied by Black Harris. Strapping on snowshoes and taking a dog to carry their supplies, they left the encampment January 1, 1827.[35]

By mid-February 1827, mild weather enticed Dan Potts and five others to leave the Weber River camp and travel south to Utah Lake to explore the countryside. Jim Bridger may have been part of this group as his description of the area and experiences were similar to Potts', who wrote that a band of Ute stole two of their horses and shot arrows into four more. Bridger had a poor opinion of the Ute who lived around Utah Lake, telling Mormon leader Brigham Young in 1847, "If they catch a man alone they are sure to rob and abuse him, if they don't kill him."[36]

The Ute at Utah Lake were the Timpanogot. Their diet consisted of fish, deer, elk, pronghorn, grouse, and waterfowl, as well as seeds, fruit, and roots. They lived in conical structures made of brush, hides, and bullrushes. They gathered in small bands, each led by a chief who was advised by a council. The Ute and Shoshone were enemies.[37]

Pictured here in 1871, Bear Lake was a favored meeting place and rendezvous site. PHOTOGRAPH BY WILLIAM HENRY JACKSON, COURTESY OF THE THE U.S. GEOGRAPHICAL SURVEY, JWH00124.

As winter relented, hoping to acquire more beaver pelts to trade at the July 1827 rendezvous, David Jackson led the brigade to the Green River on a spring beaver hunt.[38]

The Ashley supply caravan arrived at the south shore of Bear Lake in June. Although there is little information about the rendezvous, it must have been similar to other rendezvous. James Brufee, Ashley's business agent, and Hiram Scott, captain of the caravan, led sixty men to the rendezvous. Bill Sublette and his fourteen-year-old brother, Pinckney, who was in poor health, accompanied them. Bill thought life in the mountains would be just the thing for Pinckney. One hundred mules and twenty-two horses transported $22,000 in merchandise, including guns, gunpowder, lead, knives, traps, blankets, cloth, ribbon, vermillion, beads, brass nails, sugar, coffee, tobacco, and liquor. They also brought a four-pounder cannon mounted on a carriage drawn by two mules—the first wheeled vehicle to cross South Pass.[39]

Although the Ute and the Shoshone were enemies, the Ute came to the rendezvous. The mountaineers held a council with Ute and Shoshone leaders and negotiated peace between the two warring tribes. Peace was beneficial to all parties involved. News of the brokered peace eventually made its way to Mexico City, where the government protested to the American ambassador Joel Poinsett that the mountaineers had trespassed on Mexican territory.[40]

Several days before Dan Potts and his party (possibly including Jim Bridger) arrived at the rendezvous, 120 Blackfeet warriors attacked, killing a Shoshone husband and wife. Shoshone and Ute warriors as well as five mountaineers led by Bill Sublette chased the Blackfeet to a tree-covered mountain where they made a stand holding off the rendezvousers. Before the Blackfeet escaped, they killed three Shoshone and wounded Samuel Tulloch in the wrist, causing his hand to wither. The rendezvousers discovered six Blackfeet bodies. The Shoshone appreciated Sublette's bravery during the fight and gave him a buffalo robe in appreciation.[41]

Jedediah Smith and two of his men, Robert Evans and Silas Goble, arrived on July 3, 1827. Smith wrote, "My arrival caused a considerable bustle in camp, for myself and party had been given up for lost. A small Cannon brought up from St. Louis was loaded and fired for a salute."[42]

Back in August 1826, Smith led his sixteen-man brigade southwest, looking for beaver and the Rio San Buenaventura. They entered desert regions, and if it had not been for the Mojave tribe's hospitality, they might have perished. With half their horses lost and low on supplies, they crossed the Mojave Desert, climbed into the San Bernardino Mountains, then descended to California's San Bernardino Valley on November 26, 1826. Their reception was mixed. Father José Sánchez at San Gabriel Mission was hospitable. California governor José María de Echeandía was suspicious. After months of indecision, he let Smith's brigade go but told them they had to leave the same way they had come. Resupplied and with fresh horses, the brigade rode back the way they had come, but after crossing the San Bernardino Mountains, they turned north, heading up the San Joaquin Valley where they found plenty of beaver in the Sierra Nevada foothills. In May 1827, Smith tried to haul their 1,500 pounds of beaver furs to the rendezvous, but deep snow in the mountains made it impossible to cross with the furs. On May 20, 1827, Smith left his brigade encamped with the beaver packs on the Stanislaus River and, with two men, headed to the rendezvous, planning to return for the fall hunt. The three crossed the Sierra

Nevada over Ebbetts Pass and descended to Walker Lake. From there, they traveled across desolate country until, on June 27, they spied the Great Salt Lake in the distance, and from there they made their way to the Bear Lake rendezvous.[43]

The rendezvous was a success for SJS. They sold 125 packs—over 7,000 pounds—of beaver pelts at $3 per pound to Ashley's men. The beaver pelts were worth between $60,000 and $70,000 in St. Louis.[44]

By July 13, 1827, the rendezvous had ended. Leading eighteen men, Jedediah Smith headed west to rejoin his brigade in California. Bill Sublette and David Jackson joined Ashley's party returning to St. Louis. They needed to work out financial matters with William Ashley. The three partners left their clerk, Irishman Robert Campbell, in the mountains to handle business concerns.[45]

That fall, Campbell led a twenty-five-man brigade piloted by Jim Bridger on a beaver hunt to the Upper Missouri headwaters. The Blackfeet constantly harassed the trappers. Reaching Red Rock Creek near the headwaters of the Jefferson, the brigade camped near a Blackfeet encampment. Some of the mountaineers visited the Blackfeet, and Blackfeet, behaving suspiciously, entered the brigade camp. The next morning, as the brigade rode toward the Snake River, the Blackfeet followed and then fired on them. Old Pierre Tevanitagon was out too far. The Blackfeet killed him, then chopped up his body. A Flathead man was shot in the head, dying days later. The Blackfeet

Poor health led Robert Campbell to join in the fur trade in the Rocky Mountains, and he thrived as a brigade leader and businessman. PHOTOGRAPH COURTESY OF THE NATIONAL PARK SERVICE

stole one horse and 150 pounds of beaver fur. As another SJS brigade traveled from the Columbia River to the Great Salt Lake, four men left the main party to explore a few small streams. They never returned and were presumed dead.[46]

As the weather grew colder, Campbell and Bridger's brigade trapped their way through the Wasatch Mountains and returned to the Weber River. The mountaineers divided into two encampments, one on the Bear River and the other on the Weber River.[47]

Heavy snow and little game contributed to a rough winter. Adding to the mountaineers' misery, Sublette and Jackson should have returned with supplies, but heavy snow prevented them from reaching the brigades. Sublette and Jackson had met Ashley at Lexington, Missouri, back in September 1827. They sold Ashley 130 beaver packs, and he resupplied them with horses and mules and needed merchandise. They made it as far as the Wind River (probably near present-day Riverton), where they had to wait out the winter.[48]

Hudson's Bay Company man Peter Ogden and his sixty-trapper brigade encamped on the Portneuf River near its confluence with the Snake River (northwest of present-day Pocatello, Idaho). On December 24, 1827, SJS partisan Samuel Tulloch and five men with their beaver packs and merchandise loaded atop horses arrived at Ogden's encampment. On January 1, 1828, they attempted to leave for the SJS winter camp but couldn't get through the snow and returned. On January 20, 1828, Ogden wrote, "The Americans are starving on Bear River, according to report; no buffalo in that quarter; they are reduced to eat horses and dogs." Tulloch and his men made several attempts to leave, but deep snow and blizzard conditions forced them to return to the Hudson's Bay encampment.[49]

On February 16, Ogden recorded that Robert Campbell and two men arrived on dog sleds. The three men were in advance of the rest of the brigade piloted by Jim Bridger. Days later, Ogden wrote, ". . . they are strong enough in numbers." Ashley noted that Campbell had eighteen men in his brigade. Campbell's men stayed until February 23, after exchanging their dogs for horses. They planned to visit the Flathead tribe, and Ogden suspected they would be trapping at the Missouri's Three Forks.[50]

Contrary to the lore of the times, the Flatheads or Salish did not practice head shaping. The name Flathead, originating from other tribes, meant thin-headed or shaving the sides of their heads. They lived in modern-day western Montana and east-central Idaho. Acquiring horses around 1730 enabled the tribe to add buffalo as a major food source. They also hunted deer, pronghorn, elk, and other game, and added to their diet bitterroot, camas, and other plant foods. They used grass mats and hides to cover their teepees. The size of each band was fluid depending on the time of year and seasonal activity. Each band was led by a chief advised by a council. Their primary enemy was the Blackfeet. During the 1820s, Iroquois fur traders settled among the Flatheads and introduced them to Roman Catholicism.[51]

March 26, 1828, Samuel Tulloch and seven men left Ogden's camp on their trek to the Great Salt Lake camps. They were several days out and twenty miles from the Hudson's Bay camp when thirty to forty Blackfeet warriors attacked, killing three men, including Bill Sublette's younger brother, Pinckney. They stole forty-four horses, merchandise, and $4,000 of furs.[52]

Robert Campbell and Jim Bridger's brigade stayed with the Flatheads until it was time to leave for the June 1828 rendezvous at Bear Lake. Hudson's Bay traders with the Flatheads and the surrounding tribes all knew Campbell's brigade had amassed a large amount of furs.[53]

The brigade members, their wives, and children rode fast and hard. They were eighteen miles from Bear Lake's south shore, the rendezvous location, when 200 to 300 Blackfeet warriors appeared in pursuit. The warriors killed Campbell's cook, Lewis Boldue, as a running battle ensued. Women and children rode ahead as the men fought a rearguard action. The entire brigade, except for one child, made it to the protection of a willow grove. The Blackfeet lost four men, and a few mountaineers were wounded.[54]

After a four-hour fight, the mountaineers were running low on ammunition and were down to poor-quality gunpowder. Campbell and "a little Spaniard" mounted on swift horses raced through the Blackfeet and made it to the rendezvous encampment where they raised the alarm.[55] Sixty to seventy mountaineers and several hundred Shoshone warriors mounted their horses and rode toward the fight.[56]

A Flathead with the brigade, who spoke the Blackfeet language, shouted that the men at the rendezvous would soon arrive. The Blackfeet believed him and quickly left, taking $5,000 worth of beaver pelts, merchandise, and six horses.[57]

That night, the Freemen, women, and some of the mountaineers held a scalp dance. Two days later, the Shoshone held a scalp dance to honor the victory over the Blackfeet.[58]

In early June 1828, Bill Sublette and David Jackson arrived with the merchandise for the rendezvous.[59] Although there is no record, the usual festivities must have occurred.

This year, SJS had competition of sorts. Joshua Pilcher, who had been the Missouri Fur Company's field manager until the company failed in 1825, had formed a partnership with Lucien Fontenelle, William Vanderburgh, Charles Bent, and Andrew Drips to trap beaver and supply merchandise at the rendezvous. They arrived with forty-five men and pack animals hauling trade goods. They had met with difficulties. Crow had stolen most of their livestock, so they had to buy more horses from the Shoshone. They had cached their merchandise, and when they went to retrieve it, they found seeping water had ruined much of it. They were able to buy only sixteen to eighteen beaver packs.[60]

Although Jim Beckwourth embellished tales of his life, he was a skilled trapper and respected mountain man. PHOTOGRAPH COURTESY OF THE NATIONAL PARK SERVICE

SJS acquired seventy packs of beaver pelts and other furs estimated to be worth more than $35,000. Bill Sublette and his men transported the furs back to St. Louis where he remained for the winter of 1828 to 1829.[61]

In the fall of 1828, the SJS mountaineers split into brigades. Jim Bridger and Robert Campbell led a twelve-mountaineer brigade on a hunt in Crow territory, following the Powder, Tongue, and Bighorn Rivers.[62]

Jim Beckwourth, who was a brigade member, said Bridger was "as skillful a hunter as ever lived in the mountains." One evening, Beckwourth and Bridger rode away from the brigade to set their traps along a small stream. When they reached a fork in the stream, Bridger took one fork and Beckwourth the other. Beckwourth ran into a band of Crow who believed he was a long-lost member and insisted he remain with them (which he did for several years).[63]

During the winter of 1828 to 1829, Bridger and Campbell's brigade encamped with the Crow on the Wind River. Though living with the Crow, Beckwourth remained in contact with the brigade. On January 6, 1829, he signed a promissory note to SJS, witnessed by Campbell. The brigade conducted its spring beaver hunt in the upper watersheds of the Wind and Bighorn Rivers. Blackfeet killed four brigade members at Bad Pass on the Bighorn.[64]

On March 17, 1829, Bill Sublette left St. Louis for the mountains, leading fifty-four men hauling merchandise loaded on horses and mules. On July 1, they reached the rendezvous near the Popo Agie River and Wind River confluence. Neither of Sublette's partners, Jedediah Smith and David Jackson, had yet arrived.[65]

This was nineteen-year-old Joe Meek's first rendezvous. Years later, Frances Fuller Victor recorded Meek's reminiscences:

> The Summer rendezvous was always chosen in some valley where there was grass for the animals, and game for the camp. The plains along the Popo Agie, besides furnishing these necessary bounties, were bordered by picturesque mountain ranges, whose naked bluffs of red sandstone glowed in the morning and evening sun. . . . The waving grass of the plain, variegated with wild flowers . . . the grazing animals . . . the lodges of the Booshways, [SJS leaders] around which clustered the camp in motley garb and brilliant coloring; gay laughter, and the murmur of soft Indian voices, all made up a most spirited and enchanting picture, in which the eye of an artist could not fail to delight.[66]

Meek continued:

> But as the goods were opened the scene grew livelier. All were eager to purchase, most of the trappers to the full amount of their year's wages; and some of them, generally free trappers, went in debt to the company to a very considerable amount. . . .[67]

Robert Campbell, SJS's clerk, traded goods for 4,076 pounds of beaver pelts, a total of forty-five packs. After Bill Sublette ended the rendezvous around July 18, 1829, Campbell led the caravan hauling the beaver pelts back to St. Louis, and Sublette sent his brother, Milton, with a brigade to hunt beaver in the Bighorn Basin, while he and Jim Bridger led a brigade west toward Pierre's Hole to look for his partners.[68]

Jedediah Smith and one of his men, Arthur Black, had returned from the west, reaching Hudson's Bay's Flathead Post. The Hudson's Bay men informed Smith that David Jackson was in the area trapping and looking for him. Smith and Black found Jackson's brigade at the Flathead River above Flathead Lake in modern-day Montana. Together, they headed east to find Bill Sublette. On August 5, 1829, Smith and Jackson reunited with Sublette at Pierre's Hole.[69]

What had happened to Jedediah Smith and his brigade during the previous two years? On July 13, 1827, Smith led eighteen men from the Bear Lake rendezvous heading west to rejoin his brigade on California's Stanislaus River.[70]

Smith followed the same route he had taken in 1826, heading straight to the Mojave tribe who had helped on his first trip. They stayed three days with the Mojave, who acted friendly. On August 18, the brigade began crossing the Colorado River. Smith and half his men were on a raft out on the river. The rest of the men, two Indian women, their horses, and most of their supplies were on the bank waiting to cross. Suddenly, the Mojave attacked, killing the men on the riverbank and capturing the women, horses, and supplies. They attacked Smith and his remaining men, but the brigade repelled the attack and the Mojave left them alone.[71]

Smith and his men struggled across the Mojave Desert and traversed the San Bernardino Mountains into the San Bernardino Valley where they reoutfitted. Smith reached his brigade on the Stanislaus River on September 18, 1827. Father Duran at the San José mission accused Smith of claiming territory for the United States. Governor Echeandía had Smith arrested and taken to Monterey. Ship captains came to Smith's defense, and Echeandía eventually released him.[72]

Smith sold the brigade's furs to a ship captain, bought 315 horses, and he and twenty men continued their beaver hunt, heading north from San José on

December 30. Their plan was to reach Oregon's Willamette Valley, then head east. By mid-July 1828, the brigade had arrived at the north branch of the Umpqua River. They'd had no trouble with local tribes as they passed through their territories. Recently, they had been in contact with the Kelawatset.[73]

The morning of July 14, Smith and two men left to scout their route for that day. Smith left Harrison Rogers in charge, telling him not to allow Indians into camp. However, Rogers allowed a large number of Kelawatset to enter. Without warning, they attacked, killing everyone except Arthur Black who ran into the forest. When Smith and the others returned to camp, the Kelawatset fired at them, but they escaped.[74]

On August 10, Smith and his two men arrived at Hudson's Bay's Fort Vancouver on Oregon's Columbia River where they found Arthur Black. Hudson's Bay man Alexander McLeod led a party with Smith to recover Smith's furs and horses. After a three-month effort, they recovered some horses and a good amount of fur. George Simpson, Hudson's Bay governor, bought Smith's furs and recovered horses for $2,369.60.[75]

March 12, 1829, Smith and Black traveled with a Hudson's Bay party up the Columbia River to Fort Colville. From there, they traveled overland to Flathead Post where they learned David Jackson's brigade was at the Flathead River. After Smith reunited with Jackson, the brigade rode to Pierre's Hole where, on August 5, 1829, Smith and Jackson reunited with Bill Sublette.[76]

Jim Bridger considered Pierre's Hole (today's Teton Valley in Idaho) "the finest valley in the mountains." Joe Meek described the mountaineers' reunion: ". . . the trappers indulged in their noisy sports and rejoicing, ostensibly on account of the return of the long-absent Booshway."[77]

After the three partners' joyous reunion, they got down to business for the 1829 to 1830 season. Jackson's brigade would trap the Snake River country, while Smith and Sublette with Jim Bridger as pilot would take a large brigade into Blackfeet territory. After allowing their animals to rest and recover, and after preparing for the fall hunt, the SJS men divided into two brigades and left Pierre's Hole at the end of September 1829.[78]

Smith and Sublette's brigade with Bridger as pilot began their hunt by moving up the Henry's Fork of the Snake River. One morning, the Blackfeet attacked, wounding several mountaineers before they drove the warriors away.

They rode north to the Madison River headwaters where they trapped plenty of beaver but had to remain on guard as the Blackfeet continued to harass them.[79]

Joe Meek related a story that, one day, Jim Bridger was away from camp riding his horse when Blackfeet warriors ambushed him. His horse was shot and wounded, causing the horse to rear and buck. Bridger dropped his rifle, and a warrior snatched it. Bridger had to race away leaving his rifle behind. At a later camp, Bridger was inspecting the men's equipment. Checking the gun of a trapper named Mahoney, he found it very dirty.

"What would you do with a gun like that, if the Indians were to charge the camp?" Bridger asked.

"Be Jasus," Mahoney said. "I would throw it to them, and run the way ye did!"[80]

The weather grew cold that November when the brigade crossed the Madison Range to the Gallatin River headwaters, then crossed the Gallatin Range to the Yellowstone River. There the Blackfeet attacked, and Meek was separated from the brigade. He headed toward the Wind River where the brigade was going. After surviving frigid conditions for several days, two mountaineers sent out from the brigade found him.[81]

At the age of eighteen, Joe Meek signed on as a trapper with the Rocky Mountain Fur Company and spent twelve years hunting beaver. ENGRAVING BY JOHN C. BUTTRE, COURTESY OF THE BEINECKE RARE BOOK AND MANUSCRIPT LIBRARY, YALE UNIVERSITY, ZC74 870VIB.

As the brigade crossed the mountains to the Shoshone Branch of the Bighorn River, 100 horses and mules died in the deep snow. Reaching the Bighorn River, the brigade rode downriver and found Milton Sublette's forty-man brigade's encampment.[82]

After they cached their beaver pelts, a Crow war party approached. The mountaineers were apprehensive until the Crow made the sign of peace, then joined them in smoking the pipe of peace. The brigades traveled south to the Wind River where they encamped with Jackson's brigade just before Christmas.[83]

The reunited partners planned the spring beaver hunts and the 1830 rendezvous. SJS was barely making a profit. They still owed Ashley money, the price of goods and transportation costs continued to rise, and competition was on the increase. They needed to discover new beaver populations. The spring beaver hunt and summer rendezvous were critical to the company's survival.[84]

Just after Christmas, Bill Sublette and Black Harris left for St. Louis. This time they took a packtrain of dogs loaded with supplies.[85]

For the men staying in the mountains, there was not enough forage and not enough game to make it through the winter. On New Year's Day 1830, Smith and Jackson's combined brigades left the Wind River for the Powder River, 150 miles to the northeast. After two weeks of slogging through deep snow and bracing against bitter cold temperatures, they arrived at the Powder River where there was an abundance of cottonwood trees for the horses to eat the bark and plenty of buffalo to keep the people fed.[86]

By April 1830, it was time for the spring hunt. David Jackson's brigade headed for Shoshone territory, while Jim Bridger piloted Jedediah Smith's brigade into Blackfeet country where they trapped from the Tongue to the Bighorn River. When the brigade crossed the Bighorn's swollen Bovey's Fork, thirty horses carrying 300 traps were swept away. They rode through Pryor's Gap to the Yellowstone River, then crossed to the Musselshell and Judith Rivers on the Missouri. The Blackfeet constantly harassed them, stealing horses and traps. The brigade returned to Pryor's Gap then up the Bighorn River to the Wind River where they recovered the furs they had cached in December 1829.[87]

Samuel Tulloch led a party back down the Bighorn River to retrieve furs cached the previous fall. While digging out the cache, an overhanging cut bank collapsed, killing Frenchman Glaud Ponto and seriously injuring Joe Meek. The party still retrieved the furs, and Meek soon recovered.[88]

The 1830 rendezvous was held near the Popo Agie and Wind River confluence. Smith's brigade rode in with a large quantity of furs, and Jackson's brigade arrived with plenty of beaver pelts. SJS employed roughly 100 men, and all were ready to be paid. On July 16, Bill Sublette, leading eighty-one men, arrived with the merchandise hauled in wagons for the first time, creating quite a sensation. The caravan was made up of ten mule-drawn, heavy-duty Murphy wagons and two mule-drawn, light Dearborn wagons.[89]

Along with the SJS mountaineers and their families were camped bands of Indians as well as free trappers. All were ready to sell their pelts and furs, buy whatever they desired, and enjoy life. Joe Meek said, "Beaver, the currency of the mountains, was plentiful that year, and goods were high accordingly." Men spent money on merchandise as well as alcohol, gambling, tobacco, horses, and women. As always, there were games, betting, and other festivities.[90]

Smith, Jackson, and Sublette decided to sell their business. After computing their expenses, the quantity and quality of the furs, and the going price of beaver pelts in St. Louis, they believed they had enough money to pay off their debt to William Ashley and each have a tidy little profit. There were additional reasons to leave the fur business. Beaver populations were declining, and at any moment, the fad for beaver hats could vanish. The partners were tired of the Blackfeet's constant harassment, and of the competition with other American fur companies and Hudson's Bay. Besides, there were family matters to be concerned about.[91]

When news that SJS wanted to sell the company came out, a group of trappers pooled their resources to buy it. The new partners were Tom Fitzpatrick, Milton Sublette, Henry Fraeb, Jean Baptiste Gervais, and Jim Bridger. They named their partnership the Rocky Mountain Fur Company. Their agreement with SJS stated that, at the end of the rendezvous, SJS would sell to the Rocky Mountain Fur Company its remaining merchandise worth $15,532.23. On August 1, the RMFC wrote a note for that sum payable to Smith, Jackson & Sublette in beaver pelts at $3 per pound. The note was due November 1, 1831.[92]

On August 4, 1830, Jedediah Smith, David Jackson, and Bill Sublette left the rendezvous for St. Louis. They loaded the ten Murphy wagons and many pack animals with beaver pelts, and between fifty and seventy-five men were returning. Upon reaching St. Louis on October 5, they had proved wagons could cross the plains and enter the Rocky Mountains over what would become known as the Oregon Trail. William Ashley sold their furs for them, for a total of $84,499.14.[93] It was now time for Jim Bridger and his partners to prove whether their Rocky Mountain Fur Company could succeed in the fur business.

---

[1] Enzler, *Bridger,* 105, 114–115.

[2] Vestal, *Bridger,* 59–62. Blevins, *Hawks,* 45.

[3] Frances Fuller Victor, Winfred Blevins, ed., *The River of the West: The Mountain Years—The Adventures of Joe Meek,* Book 1 (Scotts Valley, CA: CreateSpace 2015), 45. Alter, *Bridger,* 110. Vestal, *Bridger,* 60–61. Utley, *Life,* 173–174, 352 n4.

[4] Osborne Russell, Aubrey Haines, ed., *Journal of a Trapper* (Lincoln, NE: University of Nebraska Press, 1955), 82. Enzler, *Bridger,* 34, 82. Blevins, *Hawks,* 44–45.

[5] Russell, Haines, ed., *Journal,* 82.

[6] Morgan, *Smith,* 157.

[7] Thomas Bonner, ed., Delmont Oswald, ed., *The Life and Adventures of James P. Beckwourth* (Lincoln, NE: University of Nebraska Press, 1972), 90, 93. Enzler, *Bridger,* 43–44. Utley, *Life,* 84. Sunder, *Sublette,* 61–62.

[8] D'Azevedo, ed., *Great Basin,* Vol. 11, 284, 289, 292–293, 295.

[9] Bonner, ed., Oswald, ed., *Beckwourth,* 93–94.

[10] Ibid, 94–95.

[11] Bonner, ed., Oswald, ed., *Beckwourth,* 96. Utley, *Life,* 84.

[12] Bonner, ed., Oswald, ed., *Beckwourth,* 96.

[13] Ibid, 97–98.

[14] Utley, *Life,* 44–45, 84–85. Enzler, *Bridger,* 46. Blevins, *Hawks,* 90, 118.

[15] Utley, *Life,* 40, 84–85. Morgan, ed., *Ashley,* 147.

[16] Morgan, ed., *Ashley,* 145.

[17] Morgan, ed., *Ashley,* 138–139, 141–143, 145. Hafen, ed., *Mountain Men,* 86–87.

[18] Morgan, ed., *Ashley,* 145. Hafen, ed., *Mountain Men,* 87.

[19] Bonner, ed., Oswald, ed., *Beckwourth,* 107.

[20] Morgan, ed., *Ashley,* 149.

[21] Bonner, ed., Oswald, ed., *Beckwourth,* 111.

[22] Morgan, ed., *Ashley,* 145, 150, 158.

[23] Jim Hardee, *Pierre's Hole: The Fur Trade History of Teton Valley, Idaho* (Pinedale, WY: Sublette County Historical Society, 2010), 143. Morgan, ed., *Ashley,* 145, 150–152.

[24] Morgan, ed., *Ashley,* 153. Alter, *Bridger,* 89.

[25] Morgan, *Smith,* 194–195.

[26] The agreement with Ashley stated forty-two men were contracted. Smith took sixteen men with him, leaving twenty-six men.

[27] Sunder, *Sublette,* 69. Enzler, *Bridger,* 48.

[28] Sunder, *Sublette,* 69. Hardee, *Pierre's Hole,* 28, 143–144. Enzler, *Bridger,* 49.

[29] Utley, *Life,* 173. Alter, *Bridger,* 78.

[30] Utley, *Life,* 93. Alter, in *Jim Bridger* on pages 76–78, writes Bridger led a trapping brigade into Yellowstone the fall of 1825. I found no other references to this.

[31] Alter, *Bridger,* 77–78.

[32] Robert Campbell, *A Narrative of Colonel Robert Campbell's Experiences in the Rocky Mountain Fur Trade From 1825 to 1835* (Scotts Valley, CA: CreateSpace 2016), 28. Enzler, *Bridger,* 51.

[33] Sunder, *Sublette,* 70. Blevins, *Hawks,* 123. Morgan, ed., *Ashley,* 163.

[34] Bonner, ed., Oswald, ed., *Beckwourth,* 134, 137.

[35] Sunder, *Sublette,* 70–71. Morgan, ed., *Ashley,* 163.

[36] Morgan, ed., *Ashley,* 167. Alter, *Bridger,* 93–94.

[37] D'Azevedo, ed., *Great Basin,* Vol. 11, 340–343, 348, 354.

[38] Morgan, ed., *Ashley,* 163.

[39] Morgan, ed., *Ashley,* 166–168. Sunder, *Sublette,* 74–75.

[40] Morgan, ed., *Ashley,* 168–169.

[41] Morgan, ed., *Ashley,* 162, 168. Bonner, ed., Oswald, ed., *Beckwourth,* 108–110.

[42] Morgan, ed., *Ashley,* 166. Utley, *Life,* 92–93.

[43] Morgan, *Smith,* 194–195. Utley, *Life,* 90–92. Hafen, ed., *Mountain Men,* 98–99.

[44] Morgan, ed., *Ashley,* 149, 176. Sunder, *Sublette,* 75.

[45] Morgan, ed., *Ashley,* 169, 310 n384. Utley, *Life,* 93–94. Chittenden, *Fur Trade,* Vol. 1, 260. Campbell, *Narrative,* 32.

[46] Alter, *Bridger,* 96. Hardee, *Pierre's Hole,* 42. Morgan, ed., *Ashley,* 186–187. Campbell, *Narrative,* 36–37.

[47] Alter, *Bridger,* 96. Morgan, ed., *Ashley,* 186, 314 n436.

[48] Alter, *Bridger,* 96, 100–101. Morgan, ed., *Ashley,* 180, 184. Chittenden, *Fur Trade,* Vol. 1, 280–281. Sunder, *Sublette,* 75.

[49] Alter, *Bridger,* 98–100. Morgan, ed., *Ashley,* 184.

[50] Alter, *Bridger,* 99–100. Morgan, ed., *Ashley,* 186.

[51] Deward Walker, Jr., volume ed., *Handbook of North American Indians: Plateau,* Vol. 12 (Washington, DC: Smithsonian Institution, 1998), 298–299, 302, 305–306, 312.

[52] Alter, *Bridger,* 100. Morgan, ed., *Ashley,* 187.

[53] Enzler, *Bridger,* 52–53. Morgan, ed., *Ashley,* 186.

[54] Morgan, ed., *Ashley,* 181, 186–187, 314 n439. Campbell, *Narrative,* 45–46. Bonner, ed., Oswald, ed., *Beckwourth,* 101–102.

[55] Beckwourth claimed he and a man named Calhoun rode for reinforcements, Bonner, ed., Oswald, ed., *Beckwourth,* 104–105.

[56] Morgan, ed., *Ashley,* 187. Campbell, *Narrative,* 46–47.

[57] Morgan, ed., *Ashley,* 187, 314 n439.

[58] Bonner, ed., Oswald, ed., *Beckwourth,* 106–107.

[59] Morgan, ed., *Ashley,* 186. Enzler, *Bridger,* 52–53.

[60] Morgan, *Smith,* 298–299. Sunder, *Sublette,* 76.

[61] Alter, *Bridger,* 104. Morgan, ed., *Ashley,* 181. Hardee, *Pierre's Hole,* 146.

[62] Campbell, *Narrative,* 48. Beckwourth said there were thirty-one men, Bonner, ed., Oswald, ed., *Beckwourth,* 142. Enzler, *Bridger,* 53.

[63] Bonner, ed., Oswald, ed., *Beckwourth,* 143–145.

[64] Enzler, *Bridger,* 53. Alter, *Bridger,* 106, 108. Morgan, *Smith,* 305–306. Campbell, *Narrative,* 49.

[65] Hardee, *Pierre's Hole,* 146–147. Hafen, ed., *Mountain Men,* 105. Enzler, *Bridger,* 53. Sunder, *Sublette,* 80.

[66] Victor, Blevins, ed., *River,* 7.

[67] Ibid, 8.

[68] Morgan, *Smith,* 306. Enzler, *Bridger,* 53. Hardee, *Pierre's Hole,* 147. Sunder, *Sublette,* 80–81.

[69] Chittenden, *Fur Trade,* Vol. 1, 287. Hafen, ed., *Mountain Men,* 105. Hardee, *Pierre's Hole,* 148.

[70] Morgan, ed., *Ashley,* 169. Utley, *Life,* 94.

[71] Hafen, ed., *Mountain Men,* 101. Chittenden, *Fur Trade,* Vol. 1, 284–285.

[72] Hafen, ed., *Mountain Men,* 102–103.

[73] Ibid, 103–104.

[74] Ibid, 104.

[75] Ibid, 105.

[76] Hafen, ed., *Mountain Men,* 105. Chittenden, *Fur Trade,* Vol. 1, 287.

[77] Hardee, *Pierre's Hole,* 150. Victor, Blevins, ed., *River,* 16.

[78] Hafen, ed., *Mountain Men,* 105. Blevins, *Hawks,* 174. Hardee, *Pierre's Hole,* 152.

[79] Hardee, *Pierre's Hole,* 152. Sunder, *Sublette,* 82. Victor, Blevins, ed., *River,* 38.

[80] Victor, Blevins, ed., *River,* 46.

[81] Victor, Blevins, ed., *River,* 29–32. Sunder, *Sublette,* 307–308.

[82] Victor, Blevins, ed., *River,* 33–34. Sunder, *Sublette,* 308. Morgan, *Smith,* 308.

[83] Morgan, *Smith,* 307–308.

[84] Sunder, *Sublette,* 83–84.

[85] Ibid, 84.

[86] Morgan, *Smith,* 313. Enzler, *Bridger,* 53.

[87] Morgan, *Smith,* 313–314. Hafen, ed., *Mountain Men,* 106.

[88] Morgan, *Smith,* 314. Victor, Blevins, ed., *River,* 41. Enzler, *Bridger,* 55.

[89] Morgan, *Smith,* 315, 343. Morgan, ed., *Ashley,* 186. Sunder, *Sublette,* 184–186.

[90] Victor, Blevins, ed., *River,* 42. Sunder, *Sublette,* 86.

[91] Sunder, *Sublette,* 86, 88.

[92] Sunder, *Sublette,* 88. Hafen, ed., *Mountain Men,* 106. Morgan, *Smith,* 320–321.

[93] Sunder, *Sublette,* 88–89. Morgan, *Smith,* 323.

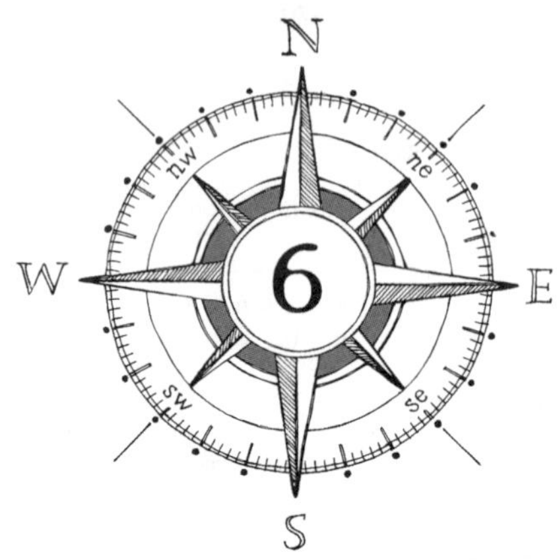

The Rocky Mountain Fur Company
1830–1834

The newly created Rocky Mountain Fur Company faced competition from the Hudson's Bay Company and John Jacob Astor's American Fur Company (AFC). Astor's company, headquartered in New York City and controlling the eastern fur trade, established a Western Department in St. Louis in 1822 and built Missouri River trading posts while absorbing competitors or driving them out of business. AFC was so large and dominant, people called it simply "the Company." Its main competitor, the Columbia Fur Company, owned Fort Tecumseh, a major trading post at the Bad River on the Missouri, as well as many smaller river posts. Astor wanted to buy the Columbia Fur Company, but its partners, including its president, Kenneth McKenzie, refused to sell. Finally, in 1827, Astor acquired the Columbia Fur Company, but it remained semiautonomous, being called the Upper Missouri Outfit, with McKenzie as its agent. The AFC contracted with Bernard Pratte & Company to manage its Western Department, bringing Pierre Chouteau, Jr. into the AFC as chief agent.[1]

In the fall of 1829, McKenzie and Chouteau sent a crew to build a post on the Missouri River's north bank six miles upriver from its confluence with the Yellowstone. The crew finished the post the following year and named it Fort Union. Fort Union and Fort Tecumseh, later renamed Fort Pierre Chouteau, Jr., then shortened to Fort Pierre, became major trading hubs on the Upper Missouri.[2]

Not far upstream from the confluence of the Yellowstone and Missouri Rivers, Fort Union was well situated for trade with various trappers and tribes. PRINT BY KARL BODMER, COURTESY OF THE BEINECKE RARE BOOK AND MANUSCRIPT LIBRARY, YALE UNIVERSITY, ZZC20 839WIG1.

Seen here in 1833, Fort Pierre Chouteau sat on a terrace on the west bank of the Missouri in present-day central South Dakota. PAINTING BY KARL BODMER, COURTESY OF THE NATIONAL ARCHIVES, 111-SC-92851.

Kenneth McKenzie believed the AFC could make money trading at the rendezvous and convinced a reluctant Pierre Chouteau to send trade caravans. In 1830, Chouteau sent a caravan from the Western Division led by Lucien Fontenelle and Andrew Drips. They failed to find the rendezvous, cached their goods on the Hams Fork on the Green River, and separated into three brigades to hunt beaver. McKenzie sent a caravan from Fort Union led by William Vanderburgh. They also failed to locate the rendezvous and went on a beaver hunt.[3]

In 1830, McKenzie moved his headquarters to Fort Union and continued with plans to build trading posts along the Upper Missouri tributaries and to send caravans to the rendezvous. People called him "King of the Upper Missouri," and since everyone called the AFC "the Company," any competitor such as the Rocky Mountain Fur Company was "the opposition."[4]

The Rocky Mountain Fur Company partners were veteran mountaineers. Irishman Tom Fitzpatrick was good at finances. Kentuckian Milton Sublette, nicknamed Thunderbolt, was Bill Sublette's brother and an experienced brigade leader. German Henry Fraeb was a seasoned trapper and one of the men who had explored the Great Salt Lake by water. French Canadian Jean Baptiste Gervais had been with the Hudson's Bay Company, leaving Peter Ogden during the 1825 Weber River confrontation. Then there was Jim Bridger, Old Gabe, who had lived in the mountains for eight years. He knew where to find beaver better than most mountaineers and was a leader of men.[5]

When the 1830 rendezvous at the Popo Agie and Wind Rivers confluence ended on August 4, 1830, the Rocky Mountain Fur Company split into two brigades. Fraeb and Gervais led thirty-four men to the Snake River. Bridger, Fitzpatrick, and Sublette led an eighty-one-man brigade to Three Forks, then to the Smith River in Blackfeet territory. Along with them rode their Indian wives and children.[6]

The brigade followed the Smith River to the Missouri above Great Falls. They had a successful beaver hunt but had to keep watch for the Blackfeet, who continued to steal traps and horses. The brigade wintered on the Yellowstone River where there was plenty of forage and buffalo. In March 1831, Fitzpatrick and an *engagé* (an indentured boatman) left for St. Louis to place the RMFC rendezvous order.[7]

Jim Bridger and Milton Sublette led the brigade to the Tongue River. There, Crow raiders stole fifty-seven horses.[8] Antoine Godin led a party on foot after the thieves. Three days later, they found the raiders and recovered their animals.[9]

The brigade rode west to the Powder River and divided there. Sublette led one party to trap along the North Platte, and Bridger led the other party to the Laramie Fork's headwaters. In early summer, the two parties rendezvoused at New Park, now North Park in northern Colorado. They rode westward to the Bear River, most likely to Cache Valley, where they held the 1831 rendezvous.[10]

Fraeb and Gervais' brigade arrived, hauling many beaver packs. Hundreds of Indians and free trappers with their families camped with the Rocky Mountain Fur Company men, waiting for the caravan. Fitzpatrick was late. The RMFC men traded what goods they had on hand. There was no alcohol or tobacco.[11]

It became obvious something had gone wrong for Fitzpatrick. Bridger and Sublette prepared a search party. Attending the rendezvous was a Crow spiritual leader. Fraeb consulted him, and he agreed to try to learn what had happened to Fitzpatrick for the price of a couple of horses. After several nights of singing, drumming, and dancing, the Crow leader fell asleep. When he awoke, he said Fitzpatrick was not dead. He was on the road, but not the right road.[12]

This was encouraging news. Fraeb, leading the search party, left the rendezvous in early August. He planned to visit last year's rendezvous site on the Wind River, thinking Fitzpatrick might have gone there by mistake. Bridger, Sublette, Gervais, and Fraeb planned to later meet on the Salmon River and winter there.[13]

Bridger and Sublette ended the rendezvous and set out, leading the RMFC brigade on the fall beaver hunt. Gervais and several *engagés* remained with the Flatheads, continuing to trade. Robert "Doc" Newell, a brigade member, wrote they rode to Grey's Fork, today's John Day River, where they had "a Scrimmage" with Blackfeet warriors.[14]

At daybreak on August 15, brigade horse herders took the livestock out to graze when a raiding party of 100 Blackfeet and 33 Cree began firing at them. Fortunately, the horses ran back to camp. A group of Cree approached as the mountaineers stood ready to use their rifles. The Cree said they were sorry for the attack, having mistaken the brigade for a Shoshone camp; then they asked for gifts. Bridger and Sublette were not deceived, but they gave the Cree a present, allowing them to depart in peace. Two brigade members were absent from camp and never returned. Fellow mountaineers believed this band had killed them. Four days later, four trappers were away from camp when the same Blackfeet and Cree attacked. The trappers repelled the warriors, who, after several hours, tired of the standoff and left.[15]

The brigade trapped from Grey's Fork to the Snake, Salmon, and Clark Fork Rivers. They traveled north to the Flathead River headwaters and then returned to the Salmon. There, they rendezvoused with the Flathead band that Gervais and the *engagés* were with. A Nez Percé band and an American Fur Company brigade also camped there.[16]

The French called the *Nimiipuu* tribe "Nez Percé" because they pierced their nasal septum. They lived in modern-day central Idaho and eastern Washington and Oregon. They were a large tribe, estimated at 6,000 people. Each village had a headman and council. Their lodges were mat-covered longhouses. When traveling, they lived in buffalo-hide teepees. They ate fish, game, vegetables, and fruit. They were renowned for their horsemanship and made annual trips to the plains of modern-day Montana to hunt buffalo. Horses were a sign of wealth, and the Nez Percé bred them for strength and speed. They were avid traders who were interested in Christianity in as far as it could give them the same power that Whites held. In 1831, along with the Flatheads, they sent a delegation to St. Louis to inquire about the White man's religion.[17]

On November 5, 1831, Henry Fraeb arrived with the missing caravan, but without Tom Fitzpatrick. (One of the caravan's forty men was twenty-one-year-old Christopher "Kit" Carson, who would become a famed scout, expedition guide, and U.S. Army officer).[18] Fraeb informed Bridger and the other partners about Fitzpatrick.[19]

Tom Fitzpatrick and an *engagé* had left for St. Louis in March 1831 to submit the RMFC merchandise order to Smith, Jackson & Sublette. Reaching Independence, Missouri, in early May, they learned the three partners were leading a caravan to Santa Fe. Fitzpatrick followed and caught up with them. They told him they would outfit his caravan in Santa Fe.[20]

On May 27, the caravan was crossing the plains between the Arkansas and Cimarron Rivers. Finding no water, Jedediah Smith and Fitzpatrick rode ahead to the south looking for water. They came upon a hollow with the possibility

A fur trading caravan was an eclectic parade of mounted company trappers, free trappers, Indians, clerks, cooks, perhaps a wealthy patron from the East or Europe, and wagons brimming with trade goods. PAINTING BY ALFRED JACOB MILLER, COURTESY OF THE WALTERS ART MUSEUM, 37.1940.51.

of water below the surface. Smith told Fitzpatrick to wait for the caravan and start digging a water hole while he scouted to the south. The caravan members never saw Jedediah Smith again. On July 4, after they arrived in Santa Fe, they learned Smith's fate. Mexican traders, who had obtained Smith's rifle and pistols from a group of Comanche, said that a hunting party had surrounded Smith. One man shot Smith in the back. He returned fire, killing their leader. The rest charged with their lances, killing him.[21]

After Smith, Jackson & Sublette outfitted Fitzpatrick, he hired forty men and led a caravan north along the Rocky Mountains' Front Range. By September, Fitzpatrick reached the North Platte where he encountered Fraeb's search party. The two partners decided Fraeb would take the caravan to the brigade's Salmon River camp, and Fitzpatrick would return to St. Louis to arrange for the 1832 rendezvous.[22]

When Henry Fraeb brought the caravan to the Salmon River encampment in early November 1831, everyone was ecstatic. Warren Ferris, with the American Fur Company, wrote, "[the] camp presented a confused scene of rioting, and debauchery for several days, after which however, the kegs of alcohol were again bunged, and all became tranquil."[23]

Thanks to the Blackfeet, the Rocky Mountain Fur Company, American Fur Company, Nez Percé, and Flathead Salmon River encampments did not enjoy a peaceful winter. Kit Carson said Blackfeet killed four or five men. In one attack, Blackfeet raiders stole twenty RMFC horses, and then, days later, they stole another eight horses from the Flathead and trader camps. Two Flatheads did kill one of the raiders. On March 1, 1832, Jim Bridger and Milton Sublette led their RMFC brigade eastward on the spring beaver hunt, trapping along the Salmon River, Henry's Fork, Lewis's Fork, and Salt River.[24]

This 1870 image shows two hunters and their dog by a large beaver dam on the Henry's Fork. PHOTOGRAPH BY WILLIAM HENRY JACKSON, COURTESY OF THE LIBRARY OF CONGRESS, LOT 3960, NO. 1 [ITEM] [P&P].

On May 15, a Company brigade discovered them. Company man Warren Ferris wrote, ". . . in a narrow bottom, beneath the walls of Gray's Creek, we found a party of trappers, headed by Bridger. Their encampment was decked with hundreds of beaver skins, now drying in the sun. . . . There were several hundred skins folded and tied up in packs. . . ."[25]

William Vanderburgh and Andrew Drips led the Company's brigade, totaling 175 men. They were well provisioned with trade goods, but they were unfamiliar with the lay of the land and where to trap beaver. Their objective was to follow the RMFC brigade and learn from them. Company men pestered the RMFC trappers for the rendezvous site, they followed trappers to their beaver locations, and they sold goods to trappers and Indians associated with the RMFC. Bridger and Sublette were angry and led their men to the Bear River, trying to elude the Company brigade. However, the Company followed, camping nearby.[26]

Violence erupted in the RMFC camp. John Gray, a Freemen Iroquois leader, was furious, believing his daughter had suffered an indignity. The quarrel exploded into a fight. Gray stabbed Milton Sublette so severely everyone believed he would die. Yet the RMFC brigade needed to continue its hunt. Bridger decided to proceed on, leaving Joe Meek to attend to Sublette until he recovered or died.[27]

The 1832 rendezvous location was in Pierre's Hole, on the west side of the Teton Range. Bridger led his brigade in that direction as they continued trapping beaver. Vanderburgh and Drips followed, continuing to trap and trade, much to Bridger's annoyance.[28]

When Bridger reached Pierre's Hole, he established the RMFC encampment in the middle of the valley, anticipating Fitzpatrick's caravan. The Company brigade soon appeared and waited for their two caravans, one led by Lucien Fontenelle out of Fort Bellevue near Fort Atkinson and the other led by Etienne Provost from Fort Union. Then Henry Fraeb and Jean Baptiste Gervais' RMFC brigade rode into the rendezvous. Many Indians, mostly Nez Percé and Flathead, and free trappers also arrived. Doc Newell estimated "in all whites and indians [*sic*] all sorts and kinds of men about 600." Whichever outfit's caravan reached the rendezvous first would make the most profit.[29]

The weather was unpleasant. Ferris wrote, "Throughout the month of June, scarcely a day passed without either rain, hail, or snow, and during the last three days of the month, a snow storm continued without intermission, the whole time, night and day; but disappeared from the earth a few hours after the sun reappeared."[30]

Joe Meek arrived with Milton Sublette. Under Meek's care, Sublette had begun to heal and regain strength. After forty days camped on the Bear River, they had ridden toward the rendezvous. Upon reaching the Green River, a Shoshone band captured them. During their council meeting, the deliberators concluded that the two men must die. One chief named Gotia disagreed with the verdict. He and a girl named Mountain Lamb helped the two men escape. (Sublette later reunited with Mountain Lamb and married her.) Meek estimated at least 1,000 people were camped at the rendezvous and had brought 2,000 to 3,000 horses and mules.[31]

Jim Bridger and his partners were tired of being shadowed by the Company. The four partners met with Vanderburgh and Drips, proposing the two outfits divide the beaver country. The Rocky Mountain Fur Company would stay in its territory and the American Fur Company would stay in its territory. Vanderburgh and Drips declined the offer.[32]

On July 3, a Company man who had been searching for the Company caravans returned to Pierre's Hole. He had not located the Company caravans, but he did find the caravan for the RMFC led by none other than Bill Sublette. The Company man reported that Tom Fitzpatrick had been with the caravan, but on June 12, at Laramie Fork on the North Platte River, he selected two horses and rode ahead of the caravan to inform the people at the rendezvous of its approach. No one had heard from Fitzpatrick since. Riders were sent to search for him. On July 8, 1832, Bill Sublette arrived with the caravan for the Rocky Mountain Fur Company.[33] He would have met with Bridger and his partners to explain his presence, as follows.

After outfitting Tom Fitzpatrick's 1831 caravan in Santa Fe, Bill Sublette and David Jackson dissolved their company. Jackson headed to California; Sublette returned to St. Louis to supply fur trade outfits. Over the 1831 to 1832 winter, Sublette prepared a caravan for the rendezvous. He led fifty men with 165 horses and mules to haul merchandise, including 450 gallons of whiskey. Robert Campbell joined him, leading his own five-man party with ten horses transporting merchandise. Fitzpatrick had returned from the mountains and planned to travel with them.[34]

The caravan left St. Louis on April 25, 1832, reaching Independence, Missouri, on May 12. There, Sublette met Nathaniel Wyeth leading a company of twenty-one men to establish a Columbia River fur trading operation. Sublette agreed to take them along. The combined party left Independence the next day. Reaching Laramie Fork on June 12, Fitzpatrick rode off and disappeared. The caravan continued and was camped near the Green River on the night of July 2 when unknown warriors attacked, stealing five horses. The following day they met a Flathead band, one of whom guided the caravan over Teton Pass to Pierre's Hole.[35]

Sublette's caravan joined the RMFC camp. His traders conducted a brisk business while Vanderburgh and Drips waited for the arrival of Fontenelle and Provost's caravans. That evening, George Nidever and a trapper named Poe returned to camp with the missing Tom Fitzpatrick, gaunt, almost unrecognizable. The encampment erupted in joy at his arrival.[36]

After leaving Sublette's caravan, Fitzpatrick had ridden westward toward Pierre's Hole. A week later, he suddenly came upon a large Gros Ventre village.[37]

The Gros Ventre were nomadic, following buffalo herds and living in teepees. Acquiring guns and horses, they increased their power and territory in modern-day southern Alberta and Saskatchewan and across northern Montana. Band members selected a leader based on his wealth and willingness to give away horses and food. A tribal council provided the leader guidance. The Gros Ventre, allies of the Blackfeet, viewed American trappers as enemies. This band had been on a two- to three-year visit with Arapaho to the south. They were now returning to their Upper Missouri homeland.[38]

Gros Ventre warriors spied Fitzpatrick and gave chase. He jumped on his fastest horse and raced toward mountains three miles distant. He was far ahead of his pursuers when he reached the foothills and rode up the slopes until his horse could go no farther. Hiding the horse in a thicket, Fitzpatrick raced uphill until he found a crevice in which to hide. The warriors discovered the horse and searched for Fitzpatrick. Eventually, they gave up and returned to their camp. The next morning, they resumed their search, coming close to Fitzpatrick but never discovering him. That night he began walking toward his destination. At daybreak, he found a hiding place and waited there until dark. He continued walking toward Pierre's Hole only at night. Crossing a river, he lost his rifle, shot, and gunpowder. By the time he arrived at Pierre's Hole, he was suffering from cold, hunger, and fatigue. Fitzpatrick's harrowing experience turned his hair gray. The Indians named him "White Hair."[39]

With much to celebrate, Bill Sublette tapped his whiskey barrels. Mountaineers and Indians had plenty of beaver pelts to trade for gunpowder, lead, and traps as well as liquor, tobacco, coffee, sugar, and other merchandise. Joe Meek recollected:

> then began the usual gay carousel; and the 'fast young men' of the mountains outvied each other in all manner of mad pranks. In the beginning of their spree many feats of horsemanship and personal strength were exhibited. . . . But the horse-racing, fine riding, wrestling, and all manlier sports, soon degraded into the baser exhibitions of a 'crazy drunk' condition."[40]

In the midst of this revelry, it became clear that dissension was stirring in Nathaniel Wyeth's camp. Many were concerned with his strict discipline and vague plans. Out of eighteen men, seven—including his brother and nephew—would not continue to trap with him. Bill Sublette agreed to take some to St. Louis, while the rest decided to stay in the mountains. Milton Sublette and Henry Fraeb planned to lead a brigade westward. Wyeth asked if he and his men could accompany them, and they agreed to take them along.[41]

A Boston-based ice merchant and inventor, Nathaniel Jarvis Wyeth came west in 1832 and within two years had inserted himself in the fur trade. ILLUSTRATION FROM *HARPER'S NEW MONTHLY MAGAZINE*, VOLUME 85, ISSUE 510, NOVEMBER 1892.

Sublette and Fraeb's brigade was leaving the rendezvous early. Besides Wyeth and his men, a few free trappers joined them, along with a small party led by Alexander Sinclair, in all totaling forty men. A homeward-bound Flathead band would also accompany them. The combined cavalcade left the rendezvous on July 17, 1832, traveling eight miles south. They were still in Pierre's Hole, two miles from Pine Creek Pass to the west, where they stopped for the night.[42]

As the mountaineers broke camp the next morning, they spied movement at the pass. They thought it might be buffalo, but as the movement came closer, they saw they were humans, some on horseback and others on foot. They believed it was a band of Blackfeet; however, they were Gros Ventre—the mountaineers later learned it was the same band that chased Tom Fitzpatrick and attacked Bill Sublette's caravan.[43]

The Gros Ventre had been visiting Arapaho relations to the south and were returning home. They had learned Fontenelle's Company caravan was to rendezvous at Pierre's Hole. They were on good terms with the Company and planned to trade with Fontenelle. As they traveled through the mountains toward Pierre's Hole, the band divided into two groups, with a smaller, faster group pushing ahead. When the advance group emerged from Pine Creek Pass, they saw the White men's camp. The Gros Ventre leader, Biahoh, believed it was Fontenelle's caravan, and the whole band—men, women, and children—approached. They were noisy and excited about the prospect of trade. As they unfurled a British flag, Biahoh, wearing a red coat and red blanket, rode toward two approaching riders from the White men's camp. Biahoh carried only a pipe of peace.[44]

When those in the camp saw the approaching Gros Ventre, they believed they were outnumbered. Nathaniel Wyeth estimated there were 200 people in the band. Milton Sublette sent a rider to the rendezvous encampment requesting help.[45]

The advancing band was a mile away when Henry Fraeb sent Antoine Godin, an Iroquois-White trapper, to determine who the band was and learn their intentions. Godin took along a Flathead friend. As the two men rode toward the band, they believed them to be the hated Blackfeet. Two years earlier, Blackfeet had killed Godin's father, and several weeks before the rendezvous, Blackfeet attacked a Flathead village, killing twelve members and stealing 1,000 horses.[46]

The two men rode up to the Gros Ventre leader Biahoh, who extended his hand to Godin. Godin held on to Biahoh's hand as the Flathead shot him point-blank. Godin grabbed Biahoh's red blanket, and they raced back to camp. The two sides began firing at each other. Gros Ventre women and children ran to the cottonwood trees along Little Pine Creek and built a hasty fortification.[47]

Bill Sublette and Robert Campbell, leading roughly 250 trappers and Nez Percé and Flathead warriors, galloped to the fight.[48] There is no record whether Jim Bridger rode with them or if he remained at the rendezvous camp to protect RMFC goods and mountaineer families.

When Sublette's force arrived, the Gros Ventre warriors retreated to their fortification. Older men escorted many of the women and children to Pine Creek Pass.[49]

The combined mountaineer and Indian force surrounded the Gros Ventre fort and began firing into it. Alexander Sinclair, Bill Sublette, Robert Campbell, and a few others entered the cottonwoods, creeping close to the fort. Sublette shot a defender. Sinclair was hit and later died. Sublette was shot in the left arm, the bullet shattering the bone.[50]

The battle raged through the afternoon. Both sides inflicted casualties. The mountaineers wanted to set fire to the fortification. The Flathead and Nez Percé argued against it; they wanted to plunder the Gros Ventre's possessions. The Gros Ventre shouted that another band planned to attack the rendezvous encampment. The mountaineers and Nez Percé and Flathead warriors raced back to their camps, learning it was a ruse. The day was over; the camps posted additional night guards. The next day, the mountaineers and warriors returned to the battlefield to find the Gros Ventre had left.[51]

The Gros Ventre killed at least eight mountaineers. The Flathead and Nez Percé lost seven men and six were wounded. The combined mountaineer and Indian force found nine Gros Ventre warrior bodies as well as those of two women and several children. Among the Gros Ventre horses rounded up were some that had been stolen from Bill Sublette as well as Tom Fitzpatrick's two horses.[52]

As friends and families cared for the wounded, the rendezvous continued in full swing. Dr. Jacob Wyeth, Nathaniel's brother who would be returning to St. Louis, attended to Bill Sublette's wound as Sublette focused on his financial concerns. Milton Sublette and his combined party resumed their journey on July 24, heading toward Pine Creek Pass.[53]

Eager to secure business for the next year's rendezvous, Bill Sublette drafted an agreement with the Rocky Mountain Fur Company. On July 25, 1832, Tom Fitzpatrick signed it on behalf of the partnership since the other partners had already left and Jim Bridger could not write. Sublette agreed to transport the RMFC furs at fifty cents per pound, then sell them in St. Louis. The profits would be used to pay off RMFC debts and purchase supplies and trade goods for the company. The RMFC agreed Sublette would be the sole supplier for the 1833 rendezvous. Soon after the signing, Bridger and Fitzpatrick led their brigade north from Pierre's Hole for the fall beaver hunt. On July 30, Sublette's caravan began its return to St. Louis with 169 beaver packs.[54]

On August 4, 1832, Vanderburgh and Drips left Pierre's Hole, leading their brigade eastward, crossing the Tetons in search of Fontenelle and Provost's caravans. To their surprise, they found a fort built on the Green River five miles upstream from Horse Creek. Benjamin Bonneville was the leader of a 100-man brigade that had built the fort. A West Point graduate and U.S. Army captain, Bonneville was on leave to enter the fur trade. He had previously met Fontenelle, who convinced him the Salmon River was a better location to winter. Bonneville took his advice and prepared to abandon the fort. He told Vanderburgh and Drips that the Company caravans' camp was a few miles farther upriver. On August 7, they arrived at the caravans' encampment. The brigade and caravans exchanged furs for trade goods and supplies. On August 12, the caravans left for Fort Union as Vanderburgh and Drips led 115 men back to Pierre's Hole. They planned to tail Bridger's brigade to compete in trade and trapping. Upon reaching Pierre's Hole, they found Bridger's trail.[55]

Jim Bridger and Tom Fitzpatrick led their eighty-man brigade north out of Pierre's Hole, trapping beaver and trading with tribes. They crossed Henry's Fork heading west to the Salmon River. From there they planned to head east to the Big Hole River, then to the Beaverhead and Jefferson Rivers.[56]

When the brigade reached the Big Hole, they discovered Vanderburgh and Drips' brigade was hot on their trail. Heading north, trying to elude their pursuers, they found beaver scarce and so was game. The Company men continued in hot pursuit. Bridger and Fitzpatrick led their brigade into the mountains, into Blackfeet territory. On September 9, the Company men came upon the RMFC's abandoned camp with fires still smoldering. On September 12, the Company brigade caught up and camped with them. On September 14, both brigades traveled together and camped by a stream upriver from the confluence of the Dearborn and Missouri Rivers.[57]

Bridger and Fitzpatrick met with Vanderburgh and Drips. Both brigades were hungry and had few beaver pelts. Bridger said they all should find enough game and beaver in the Missouri's Three Forks country.[58]

Whether Vanderburgh and Drips told Bridger and Fitzpatrick their plans or not, on September 16, during a severe sleet storm, the Company brigade divided. Vanderburgh led fifty men following the Missouri upriver straight south, while Drips and fifty men followed the RMFC brigade to the southeast and then west to Three Forks.[59]

The RMFC and Company brigades reached Three Forks on October 1; there they separated. Drips followed the Jefferson upriver, while Bridger and Fitzpatrick took the Gallatin River. After several days of trapping, the RMFC brigade had caught few beavers, and several brushes with Blackfeet war parties caused alarm. Bridger and Fitzpatrick regrouped and led the brigade to the Madison River. On October 6, they rode upriver a few miles when they encountered Vanderburgh's brigade's encampment and pitched camp near them.[60]

The weather was bad. The prairie was so wet and muddy, the brigades remained in camp. The men amused themselves with a variety of activities, cardplaying the most popular. Warren Ferris said, ". . . the stentorian voices of the hardy hunters, were occasionally heard, practicing that fashionable folly and crime, profane swearing."[61]

By October 11, the weather improved enough for the RMFC brigade to continue hunting beaver up the Madison. The Company brigade remained in camp, waiting for several hunters to return. Vanderburgh planned to follow the Madison downriver.[62]

Bridger and Fitzpatrick always took precautions, watchful for robbery or attack. In the evening, the horses were brought into camp and picketed, with guards stationed around the perimeter. Before daybreak, Bridger or Fitzpatrick would ride his horse a half mile from camp to the front and rear, surveying the countryside. After determining all was clear, they allowed the herders to take the livestock out to graze. When the brigade was on the move, scouts rode in advance and on the flanks of the main body.[63]

The RMFC brigade crossed to the Gallatin River, following it to its headwaters. There they met Bill Craig leading several RMFC hunters. The brigade continued its beaver hunt, crossing back to the Madison and then on to Pierre's Fork of the Jefferson River where they encountered a Peigan Blackfeet band numbering sixty warriors who made signs of peace. Bridger and Fitzpatrick invited two chiefs to enter the camp. The chiefs said all Peigan chiefs had met in council and decided not to rob and kill Whites anymore. They said they would visit the RMFC winter encampment on the Salmon River to trade. They also said to inform the Flathead they would pay them a visit in the spring "and if possible exterminate their race." They warned that a party of more than 100 Blood Blackfeet was two days ahead of them who might want to "show fight." The Peigan camped near the brigade that night. The next morning, Bridger and Fitzpatrick gave them presents and they departed pleased.[64]

The next day, Joe Meek and several other mountaineers rode out from camp and came upon some unarmed Blackfeet along a lake. Meek said that for their own amusement, they began shooting at the Blackfeet who had no option but to jump in the lake while the mountaineers laughed until a large force of mounted Blackfeet arrived, chasing the mountaineers back to camp.[65]

The Blackfeet halted at the edge of an open area near rocky cliffs. These were the Blood Blackfeet that the Peigan had told Bridger and Fitzpatrick about. Their leader was Pe-to-pee-kiss, Eagle Ribs, who claimed he had killed and scalped eleven White men.[66]

The two parties fired at each other until the Bloods waved a white flag. Eagle Ribs, holding the pipe of peace, and another leader, escorted by several warriors, advanced from the Bloods' lines. An equal number of brigade members did the same, including a young Mexican named Loretto and his wife who held their infant. The woman, a Blackfeet, had been previously captured by the Crow. Loretto had ransomed her, and she became his wife. She would act as interpreter.[67]

As the two parties approached each other, the woman recognized one of the Blood warriors as her brother. Handing the infant to Loretto, she rushed into her brother's open arms. The members of the two sides sat and began to smoke and talk. The Bloods said Kenneth McKenzie with the American Fur Company told them if they waved a white flag, the Whites would not molest them and allow them to enter their camp to trade.[68]

Jim Bridger had remained in camp but now slowly rode his horse toward the smoking group. His rifle lay across his saddle's pommel. Eagle Ribs stood and walked toward Bridger with his hand extended. Believing Eagle Ribs' movement was sinister, Bridger cocked the rifle's hammer. Eagle Ribs heard the hammer click and in a swift motion grabbed the rifle barrel, forcing it toward the ground. The rifle discharged. Two arrows slammed into Bridger's lower back. Eagle Ribs snatched Bridger's rifle and, using it as a club, knocked him to the ground. Eagle Ribs swung into the saddle and, still clutching Bridger's rifle, raced Bridger's horse back to the Bloods who took positions in the rocks.[69]

As both sides began firing, the brother hauled Loretto's wife to the Bloods' position. Loretto, holding the infant and ignoring bullets and arrows, ran to his wife and gave her their child. The Bloods, respecting his act of courage, did not kill him. Eagle Ribs said he was a madman, but he could go in peace. Loretto wanted his wife to go with him, but the brother would not allow it. His wife begged him to go before the Bloods changed their minds and killed him. Dejected, Loretto returned

Blood leader Pe-to-pee-kiss or Eagle Ribs, show here in 1832 wearing a headdress of buffalo horns and ermine skins, got the better of Jim Bridger in an encounter near the Jefferson River in present-day southwest Montana. PAINTING BY GEORGE CATLIN, COURTESY OF THE SMITHSONIAN AMERICAN ART MUSEUM, 1985.66.152.

to the brigade. Months later, he left the RMFC, recovered his wife, and the two of them worked as interpreters at a Company post.[70]

Firing lasted until evening when the Bloods rode away. The mountaineers removed one three-inch steel arrowhead from Bridger's backside, but the other was too deep, so they left it in place. Fitzpatrick wrote to Robert Campbell, stating Bridger had been shot with two arrows, and they lost a woman, a horse, and "the gun you sold Bridger."[71]

Meeting Bridger later, Black Harris allegedly said, "Hulloa! Bridger, what's the matter now?"

"Only some feathers in my ass," Bridger replied.[72]

Several days after the Blackfeet encounter, Bridger and Fitzpatrick's brigade and Vanderburgh's brigade met and camped together in the headwaters of the Jefferson River.[73] The Company men told a sad tale.

Their beaver hunt had taken them up a tributary of the Jefferson, the Philanthropy, today's Ruby River. On October 14, hunters returned to camp reporting they had seen Indians, and they did not want to go back out. Vanderburgh decided to investigate, and six men accompanied him.[74]

They were six miles from camp, crossing a deep gully, when more than 100 Blackfeet warriors surrounded them, firing a twenty-musket volley. Vanderburgh's horse was killed, and the horse ridden by Pilau, a Frenchman, was wounded, throwing him to the ground where warriors killed him. The other five men, some wounded, including Warren Ferris, raced their horses back to camp. Surrounded, Vanderburgh shot the closest warrior. Ferris said, "The Indians immediately fired a volley upon him—he fell—they uttered a loud and shrill yell of exultation. . . ." Several days later, a small party visited the ambush site and buried Pilau, but they could not find Vanderburgh. Months later, some Flathead and Pend d'Oreille told Company men that they had found Vanderburgh's bones. The Blackfeet had cut his body to pieces and thrown them in the river. The Flathead and Pend d'Oreille had collected and buried his bones.[75]

Years later, Eagle Ribs admitted his Blood warriors had ambushed Vanderburgh's men. This was the same Eagle Ribs whom days later Bridger saw make a movement, causing him to cock his rifle. Eagle Ribs claimed both Vanderburgh and Bridger were the aggressors.[76]

The RMFC and Company brigades traveled together west to the forks of the Salmon River to encamp for the winter. Since temperatures were relatively mild in the Salmon River area, Flathead, Nez Percé, and Pend d'Oreille tribes established their winter villages there. Captain Benjamin Bonneville's brigade arrived and built a series of temporary forts. The American Fur Company brigades encamped along the river as did the Rocky Mountain Fur Company brigades, moving to new locations as game and grass became scarce. On December 1, 1832, five men left the RMFC encampment to hunt but never returned. A search party found their trail but also the trail of an Indian party that appeared to be following them. They concluded Indians had killed the hunters.[77]

All five Rocky Mountain Fur Company partners met in January 1833 to plan the spring beaver hunt. Toward January's end, Milton Sublette and Jean Baptiste Gervais led a thirty-man brigade to the mouth of the Portneuf on the Snake River. Jim Bridger, Tom Fitzpatrick, and Henry Fraeb led sixty men to the Green River where they split. Fitzpatrick's brigade remained in the area, while Bridger and Fraeb led their brigades to the Medicine Bow River's east fork. The two brigades reunited on the North Platte in late May 1833. They had successful beaver hunts and cached forty beaver packs. Unfortunately for the trappers, Arikara had stolen sixty of Bridger and Fraeb's horses.[78]

Bridger, Fitzpatrick, and Fraeb decided Fraeb would ride downriver with two men to find either Sublette or Campbell's caravan. Fraeb's party soon encountered Louis Vasquez and two men. Robert Campbell, leading a forty-four man, 100-mule caravan, had sent them ahead to find a RMFC brigade.[79]

The brigade and caravan camped together on the North Platte six miles upriver from the forks of the Laramie River. Campbell informed Bridger, Fitzpatrick, and Fraeb that Bill Sublette and he had formed a partnership to supply the rendezvous. The RMFC partners bought all of Campbell's items except ten mules, ten barrels of liquor, and two bales of goods.[80]

St. Louis businessman Edmund Christy and Dr. Benjamin Harrison, son of General William Henry Harrison who would become president in 1841, accompanied Campbell. The elder Harrison had sent his son west to keep him from whiskey. Also traveling with Campbell was British adventurer William Drummond Stewart.[81]

The 1833 rendezvous was to be held in July on the Green River. But the brigade and caravan men were ready to celebrate at this impromptu rendezvous on the North Platte, which quickly degenerated into a drunken spree. The next day, the caravan and Fitzpatrick's brigade rode toward the official rendezvous site, while Bridger and Fraeb led their brigades on a beaver hunt in the Laramie and Medicine Bow Mountains of current-day Wyoming.[82]

Bridger and Fraeb's brigades experienced excitement and hardships in addition to trapping beaver and eluding Indians. For example, Bridger's men found a "Gold Canyon" along the Chugwater River when they washed the riverbank soil in pans and, for a time, believed they had found gold dust. Then, during a rainstorm, several men gathered in Fraeb's tent. A clerk named Guthrie was leaning against a tent pole when lightning struck, killing him. Later, John Hawken, nephew of the St. Louis gunsmith Hawken brothers, disliked a campsite Bridger had selected at the bottom of a hill. Hawken believed it was a poor location to defend, but Bridger disagreed. To prove his point, Hawken climbed the hill and dislodged a rock that rolled into camp and through a lodge, breaking a gun and injuring a Frenchman's leg. Bridger charged Hawken for the broken gun and damaged equipment, adding $10 for injuring the man.[83]

By November 1833, Bridger and Fraeb's brigades had returned to Ham's Fork on the Green River. There they joined Fitzpatrick's brigade.[84] Fitzpatrick updated them on what had happened at the rendezvous and to his brigade.

On July 5, 1833, Fitzpatrick's brigade and Campbell's caravan arrived at the Green River rendezvous. They cornered most of the beaver pelts before Lucien Fontenelle's Company caravan arrived. By July 15, the brigades of Benjamin Bonneville, Nathaniel Wyeth, the American Fur Company, and the Rocky Mountain Fur Company had arrived. On July 22, Jean Baptiste Gervais and Edmund Christy, whom the RMFC took on as a partner for one year, left the rendezvous, leading a thirty-man brigade to the Great Salt Lake.[85]

The Rocky Mountain Fur Company brigades acquired sixty-one packs worth approximately $21,000. Deducting their debt to Bill Sublette, transportation costs, purchase of supplies and goods, salaries for fifty-five employees, the cost of replacing stolen horses, and other expenses, they were in debt to Bill Sublette for $12,000. Tom Fitzpatrick and Milton Sublette made a deal with Nathaniel Wyeth to supply the RMFC a small amount of goods for the

1834 rendezvous for a cheaper price than Bill Sublette, approximately $6,500, considerably less than the $15,000 Sublette was charging. They each agreed to a $500 bond if either defaulted.[86]

Robert Campbell planned to return to St. Louis by way of the Bighorn River to the Yellowstone River, then down the Missouri. He told the mountaineers that Bill Sublette was building a fort at the confluence of the Yellowstone and Missouri to compete with the Company's Fort Union. Fitzpatrick and Milton Sublette's brigade accompanied Campbell's caravan to the Bighorn River. William Stewart and Benjamin Harrison tagged along, as did Nathaniel Wyeth and his men. On August 4, Benjamin Bonneville's brigade caught up with them, and by August 12, the cavalcade had traversed Bad Pass and was far enough down the Bighorn River where they could travel by water. There, they built bull boats. Milton Sublette was leaving with Campbell. Bonneville was sending back thirty-six men with his furs, but he would remain in the mountains with four men and rejoin his remaining brigades. The bull boat flotilla paddled down the Bighorn on August 15, as Fitzpatrick led his thirty-man brigade, including Stewart and Harrison, eastward.[87]

Reaching the Tongue River on September 5, Fitzpatrick's brigade encountered a large Crow village. The chief invited Fitzpatrick to camp with them, but he declined, establishing camp three miles away. He left Stewart in charge while he and several men rode to the Crow village to meet with the chief. While Fitzpatrick was away, friendly-acting Crow entered the camp. On a prearranged signal, they overpowered the mountaineers and ransacked the camp, taking the horses and mules, weapons, ammunition, traps, beaver pelts, and anything they liked. They were kind enough not to hurt anyone.[88]

As Fitzpatrick and his men returned to camp, they encountered warriors who stopped them and took their horses, weapons, and most of their clothes. An angry Fitzpatrick walked back to camp, becoming more furious when he saw the brigade had been looted. Returning to the Crow village, he demanded the chief return their possessions. The chief replied he had nothing to do with the robbery. The chief later recovered and returned to Fitzpatrick the stolen livestock, weapons, some ammunition, and some traps and equipment.[89]

The American Fur Company had three men working with the Crow. Samuel Winters was in the village. Another was Samuel Tulloch, former Smith, Jackson

& Sublette employee, who, in 1832, had built Fort Cass, a Company post below the Bighorn River on the Yellowstone. The third was Jim Beckwourth, who was in the village at the time. Fitzpatrick wrote William Ashley he believed the Company had encouraged the theft and "the agent of these people who was there present did not pretend to deny it." The agent was Beckwourth, who claimed he was innocent and had saved the brigade from being massacred. The Crow did not return Fitzpatrick's beaver pelts but traded them to the Company. Tulloch wrote about the furs to Kenneth McKenzie, who replied, "The 43 beaver skins traded, marked, 'R. M. F. Co.,' I would in the present instance give up if Mr. Fitzpatrick wishes to have them, on his paying the price the articles traded for them were worth on their arrival in the Crow village, and the expense of bringing the beaver in and securing it."[90]

Fitzpatrick led the brigade out of Crow territory as raiders continued to steal livestock. They hunted beaver until meeting Bridger and Fraeb at Ham's Fork.[91]

After the Rocky Mountain Fur Company men reunited, Henry Fraeb led a twenty-man brigade down the Green River to hunt beaver in present-day Colorado. Fitzpatrick wrote a letter to William Ashley describing the American Fur Company outrages. Another letter was to Milton Sublette concerning the RMFC's financial situation: they had acquired only twenty-three beaver packs. Fitzpatrick was concerned that Wyeth might not meet his obligations to supply their needed merchandise. He also warned Ashley not to trust the Crows, and he wrote that he was moving the 1834 rendezvous to Sandy Creek on the Green River. Fitzpatrick sent the letters to St. Louis with Black Harris and Benjamin Harrison.[92]

Bridger and Fitzpatrick led their brigade southeast to the confluence of the Little Snake River and Little Bear River, now the Yampa River, in present-day Colorado, where they established their 1833 to 1834 winter encampment. Toward winter's end, Fitzpatrick sent Bill Sublette their merchandise order for the 1834 rendezvous. In late March, Stephen Lee, leading a Taos trading party that included Kit Carson, arrived at the encampment. Lee traded his goods for Bridger and Fitzpatrick's beaver pelts. Fitzpatrick led his brigade on a spring beaver hunt. Carson went with them, while Bridger and his men, including William Stewart, rode with Lee to Taos.[93]

Taos was a small Mexican town northeast of Santa Fe that some American fur traders and trappers used as a base of operation. Trappers sent furs from there to St. Louis in returning caravans.[94] For Jim Bridger and many of his men, Taos was their first experience of town life since leaving St. Louis, and they most likely enjoyed what Taos had to offer. However, there were beaver to trap, and Bridger was soon leading the brigade on its spring beaver hunt.

Bridger hired an Ioway Indian named Marshall to work as a camp keeper. Marshall refused to do his duties, so Bridger fired him. William Stewart felt sorry for Marshall and hired him, but soon Marshall would not work for him either, and Stewart threatened to fire him. The next morning, Marshall was gone, taking two horses, one being Stewart's prized racehorse Otholoho, and Stewart's favorite rifle. In a fit of rage, Stewart said, "I'd give $500 for his scalp." Mark Head and another mountaineer rode from camp, returning that night with the missing horses and Stewart's rifle with Marshall's scalp dangling from its barrel. Stewart was horrified that they had believed what he'd said and killed the man. He never wanted to ride Otholoho again and gave the horse to Bridger.[95]

Bridger led the brigade north to the Laramie River where they had a successful beaver hunt. Afterwards, they traveled south of the Medicine Bow River for a successful buffalo hunt. At the headwaters of the Laramie, they found Kit Carson and three other trappers from Fitzpatrick's brigade who joined them to ride to the 1834 Green River rendezvous.[96]

Scottish Baronet William Drummond Stewart commissioned painter Alfred Jacob Miller to accompany him in the West, capturing scenes of the fur trade and rendezvous era. PAINTING BY ALFRED JACOB MILLER, FROM WIKIMEDIA.

Eager to reach the rendezvous, Carson and Stewart rode ahead, arriving the night of June 24, 1834. Bridger's brigade arrived the next day. Fitzpatrick told Bridger good and bad news. First the bad news: Bill Sublette had demanded full payment of their debt, which they could not pay, so the Rocky

Mountain Fur Company was no more. The good news was Bridger was partner in a new company: Fitzpatrick, Sublette, & Bridger.[97]

The events leading to the Rocky Mountain Fur Company's demise revolved around Bill Sublette, who held all RMFC debt. In 1833, Sublette and Robert Campbell had formed a partnership to supply merchandize to the RMFC and to build trading posts on the Upper Missouri in direct competition with the American Fur Company. While Campbell led a caravan overland to the 1833 rendezvous, Sublette ascended the Missouri River and established thirteen trading posts. The farthest upriver post was Fort William, built three miles downriver from the confluence of the Yellowstone and Missouri. The Company's Fort Union was on the Missouri upriver from the confluence.[98]

On August 30, 1833, Robert Campbell, Milton Sublette, Nathaniel Wyeth, and their men arrived in bull boats at Fort William. In mid-September, leaving Campbell in charge of Fort William, Bill and Milton, who was suffering from a leg injury, left for St. Louis on Bill's keelboat. During the downriver journey, Milton may have told Bill about the Rocky Mountain Fur Company deal with Wyeth to supply goods at a reduced price. Holding all the RMFC debt, Sublette would not want to lose control over the RMFC, which could happen if they incurred additional debt with Wyeth. Meanwhile, Milton's leg was not healing, and when the brothers reached St. Louis, Bernard Farrar, a prominent doctor, treated him.[99]

In January 1834, Bill and Milton traveled to New York City where Bill met with American Fur Company representatives. They agreed Sublette & Campbell would sell the American Fur Company their Missouri River trading posts, and the American Fur Company would not trap or trade in the mountains for one year. Part of the agreement was likely that Sublette would call in the Rocky Mountain Fur Company debt, causing its bankruptcy. In a letter from brother Hugh Campbell to Robert, he wrote concerning the agreement, ". . . but with regard to the importance of setting at rest all competition (unprofitable to both parties) . . . I think the compromise is excellent."[100]

The Sublette brothers returned to St. Louis in February. Black Harris and Benjamin Harrison arrived with Fitzpatrick's letter for Milton. Bill read it and would have discussed with Harris and Harrison the situation in the mountains. Fitzpatrick's letter must have convinced Bill he needed to lead the caravan for the 1834 rendezvous and to leave as soon as possible to demand payment of the RMFC debt before Wyeth could affect it and possibly help sustain the RMFC as a viable business. On April 5, 1834, Bill wrote Robert Campbell, "the arrangement with Captn. Wyeth likely to operate against the goodness of the debt due by the company."[101] Sublette needed to reach the rendezvous before Wyeth, demand the debt payment, and bring an end to the Rocky Mountain Fur Company.

Sublette prepared his caravan, hired thirty-five men, and left for the rendezvous the end of April. Other caravans were also heading west. Michele Cerré led a caravan for Benjamin Bonneville, and Etienne Provost led an American Fur Company caravan for the partnership of Drips & Fontenelle.[102]

Milton Sublette honored his commitment to join Wyeth's caravan, but on May 8, he turned back for St. Louis when his leg problem flared up. Wyeth was escorting Thomas Nuttall, a botanist, and John Townsend, an ornithologist, as well as Methodist ministers Jason Lee and his nephew Daniel Lee bound for Oregon as missionaries to the Flathead and Nez Percé.[103]

Wyeth's caravan had a head start on Sublette's, but by May 11, Sublette overtook Wyeth and was soon two days ahead. Wyeth sent two express riders to Fitzpatrick with letters asking him not to sell his furs or buy merchandise until he reached the rendezvous.[104]

Sublette planned to build a trading post at the Laramie Fork on the North Platte River. When his caravan arrived there May 30, he named the site Fort William and left thirteen men to build the post, later to be renamed Fort Laramie.[105]

On June 13, 1834, Sublette reached the rendezvous on the Green River near Ham's Fork. Two days later, Tom Fitzpatrick rode into Sublette's camp to tell him the rendezvous was moving to a site south of Ham's Fork. Sublette told Fitzpatrick he was demanding repayment of the Rocky Mountain Fur Company's debt. The RMFC did not have enough furs to cover the payment. Bill Sublette bankrupted the Rocky Mountain Fur Company, and it was no more.[106]

Unknown to the June 1834 rendezvous attendees, that same month, John Jacob Astor sold the American Fur Company's Western Department to Pratte, Chouteau, & Company. People would still refer to it as the American Fur Company or just the Company.[107]

---

[1] Robert Athearn, *Forts of the Upper Missouri* (Lincoln, NE: University of Nebraska Press, 1967), 19. Schuler, *Fort Pierre,* 12–13.

[2] Morgan, ed., *Ashley,* 175. Barbour, *Fort Union,* 39. Schuler, *Fort Pierre,* 15.

[3] Warren Angus Ferris, *Life in the Rocky Mountains* (Morrisville, NC: Adansonia Press, Lulu.com, 2018), 26–27. Utley, *Life,* 133–134.

[4] Bill Markley, Paul Andrew Hutton, ed., "Kenneth McKenzie, King of the Upper Missouri," *Roundup!* (Chyenne, WY: La Frontera Publishing, 2010), 125. Chittenden, *Fur Trade,* Vol. 1, 378. Barbour, *Fort Union,* 44.

[5] Enzler, *Bridger,* 57.

[6] Robert Newell, Dorothy Johansen, ed, *Robert Newell's Memoranda: Travels in the Territory of Missourie…* (Portland, OR: Champoeg Press, 1959), 31. Enzler, *Bridger,* 58. Alter, *Bridger,* 113.

[7] Newell, Johansen, ed, *Memoranda,* 31–32. Enzler, *Bridger,* 58. Alter, *Bridger,* 113–114.

[8] This is Newell's number. Meek said the horses numbered 300.

[9] Newell, Johansen, ed, *Memoranda,* 32. Victor, Blevins, ed., *River,* 49–50.

[10] Newell, Johansen, ed, *Memoranda,* 32, 41n8. Enzler, *Bridger,* 59.

[11] Enzler, *Bridger,* 59.

[12] Victor, Blevins, ed., *River,* 51–52.

[13] Don Berry, *A Majority of Scoundrels: An Informal History of the Rocky Mountain Fur Company* (Sausalito, CA: Comstock Editions, Inc., 1961), 269, 277.

[14] Newell, Johansen, ed, *Memoranda,* 32. Ferris, *Rocky Mountains,* 60.

[15] Ferris, *Rocky Mountains,* 60–62.

[16] Newell, Johansen, ed, *Memoranda,* 32. Ferris, *Rocky Mountains,* 60.

[17] Walker, Jr., vol. ed., *Plateau,* Vol. 12, 420–421, 425, 427, 429, 433, 437.

[18] In April 1832, Carson left the RMFC to work for John Gnat. Hafen, ed., *Mountain Men,* 168.

[19] Alter, *Bridger,* 117. Enzler, *Bridger,* 61.

[20] Hafen, ed., *Mountain Men,* 240. Morgan, *Smith,* 327–328.

[21] Morgan, *Smith,* 329–330.

[22] Hafen, ed., *Mountain Men,* 240–241. Morgan, *Smith,* 436n51. Berry, *Scoundrels,* 269, 276.

[23] Ferris, *Rocky Mountains,* 63.

[24] Ferris, *Rocky Mountains,* 64–65. Alter, *Bridger,* 117–118. Newell, Johansen, ed, *Memoranda,* 32.

[25] Ferris, *Rocky Mountains,* 72.

[26] Newell, Johansen, ed, *Memoranda,* 32. Victor, Blevins, ed., *River,* 54.

[27] Victor, Blevins, ed., *River,* 55. Enzler, *Bridger,* 62.

[28] Berry, *Scoundrels,* 280.

[29] Alter, *Bridger,* 119. Berry, *Scoundrels,* 280, 282. Ferris, *Rocky Mountains,* 75. Newell, Johansen, ed, *Memoranda,* 32.

[30] Ferris, *Rocky Mountains,* 75.

[31] Victor, Blevins, ed., *River,* 55–58, 60.

[32] Ibid, 58.

[33] Don Johnson, ed., *The Journals of Captain Nathaniel J. Wyeth's Expeditions to the Oregon Country, 1831–1836* (Fairfield, WA: Ye Galleon Press, 1997), 14–15. Sunder, *Sublette,* 105. Ferris, *Rocky Mountains,* 75–76. Hafen, ed., *Mountain Men,* 241.

[34] Campbell, *Narrative,* 102–103. Sunder, *Sublette,* 99–100, 102–103.

[35] Sunder, *Sublette,* 103–107. Johnson, ed., *Wyeth,* 11, 14.

[36] Sunder, *Sublette,* 108. Berry, *Scoundrels,* 282. Hardee, *Pierre's Hole,* 164, 172, 182. Ferris, *Rocky Mountains,* 76. Victor, Blevins, ed., *River,* 59.

[37] Milo Quaife, ed., *Adventures of a Mountain Man: The Narrative of Zenas Leonard* (Lincoln, NE: University of Nebraska Press, 1978), 59–60. Ferris, *Rocky Mountains,* 76.

[38] DeMallie, editor, *Plains,* Vol. 13, Part 2, 677–679, 685. Campbell, *Narrative,* 55–56.

[39] Quaife, ed., *Leonard,* 61, 63–64. Ferris, *Rocky Mountains,* 76. Hafen, ed., *Mountain Men,* 241–242. Berry, *Scoundrels,* 286.

[40] Victor, Blevins, ed., *River,* 60–61. Hardee, *Pierre's Hole,* 171, 274–277. Berry, *Scoundrels,* 287.

[41] Johnson, ed., *Wyeth,* 15, 101 n8. Berry, *Scoundrels,* 290. Hardee, *Pierre's Hole,* 176. Sunder, *Sublette,* 108. Hafen, ed., *Mountain Men,* 317.

[42] Hardee, *Pierre's Hole,* 246–247.

[43] Ibid, 247, 249, 259.

[44] Ibid, 250, 252.

[45] Johnson, ed., *Wyeth,* 15. Hardee, *Pierre's Hole,* 251.

[46] Hardee, *Pierre's Hole,* 251–253.
[47] Ibid, 253–254.
[48] Ibid.
[49] Ibid, 225, 254.
[50] Hardee, *Pierre's Hole,* 255. Campbell, *Narrative,* 60.
[51] Hardee, *Pierre's Hole,* 255.
[52] Hardee, *Pierre's Hole,* 257, 259. Chittenden, *Fur Trade,* Vol. 2, 661.
[53] Hardee, *Pierre's Hole,* 271. Sunder, *Sublette,* 110. Johnson, ed., *Wyeth,* 15.
[54] Berry, *Scoundrels,* 297–298. Sunder, *Sublette,* 112.
[55] Washington Irving, *The Adventures of Captain Bonneville* (Washington, D.C.: National Geographic Society, 2003), 65. Hafen, ed., *Mountain Men,* 274, 276–277, 366. Hardee, *Pierre's Hole,* 280–282. Robertson, *Struggle,* 77. Ferris, *Rocky Mountains,* 78–79. Berry, *Scoundrels,* 282. Alter, *Bridger,* 127.
[56] Ferris, *Rocky Mountains,* 84. Newell, Johansen, ed, *Memoranda,* 32. Alter, *Bridger,* 126.
[57] Alter, *Bridger,* 127. Ferris, *Rocky Mountains,* 83–84. Irving, *Bonneville,* 65–66.
[58] Alter, *Bridger,* 127–128.
[59] Ferris, *Rocky Mountains,* 85.
[60] Ferris, *Rocky Mountains,* 87. Chittenden, *Fur Trade,* Vol. 2, 667.
[61] Ferris, *Rocky Mountains,* 87.
[62] Ibid.
[63] Irving, *Bonneville,* 67.
[64] Newell, Johansen, ed, *Memoranda,* 32. Ferris, *Rocky Mountains,* 92.
[65] Victor, Blevins, ed., *River,* 78.
[66] Earl of Southesk (James Carnegie), *Saskatchewan and the Rocky Mountains: A Diary and Narrative of Travel...* (Toronto, Canada: James Campbell and Son, 1875), 160. Ferris, *Rocky Mountains,* 92. Irving, *Bonneville,* 67.
[67] Ferris, *Rocky Mountains,* 92. Irving, *Bonneville,* 68.
[68] Ferris, *Rocky Mountains,* 92. Irving, *Bonneville,* 68.
[69] Southesk, *Saskatchewan,* 161. Victor, Blevins, ed., *River,* 79. Irving, *Bonneville,* 68.
[70] Irving, *Bonneville,* 68–69.
[71] Irving, *Bonneville,* 69. Enzler, *Bridger,* 71–73.
[72] Southesk, *Saskatchewan,* 161–162.
[73] Ferris, *Rocky Mountains,* 91–92.
[74] Ibid, 87–88.
[75] Ferris, *Rocky Mountains,* 88–92. Southesk, *Saskatchewan,* 161.
[76] Southesk, *Saskatchewan,* 160–161.
[77] Ferris, *Rocky Mountains,* 92–93, 96. Newell, Johansen, ed, *Memoranda,* 32. Alter, *Bridger,* 132. Robertson, *Struggle,* 32.
[78] Alter, *Bridger,* 133. Enzler, *Bridger,* 74. Victor, Blevins, ed., *River,* 80. Johnson, ed., *Wyeth,* 110.
[79] Charles Larpenteur, Elliot Coues, ed. *Forty Years A Fur Trader: The Personal Narrative of Charles Larpenteur, 1833–1872,* (Minneapolis, MN: Ross & Haines, Inc., 1962), 15, 25. Enzler, *Bridger,* 74.
[80] Larpenteur, Coues, ed. *Trader,* 25. Campbell, *Narrative,* 64–65.
[81] Larpenteur, Coues, ed. *Trader,* 16–17. Berry, *Scoundrels,* 344.
[82] Larpenteur, Coues, ed. *Trader,* 27, 74–75.
[83] Enzler, *Bridger,* 75–76.
[84] Ibid, 77.
[85] Larpenteur, Coues, ed. *Trader,* 30, 36–38. Berry, *Scoundrels,* 346, 350. Johnson, ed., *Wyeth,* 57. Irving, *Bonneville,* 119. Robertson, *Struggle,* 77. Enzler, *Bridger,* 82.
[86] Berry, *Scoundrels,* 348–350, 356–357.
[87] Berry, *Scoundrels,* 351–352, 364. Johnson, ed., *Wyeth,* 61. Irving, *Bonneville,* 132, 134–135, 159. Chittenden, *Fur Trade,* Vol. 1, 351.
[88] Irving, *Bonneville,* 159–160. Berry, *Scoundrels,* 364–366. Chittenden, *Fur Trade,* Vol. 1, 351.
[89] Irving, *Bonneville,* 160. Berry, *Scoundrels,* 365.
[90] Bonner, ed., Oswald, ed., *Beckwourth,* 274–284. Berry, *Scoundrels,* 365–366. Robertson, *Struggle,* 89. Chittenden, *Fur Trade,* Vol. 1, 302, 351.
[91] Berry, *Scoundrels,* 366.
[92] Ibid, 350, 380–381.
[93] Milo Quaife, ed., *Kit Carson's Autobiography* (Chicago, IL: R. R. Donnelley & Sons Co., 1935) 33, 37. Enzler, *Bridger,* 77.
[94] Donlin, *Fur,* 259.

[95] David Brown, *Three Years in the Rocky Mountains* (Cincinnati, OH: Cincinnati Daily Morning Atlas, 1845), 26–30. Miller, Ross, ed., *Miller,* 159. Enzler, *Bridger,* 78.

[96] Enzler, *Bridger,* 81. Quaife, ed., *Carson,* 37, 39.

[97] Dale Morgan, ed., and Eleanor Harris, ed., *The Rocky Mountain Journals of William Marshall Anderson: The West in 1834,* (Lincoln: NE: University of Nebraska Press, 1987), 147. Enzler, *Bridger,* 83.

[98] Sunder, *Sublette,* 116–117, 126, 128, 130. Robertson, *Struggle,* 230.

[99] Sunder, *Sublette,* 128–129, 131.

[100] Sunder, *Sublette,* 134. Berry, *Scoundrels,* 378. Utley, *Life,* 145.

[101] Sunder, *Sublette,* 137. Berry, *Scoundrels,* 380–381.

[102] Bernard DeVoto, *Across the Wide Missouri* (New York, NY: Houghton Mifflin Co., 1947), 190. Sunder, *Sublette,* 137–138. Morgan, Harris, eds., *Anderson,* 73, 282, 347.

[103] Johnson, ed. *Wyeth,* 71. Sunder, *Sublette,* 139. DeVoto, *Missouri,* 12–13.

[104] Johnson, ed. *Wyeth,* 71, 123.

[105] Enzler, *Bridger,* 82. Morgan, Harris, eds., *Anderson,* 110. Sunder, *Sublette,* 140.

[106] Enzler, *Bridger,* 82. Sunder, *Sublette,* 140. Berry, *Scoundrels,* 397.

[107] Sunder, *Sublette,* 134. Utley, *Life,* 145.

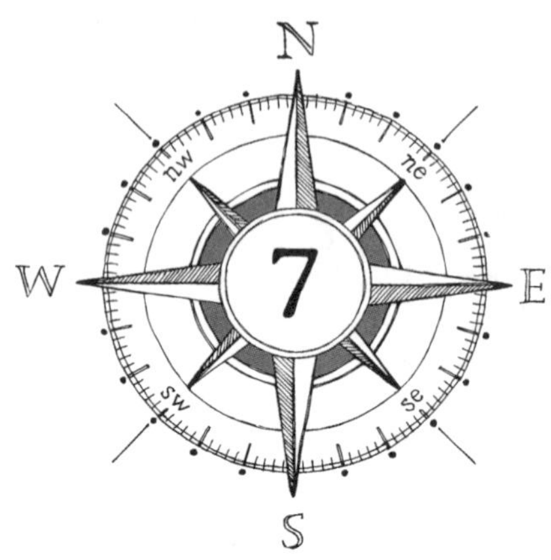

Fontenelle, Fitzpatrick & Company
1834–1836

When Jim Bridger arrived at the 1834 Green River rendezvous, on June 25, the Rocky Mountain Fur Company was a thing of the past, and he was a partner in a new company, Fitzpatrick, Sublette, & Bridger. "Sublette" referred to Milton Sublette who was back in St. Louis. Tom Fitzpatrick had made all the decisions for the three partners.

Irishman Thomas Fitzpatrick was well educated and adventurous. His skills as a trapper, businessman, and treaty negotiator earned respect from all corners. ILLUSTRATION COURTESY OF THE NATIONAL PARK SERVICE.

Nathaniel Wyeth had ridden ahead of his caravan, arriving at the rendezvous on June 18, and found Fitzpatrick, but it was too late. Fitzpatrick had traded the Rocky Mountain Fur Company furs to Bill Sublette to help cover the company's debt. Wyeth wrote, "much to my astonishment the goods which I had contracted to bring up to the Rocky Mountain fur Co. were refused by those gentlemen." Fitzpatrick paid Wyeth the $500 penalty and money Wyeth had advanced to Milton Sublette. Wyeth was angry, telling the RMFC partners, "Gentlemen, I will roll a stone into your garden that you will never be able to get out." Wyeth planned to take his goods west to the confluence of the Snake and Portneuf Rivers and build a fort to trade with the tribes. He would name it Fort Hall.[1]

A whirlwind of deals ensued on June 20, 1834.

First, Henry Fraeb left the partnership, selling his interest to Milton Sublette, Fitzpatrick, Gervais, and Bridger for forty horses, forty traps, eight guns, and $1,000 of merchandise.

Second, Jean Baptiste Gervais left the partnership for twenty horses, thirty traps, and $500 of merchandise.

Third, the partners wrote and signed a two-part notice. The first part let all know of the dissolution of the Rocky Mountain Fur Company and requested that anyone the company owed money to or who owed the company money should conduct their business with them as soon as possible. The second part notified that the former business would be conducted by a new company named Fitzpatrick, Sublette, & Bridger. Milton Sublette was not there, but someone signed for him. Bridger could not write, so an X was made for his signature. Either someone made it for him on June 20 or he made his mark after his arrival on June 25.[2]

When Bridger's brigade arrived, the rendezvous was in full swing. William Anderson estimated more than 1,500 people attended, writing on June 27, "Nothing in the camps, now but drunken songs & brawls day or night." Betting on horse races was a major form of entertainment. Bridger riding Otholoho was a big winner, and he claimed he made lots of money betting on his own horse and valuing him at $3,000.[3]

Nathaniel Wyeth led his caravan west on July 2. William Stewart joined them, wanting to see the country and hoping to board a ship bound for Great Britain. On July 9, having done the damage he had come to do, Bill Sublette and his caravan, hauling sixty beaver packs, left for St. Louis.[4]

Bridger and Fitzpatrick wanted nothing to do with Bill Sublette as their supplier, and Fitzpatrick had burned their bridges with Wyeth. To have an outlet for their beaver pelts and a source for trade goods and supplies, on August 3 they partnered with Lucien Fontenelle and Andrew Drips, whose company Pratte, Chouteau, & Company supplied. The weeks-old company Fitzpatrick,

Sublette, & Bridger was replaced by Fontenelle, Fitzpatrick & Company. Etienne Provost's Company caravan arrived and resupplied them.[5]

On August 6, 1834, Bridger's fifty-man brigade, including Kit Carson and Joe Meek, left the rendezvous. Anderson wrote of Bridger's men, "There are many brave, rough fellows among them, whom I most heartily wish well—They have been kind and accommodating to me, a stranger—I have been hungry in the desert and they have given me elk and buffalo meat." Andrew Drips led his brigade away from the rendezvous, but it's not known in what direction. The following day, Fitzpatrick and Fontenelle joined Provost's caravan and began their journey to St. Louis. Bridger led a brigade toward the headwaters of the Gallatin, Madison, and Jefferson Rivers—Blackfeet territory.[6]

Sometime during the years 1834 and 1835, Jim Bridger married a Flathead girl, giving her the English name Cora. Grenville Dodge wrote she was the daughter of a chief. Bridger biographer Gene Caesar wrote that Bridger had married the daughter of the first chief, but he cited no sources. Another Bridger biographer, J. Cecil Alter, believed Cora was the daughter of Chief Insillah. Samuel Parker wrote that Insillah was the most influential Flathead chief.[7]

The Blackfeet harassed Bridger's trappers. "Five of our men were killed," Kit Carson said. "A trapper could hardly go a mile from camp without being fired upon." Bridger led the brigade out of Blackfeet territory, hunting beaver along Pierre's Fork, today's Teton River. There they met Doc Newell leading a Fontenelle, Fitzpatrick & Co. brigade that was returning from trading with the Flathead. The two brigades traveled along Henry's Fork, reaching the Snake River in November 1834, where they established their winter camp sixty miles upriver from Nathaniel Wyeth's Fort Hall.[8]

On January 20, 1835, twelve of Bridger's men left the brigade and were hired by Captain Joseph Thing, Wyeth's second in command. In March, they would be part of a seventeen-man brigade led by Joseph Gale.[9]

It was relatively peaceful in Bridger's winter camp until early February when Blackfeet raiders on snowshoes stole eighteen horses, including Bridger's favorite, Otholoho. Upset at losing his valuable horse, Bridger led a posse of twelve to fifteen men including Joe Meek, Isaac Rose, and Kit Carson. They followed the raiders through deep snow fifty miles into the mountains. The Blackfeet glided on snowshoes while Bridger's men trudged through the snow.[10]

The men walked single file through deep snow. Bridger was in the lead when he spied smoke rising above the trees ahead. He rushed forward as the others followed. Coming to a clearing, he saw the Blackfeet had stopped to eat. When they saw him running at them, they began strapping on their snowshoes. One warrior nocked an arrow to shoot Bridger, but he was faster and shot the warrior, shouting, "Come on boys, let's give them hail Columbia!" Several mountaineers shot before the Blackfeet disappeared into the trees, taking a hill-side defensive position.[11]

The posse called to the raiders for a parley to which they agreed. Each side sent one man to walk out between the two sides to talk. The Blackfeet negotiator claimed they thought the brigade's stolen horses belonged to Shoshone. They did not want to steal from Whites. The White negotiator replied if the Blackfeet were truly friendly, they would put down their weapons to smoke and talk. They agreed to this. Each side left one man to guard their weapons while everyone else sat to smoke and talk.[12]

The Blackfeet agreed to return the horses and sent word to the herd guards to bring them to the mountaineers. They led forward the five worst horses, stating these were all they were willing to return. This was unacceptable to Bridger's men. The talks were over. Each side went for their weapons and fighting resumed.[13]

Kit Carson and Mark Head had advanced beyond the other mountaineers when they came upon two Blackfeet warriors, one in front of Carson and the other in front of Head. Carson saw the warrior in front of Head raise his gun to shoot Head. Taking his eye off the warrior in front of him, Carson shot, killing the man aiming at Head. Carson glanced back at the warrior in front of him who was aiming his gun at Carson's chest. Carson dove to the side as the warrior fired. The bullet grazed Carson's neck then passed through his shoulder.[14]

The fighting lasted until nightfall when the mountaineers broke off and established camp a mile away. Next morning, they returned to the scene of the fight, but the Blackfeet now outnumbered the mountaineers, and they could not recover the horses. The mountaineers returned to their encampment, and Bridger organized a thirty-man posse and led them to the scene of the fight only to find the Blackfeet and their horses were long gone.[15]

Bridger's men bought replacement horses from the Nez Percé, and they were soon on the spring beaver hunt. They had a successful hunt trapping along the Snake and then the Green River.[16]

From May into August, people arrived at Horse Creek on the Green River for the 1835 rendezvous. Roughly 300 mountaineers, along with large bands of Ute, Shoshone, Nez Percé, and Flathead, waited for the caravan.[17]

Bridger's brigade arrived around May 31 and established the Fontenelle, Fitzpatrick & Co. encampment. Andrew Drips rode in with his F, F & Co. brigade, and a Hudson's Bay Company brigade led by Francis Ermatinger appeared, accompanied by William Stewart. Nathaniel Wyeth did not attend; he was managing his business ventures from his new Fort William near the confluence of the Columbia and Willamette Rivers in western Oregon. Captain Benjamin Bonneville also skipped the rendezvous. Leaving a brigade in the mountains, Bonneville and the remainder of his men returned to the States.[18]

Waiting for the F, F & Co. caravan, the mountaineers and their families, as well as members of the various Indian bands, visited, feasted, played games, wrestled, raced their horses, and gambled.[19]

Tom Fitzpatrick, guiding the caravan, arrived on August 12, 1835. Accompanying him were two missionaries to the Flathead and Nez Percé, Congregationalist Reverend Samuel Parker and Presbyterian Doctor Marcus Whitman. Parker wrote:

> In the afternoon, we came to the Green river, a branch of the Colorado, in latitude 42°, here the caravan hold their rendezvous. This is a widely extended valley, which is pleasant, with a soil sufficiently fertile for cultivation, if the climate was not so cold. Like the country we have passed through, it is almost entirely prairie, with some woods skirting the streams of water.[20]

Fitzpatrick updated Bridger on the latest news. Bill Sublette and Robert Campbell had sold them Fort William on the North Platte and Laramie Rivers where they had established a good trade with the Lakota. Lucien Fontenelle had a late start with the caravan leaving Liberty, Missouri, on May 15. Asiatic cholera, a new disease sweeping through America, hit the caravan. Many became ill and three died. If it wasn't for Dr. Whitman's medical care, more would have died. Reaching Fort William, Fontenelle remained there. Probably the worst news was the St. Louis price for beaver fur had dropped. Hatters were using cheaper materials, and more men chose silk hats.[21]

Marcus Whitman's missionary work brought him to the Oregon Country, but his skills as a medical doctor were in high demand. ILLUSTRATION FROM *HOW MARCUS WHITMAN SAVED OREGON*, BY OLIVER W. NIXON, 1895, COURTESY OF PROJECT GUTENBERG.

The Blackfeet arrowhead lodged in Bridger's backside had been plaguing him since October 1832. Whitman agreed to attempt to remove it. Parker wrote:

> It was a difficult operation, because the arrow was hooked at the point by striking a large bone, and a cartilaginous substance had grown around it. The Doctor pursued the operation with great self-possession and perseverance; and his patient manifested equal firmness. The Indians looked on meanwhile, with countenances indicating wonder, and in their own peculiar manner expressed great astonishment when it was extracted.

The doctor was soon examining everyone with medical needs.[22]

One evening, Joseph Chouinard challenged anyone to fight. Chouinard, a large, powerful Frenchman in Andrew Drips' brigade, called himself "the great bully of the mountains" and whipped anyone who displeased him. Riding his horse through camp while resting the butt of his rifle on his knee, he shouted he had no trouble flogging Frenchmen, and as for Americans, they were children, and he would flog them with a switch. Kit Carson confronted him, saying he was the worst American, and if Chouinard didn't stop his threats he would rip his guts. Chouinard said nothing, rode his horse out to the front of the camp, and waited for Carson. Smiling to himself, Carson grabbed his pistol, mounted his horse, and galloped out to Chouinard. Carson reined in his horse so close to Chouinard's, the two animals touched. Carson demanded to know if Chouinard intended to shoot him. "No," said Chouinard, as he raised his rifle to shoot. Both fired simultaneously. Chouinard's bullet passed Carson's head, cutting his hair and gunpowder burning his eye. Carson's bullet hit Chouinard's hand, came out at the wrist, then passed through his arm above the elbow. Carson returned to his lodge for another pistol. Chouinard begged for his life, and Carson relented. Years later, Carson said, "During the remainder of our stay in camp we had no more bother with this French bully."[23]

Christopher "Kit" Carson was known for his courage, tenacity, and fighting skills. PHOTOGRAPH FROM THE BRADY-HANDY COLLECTION, COURTESY OF THE LIBRARY OF CONGRESS, LC-DIG-CWPBH-00514.

Samuel Parker noted the mountaineers would "squander away their wages in ornaments for their women and children," Dr. Marcus Whitman and Parker met with Flathead and Nez Percé leaders, believing these tribes sincerely wanted to learn about Christianity. They would need additional teachers, and the two ministers devised a plan. Whitman would return to the East to recruit more workers, while Parker accompanied the Flathead and Nez Percé to their home territory to start teaching them. The missionaries presented the plan to the Flathead and Nez Percé leaders, who agreed to it.[24]

On August 21, 1835, Jim Bridger led his fifty-man brigade away from the rendezvous for the fall beaver hunt in Blackfeet territory. Samuel Parker with the Flathead and Nez Percé bands joined Bridger's brigade. On August 27,

Tom Fitzpatrick, taking with him William Stewart and Marcus Whitman, would lead the trade caravan on its eastward return.[25]

As Bridger's brigade and the Flathead and Nez Percé bands rode north into Jackson Hole, Parker noted the Indians' order of travel, "The first chief leads the way, the next chiefs follow, then the common men, and after these the women and children. The place assigned me was with the first chief."[26]

August 23 was a sabbath day, and Bridger allowed a day of rest. That afternoon, Parker held a church service. The congregation sat on the ground above a deep, narrow defile. Above them rose snowcapped mountains. The men conducted themselves well and paid attention to the sermon. Parker admonished them, saying they were unfit for heaven unless they had a change of heart. The service ended abruptly when a buffalo herd appeared, and the men rushed to their horses to give chase. They killed twenty-five buffalo, and everyone feasted that evening. Parker rebuked the sabbath breakers before devouring a tenderloin cut.[27]

On August 28, the brigade and the Flathead and Nez Percé bands began crossing over a mountain pass to the west that would bring them to Pierre's Hole. Indian hunters found a small buffalo herd and chased it toward the cavalcade. The buffalo raced through the column. One ran over a horse ridden by a child, and the horse threw the child down a steep slope. Fortunately, the child was only slightly hurt. Another buffalo injured a packhorse. Crossing the mountain pass, the travelers descended into Pierre's Hole.[28]

On Sunday, August 30, Parker remained with the Flathead and Nez Percé who would be heading west to their home territory. Bridger led his brigade to the northeast to hunt beaver in Blackfeet territory. The Flathead's first chief, his family, and some of his followers rode with Bridger's brigade to hunt buffalo.[29]

It was early September when Bridger's brigade, now numbering sixty men, along with the twenty-member Flathead band, reached Henry's Lake west of Yellowstone. There they encamped and sent out small trapping parties.[30]

On September 9, fourteen of Bridger's trappers, including Kit Carson and Joe Meek, were in the Madison River headwaters when they spied a camp of White men and raced to it at full gallop. This was Nathaniel Wyeth's brigade led by Joseph Gale out of Fort Hall. Many of the men were those who had left Bridger to work for Wyeth in January 1835. Bridger's men stayed with Gale's brigade that evening, telling each other yarns and exchanging news.[31]

Gale's brigade began with twenty-four men but experienced a lot of trouble along the way. One man drowned crossing a river. Sixty naked warriors attacked, wounding two men, stealing six horses, and killing three more. The brigade lost two rifles crossing a river. When they entered territory new to Gale, he would not listen to mountaineers who knew it well. He was argumentative and tyrannical. Three men quit and left the brigade but not before one of them gave Gale a sound beating. A fifty-eight-year-old man disappeared while out trapping. On August 22, four trappers and one camp keeper dropped behind the brigade, and when out of sight, rode away.[32]

On the morning of September 10, eight of Bridger's men left Gale's camp, riding downstream to set traps, but within an hour they came galloping back chased by eighty Blackfeet warriors. The warriors climbed the bluffs overlooking the camp and fired into it, wounding the trappers' heads, shoulders, and arms but killing no one. They killed two horses and a mule and severely wounded five additional animals. The trappers took cover in thick brush. The Blackfeet set fire to it, hoping to drive out the trappers. Flames roared through the overhead tree canopy while the men below set counterfires to stop the brushfire advance. By 4 P.M., the Blackfeet had enough. A leader stood on a rock ledge, and grasping the edges of his robe, raised it high then smacked the ground with it three times. The firing stopped and the Blackfeet rode away in silence.[33]

Gale and Bridger's men broke camp and rode to join Bridger's brigade on the Madison River. One trapper had been shot in the shoulder. Bridger worked on the man, probing for the ball and then extracting it. Bridger's patient would recover. Gale's brigade was so disabled by loss of men and livestock that Bridger told them they could travel with him to the Snake River where both groups planned to winter.[34]

At sunrise on September 11, an alarm was shouted, "Blackfeet!" Thirty warriors stood lined on a ridgetop. In the center, one of them held a pole with an American flag attached. Bridger led twenty-nine trappers on foot toward the Blackfeet. When they were 300 yards apart, the Blackfeet motioned for Bridger's men to stop and for only two to advance to parley with two of their representatives. Bridger sent two men who spoke Blackfeet. Both sides sat while the four men smoked and talked between the lines. A half hour later, they returned to their respective sides. The White negotiators said the Blackfeet were

Many western tribes held the custom of sharing a pipe of peace as a greeting and as a prelude to discussions and negotiations. PAINTING BY ALFRED JACOB MILLER, COURTESY OF THE WALTERS ART MUSEUM, 37.1940.186.

Peigan, numbering forty-five and well-armed. All they wanted was peace with the Whites. Bridger invited them into camp. There they again smoked the pipe of peace and received friendly treatment from Bridger's men. The chief warned that several Blood parties were in the area. The Peigan stayed throughout the day, and when evening came, they left except one who wanted to spend the night.[35]

On September 13, Bridger led the brigades westward twenty miles and camped on a divide. A French trapper decided to ride ahead and set a few traps. His friends tried to talk him out of it, but he left anyway. He was several miles from camp when Blackfeet warriors shot and scalped him. The next day, the brigades followed the streams to the west. Small parties tried to trap, but Blackfeet warriors harassed them.[36]

They were hunting beaver in the Jefferson River watershed when Flathead Indians visited and said their village was located on the Beaverhead River, a tributary of the Jefferson. On September 19, the brigades rode to the Flathead and Pend d'Oreille village of 180 lodges and camped with them. Francis Ermatinger's Hudson's Bay brigade was there trading for beaver pelts. The next day, everyone moved twelve miles upriver and joined a 130-lodge village of Flathead and Pend d'Oreille. After several days of visiting, Bridger led the brigades to the southeast continuing to hunt beaver. Plenty of buffalo grazed

Titled "Trappers making their escape from hostile Blackfeet," this painting documents a routine hazard of life during the fur trade. PAINTING BY ALFRED JACOB MILLER, COURTESY OF THE BEINECKE RARE BOOK AND MANUSCRIPT LIBRARY, YALE UNIVERSITY, WA MSS 342.

in the Jefferson River valley and the men hunted them, but they had to be wary of the ever-present Blackfeet.[37]

Joseph Gale did not like being dependent on Bridger for horses and mules. He selected Osborne Russell to ride alone to Fort Hall to bring back horses. Bridger and his men advised Russell not to attempt the ride, but he did not want Gale to call him a coward and rode off on September 30.[38]

By October 19, 1835, Bridger and Gale's brigades had separated on their approach to the Snake River. Bridger headed to the confluence of Henry's Fork and the Snake River, and Gale followed the Snake downriver to Fort Hall. Bridger's brigade settled in for the winter fifteen miles north of the fort on Blackfoot Creek.[39]

Mary Ann, the daughter of Jim and Cora Bridger, was born during the winter, in either 1835 or 1836.[40] Nothing has been written about her early life, but she likely had a healthy and happy childhood.

That winter, Kit Carson and a few others left Bridger to join Thomas McKay's Hudson's Bay brigade bound for waterways flowing into the Great Basin. In February 1836, Osborne Russell joined Bridger's brigade. After Gale had sent him to Fort Hall for horses, he had not returned, and everyone presumed him dead. Gale had given him faulty directions. After traveling in the wrong direction, he had to backtrack. At times he was low on water and food. Bannock and later Shoshone helped him. He reached Fort Hall on October 20, 1835, and on December 20, Nathaniel Wyeth discharged Russell and his fellow brigade members.[41]

The quality of the food supply for Bridger's brigade was poor. Hunters had driven the buffalo herds over the divide, and deep snow prevented their return. All that was available were tough, old, solitary bull buffalos.[42]

On March 28, 1836, Bridger's brigade left on its spring beaver hunt. The party traveled up the Snake River to Lewis' Fork, then rode in a southerly direction, reaching the Bear River in early May. There they found Andrew Drips' 120-man brigade, along with 400 Shoshone and Bannock lodges and 100 Flathead and Nez Percé lodges. The brigades and tribes traveled to Ham's Fork on the Green River. There, they found insufficient grass for the horse herds; the bands needed to spread out. Bridger told them to gather at Horse Creek by July 1, when he expected the caravan's arrival.[43]

On June 28, 1836, Bridger and Drips' brigades established their encampment along the Green River north of Horse Creek and built a temporary eighteen-foot-square log trading hut. The men set up their tents to the right and left of the hut. Other mountaineers located their camps upriver of the F, F & Co. men. The Shoshone and Bannock encampment stretched three miles upriver from the mouth of Horse Creek. The Flathead and Nez Percé camp was also along Horse Creek, six miles from its mouth.[44]

Leading a small party, Nathaniel Wyeth arrived on July 1. He was returning East and had agreed to sell Fort Hall to the Hudson's Bay Company. The transaction would be complete the following year. Kit Carson rode in with Thomas McKay's Hudson's Bay brigade. Upon reaching the rendezvous, he resigned from that brigade.[45]

A messenger from the caravan arrived to announce it would reach the rendezvous in a couple of days. Tom Fitzpatrick led the caravan, and Reverend

Marcus Whitman accompanied it, bringing additional missionaries, two of whom were women. Joe Meek and six other mountaineers were excited to meet the women, and twelve Nez Percé were eager to meet the missionaries. The Nez Percé also had a letter from Samuel Parker for Whitman. The nineteen men rode off to greet the travelers along the trail.[46]

The caravan reached the rendezvous on July 3. It was large—400 horses and mules, twenty carts loaded with supplies, all managed by seventy *engagés*. Black Harris was along to assist Fitzpatrick. The past winter, Blackfeet had shot Fitzpatrick in the hand and ruined it. Indians gave him a new name: "Broken Hand."[47]

F, F & Co. partners Lucien Fontenelle and Milton Sublette arrived, too. Milton's damaged left leg had grown worse, and on February 4, 1835, Dr. Bernard Farrar had amputated it in St. Louis. Milton got around using a cork leg. He would return to Fort William where he would later die on April 5, 1837. Joshua Pilcher, representative of Pratte, Chouteau, & Company, which people still referred to as the Company, was with them. Captain William Stewart rode along with a German gentleman, Mr. Sillem, three servants, two dogs, and two blooded horses to race.[48]

The Protestant revival known as the Second Great Awakening spurred Narcissa Prentiss to become a missionary. She then married Marcus Whitman, and the couple traveled west to begin their work among the tribes. ILLUSTRATION FROM *HOW MARCUS WHITMAN SAVED OREGON,* BY OLIVER W. NIXON, 1895, COURTESY OF PROJECT GUTENBERG.

The arrivals who caused the most excitement were the missionaries. Marcus Whitman and his bride of February, Narcissa, and Reverend Henry Spalding and his wife, Eliza, were traveling to Oregon to teach the tribes about Jesus. Along with them was William Gray, their secular agent, and two employees. They brought with them two wagons, fourteen horses, six mules, and fifteen head of beef and milk cattle.[49]

Jim Bridger must have greeted Whitman warmly, who then would have introduced Bridger to Narcissa and the other members of the missionary party. Narcissa and Eliza were the first White women to reach the Rocky Mountains. Most of the Indians had never seen White women, and for many mountaineers it had been years.[50] Narcissa wrote to her sister Julia:

> As soon as I alighted from my horse I was met by a company of matron women. One after another shaking hands and salluting [*sic*] me with a most hearty kiss. This was unexpected and affected me very much. They gave Sister Spaulding the same salutation. After we had been seated awhile in the midst of the gazing throng, one of the chiefs whom we had seen before came with his wife and very politely introduced her to us. They say they all like us very much and thank God that they have seen us, and that we have come to live with them.[51]

William Gray estimated 1,500 people attended the rendezvous. Six days after the missionaries' arrival, the Flathead, Nez Percé, Shoshone, and Bannock put on a procession. Painted men carrying their weapons rode past the mission camp. The women were dressed in their finest, decorated with much beadwork. People sang and played musical instruments. Once the procession ended, they thronged the mission camp to visit the missionaries.[52]

For the Fontenelle, Fitzpatrick & Company partners, there were business matters to address. Pratte, Chouteau, & Company wanted to buy them out. The Company's representative, Joshua Pilcher, met with Bridger, Fitzpatrick, Milton Sublette, Fontenelle, and Drips, and made them an offer they couldn't refuse. They agreed to sell Fort William, soon to be renamed Fort Laramie. The Company bought all their merchandise. The partners and their men were retained as employees of the Company and were renamed the Rocky Mountain Outfit.[53]

The Company was now the dominant American fur trader in the Upper Missouri and northern Rocky Mountains. The Company had won.

---

[1] Berry, *Scoundrels,* 397. Johnson, ed. *Wyeth,* 75, 124. Enzler, *Bridger,* 82. Victor, Blevins, ed., *River,* 105. Robertson, *Struggle,* 122.

[2] Alter, *Bridger,* 147–148. Chittenden, *Fur Trade,* Vol. 1 and 2, 304, unnumbered page between 864–865.

[3] Morgan, Harris, eds., *Anderson,* 135, 146–147. Enzler, *Bridger,* 85.

[4] Morgan, Harris, eds., *Anderson,* 356. Alter, *Bridger,* 149.
[5] Alter, *Bridger,* 149. Chittenden, *Fur Trade,* Vol. 1, 305. Morgan, Harris, eds., *Anderson,* 309, 347.
[6] Quaife, ed., *Carson,* 39. Victor, Blevins, ed., *River,* 107. Morgan, Harris, eds., *Anderson,* 174–176, 214, 295, 309. Hafen, ed., *Mountain Men,* 170.
[7] Gene Caesar, *King of the Mountain Men: The Life of Jim Bridger* (New York, NY: E. P. Dutton Co., 1961), 162–163. Samuel Parker, *Journal of an exploring tour beyond the Rocky Mountains...* (Ithaca, NY: Andrus, Woodruff, & Gauntlett, 1844), 81. Dodge, *Bridger,* 21. Alter, *Bridger,* 156. Enzler, *Bridger,* 85.
[8] Osborne Russell, Aubrey Haines, ed., *Journal of a Trapper* (Lincoln, NE: University of Nebraska Press, 1955), 8. Newell, Johansen, ed, *Memoranda,* 33. Enzler, *Bridger,* 87. Quaife, ed., *Carson,* 40.
[9] Russell, Haines, ed., *Journal,* 9.
[10] James Marsh, *Four Years in the Rockies, or the Adventures of Isaac P. Rose* (New Castle, PA: Printed by W. B. Thomas, 1884), 70–71. Quaife, ed., *Carson,* 40. Victor, Blevins, ed., *River,* 85.
[11] Marsh, *Rose,* 71.
[12] Quaife, ed., *Carson,* 40–41.
[13] Ibid, 41.
[14] Ibid.
[15] Ibid, 42.
[16] Quaife, ed., *Carson,* 42. Victor, Blevins, ed., *River,* 86.
[17] Enzler, *Bridger,* 88. DeVoto, *Missouri,* 58. Parker, *Journal,* 79–80. Ferris, *Rocky Mountains,* 143.
[18] Alter, *Bridger,* 151. Quaife, ed., *Carson,* 42. Russell, Haines, ed., *Journal,* 13–14. Robertson, *Struggle,* 252. Irving, *Bonneville,* 281, 288.
[19] DeVoto, *Missouri,* 226.
[20] DeVoto, *Missouri,* 221. Parker, *Journal,* 79.
[21] Hafen, ed., *Mountain Men,* 244. Larpenteur, Coues, ed. *Trader,* 23. Chittenden, *Fur Trade,* Vol. 1, 305. DeVoto, *Missouri,* 218, 220. Enzler, *Bridger,* 89.
[22] Parker, *Journal,* 80–81.
[23] Quaife, ed., *Carson,* 42–44. Marsh, *Rose,* 152. Parker, *Journal,* 84. Utley, *Life,* 128, 350–351 n11.
[24] Parker, *Journal,* 82–83, 85.
[25] Parker, *Journal,* 86–87. Morgan, Harris, eds., *Anderson,* 357. DeVoto, *Missouri,* 235.
[26] Parker, *Journal,* 87–88.
[27] Parker, *Journal,* 88. Victor, Blevins, ed., *River,* 126.
[28] Parker, *Journal,* 93–94.
[29] Ibid, 97.
[30] Russell, Haines, ed., *Journal,* 30. Enzler, *Bridger,* 91.
[31] Russell, Haines, ed., *Journal,* 12, 30. Victor, Blevins, ed., *River,* 107.
[32] Russell, Haines, ed., *Journal,* 14-17, 20–21, 28–30.
[33] Russell, Haines, ed., *Journal,* 30–31. Marsh, *Rose,* 60, 62.
[34] Russell, Haines, ed., *Journal,* 31. Marsh, *Rose,* 60–61.
[35] Russell, Haines, ed., *Journal,* 31–32.
[36] Ibid, 32.
[37] Ibid, 33–34.
[38] Ibid, 34.
[39] Ibid, 38–39.
[40] Enzler, *Bridger,* 93.
[41] Quaife, ed., *Carson,* 45. Russell, Haines, ed., *Journal,* 36–39.
[42] Russell, Haines, ed., *Journal,* 37–38.
[43] Ibid, 39, 41.
[44] William Gray, *A History of Oregon, 1792–1849, Drawn from Personal Observation and Authentic Information* (Portland, OR: Harris & Holman, 1870), 121–122. Russell, Haines, ed., *Journal,* 41.
[45] DeVoto, *Missouri,* 258. Russell, Haines, ed., *Journal,* 41. Quaife, ed., *Carson,* 47.
[46] Gray, *Oregon,* 119. Victor, Blevins, ed., *River,* 138.
[47] DeVoto, *Missouri,* 244. Enzler, *Bridger,* 95.
[48] Utley, *Life,* 164. Morgan, Harris, eds., *Anderson,* 368–369. *Missouri,* 244, 414–415 n1.
[49] DeVoto, *Missouri,* 251, 246–247. Gray, *Oregon,* 112.
[50] Alter, *Bridger,* 161. Russell, Haines, ed., *Journal,* 41. DeVoto, *Missouri,* 247.

[51] "Letters and Journal of Mrs. Narcissa Prentiss Whitman, 1836," Library of Western Fur Trade Historical Source Documents, Mountain Men and the Fur Trade, accessed November 22, 2023, http://user.xmission.com/~drudy/mtman/html/nwhitman.html#3.

[52] Gray, *Oregon,* 122–123.

[53] Douglas McChristian, *Fort Laramie: Military Bastion of the High Plains* (Norman, OK: University of Oklahoma Press, 2008), 28. Hafen, ed., *Mountain Men,* 43, 244–245. Morgan, Harris, eds., *Anderson,* 304, 310.

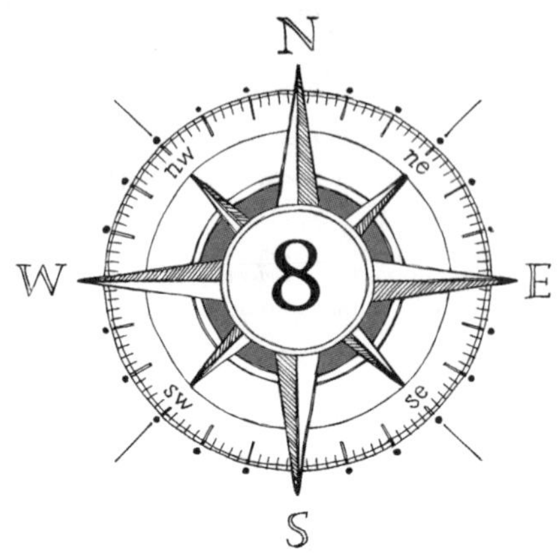

The Rocky Mountain Outfit

1836–1839

Jim Bridger, now thirty-two years old, was content. All he wanted was to continue his lifestyle. He had no desire to return to the eastern settlements. He had a wife and child, men to lead, and country to explore. He was employed, receiving a salary, and could continue the adventure he enjoyed.

The 1836 rendezvous ended on July 16. Tom Fitzpatrick led the fur-laden caravan eastward. Milton Sublette, Joshua Pilcher, Lucien Fontenelle, and likely Captain William Stewart's party accompanied the caravan. The Whitman and Spalding party left for Oregon Country with the Hudson's Bay brigade. Nathaniel Wyeth led his party toward Taos. From there, they planned to return to the States. Andrew Drips took his brigade toward the Snake River.[1]

Bridger planned to lead his sixty-man brigade and their families to Yellowstone Lake in Blackfeet territory. On July 24, 1836, he sent an advance party of fifteen trappers and two camp keepers to hunt beaver in the lake's vicinity. On August 16, Bridger, leading the brigade, arrived at the southern inlet of Yellowstone Lake, joining the advance party.[2]

The brigade traveled along the lake's eastern shore and camped on a small prairie near the northern outlet. Hot springs bubbled nearby. Osborne Russell wrote, "Near these was an opening in the ground about 8 inches in diameter from which hot steam issues continuously. . . ."[3]

Bridger sent small parties to hunt beaver as the main camp moved to Gardner's Hole (part of the Swan Flats area in today's Yellowstone National Park). After the trapping parties returned on August 27, the brigade traveled north along the Yellowstone River. Bridger, again, sent out trapping parties while he led twenty-five camp keepers downriver. On September 1, ten Delaware Indian trappers joined Bridger's brigade for protection. By September 5, the brigade reached the Stillwater River in modern-day Montana.[4]

Delaware or Lenape trappers from the East had been originally hired by the British North West Company. After the North West Company and Hudson's Bay Company merged, they continued on with the new Hudson's Bay Company or worked as free trappers.[5]

On September 7, they encamped on Rock Creek (between the Stillwater and the Clark's Fork of the Yellowstone near today's town of Red Lodge). Blackfeet war parties were in the area. Isaac Rose and a French trapper named Bodah or Godis rode from camp to inspect Bodah's traps. The two men were out of each other's eyesight when Blackfeet killed Bodah. Rose returned to camp and told of Bodah's death, when Joe Meek and Dave Crow arrived reporting to Bridger that Blackfeet had attacked them on Pryor Creek.[6]

The next day, the brigade traveled downstream and encamped where Rock Creek joins the Clark's Fork of the Yellowstone. The following morning, two trappers named Green and Howell rode downriver to set traps. Sixty Blackfeet attempted to surround them. The two men rode their horses into the stream to escape. Two balls hit Howell in the chest, but he rode on. A half mile from camp, he collapsed off his horse. Green rode to camp and returned with men to bring Howell back. He died in great agony about twenty hours later.[7]

An hour after Howell had been brought to camp, Bridger led a party after the Blackfeet, who retreated to an island where they built a fortification out of downed timber. The Blackfeet killed one of Bridger's men, a Nez Percé, and Mark Head received a flesh wound to one arm. The fight lasted until nightfall, when Bridger and his men returned to camp. The next morning, they found the Blackfeet had left.[8]

On September 11, the brigade traveled to Pryor Creek where they encamped. On September 19, they returned to the Clark's Fork while small parties trapped the nearby streams. There was little sign of Blackfeet, and beaver

Enemy tribes sometimes battled indirectly. Here, Blackfeet men set fire to buffalo grazing range in Crow territory. PAINTING BY CHARLES M. RUSSELL, COURTESY OF THE BEINECKE RARE BOOK AND MANUSCRIPT LIBRARY, YALE UNIVERSITY, WA PRINTS 360.

hunting was good. During the second half of September, bands of Crow traveled through the area, intent on raiding Blackfeet villages for horses.[9]

Joe Meek had a run-in with a band of Crow led by a chief named The Bold. Meek was trapping along Rock Creek when Crow warriors captured him. The Bold asked Meek where his brigade was, the number of men, and their leader. Meek told him the Blanket Chief, the Crows' name for Bridger, led the brigade, and he gave a lower number of men than were in the brigade. The Bold believed he might be able to kill the trappers and take their possessions.[10]

Meek led the Crow to the brigade's encampment. When they saw its size and realized Meek had lied, some wanted to kill him, but The Bold prevented it. The brigade's herd guard was about 200 yards away. The Bold told Meek to call him to come toward them, but Meek shouted to tell Bridger that the Crow planned to kill him and to negotiate for him. The guard rode to camp and reported to Bridger. Alone, Bridger rode out to parley with the advancing Crow. But first, he instructed five men to follow the bottom of a nearby ravine to a point where they would be between any Crow negotiators and the main Crow party.[11]

When Bridger was 300 yards from the Crow, he stopped and shouted for The Bold to send a leader to smoke with him. The Bold sent his second in command, Little Gun, who rode out to meet Bridger. Following the Crow customs of war, when Little Gun was 100 yards from Bridger, he dismounted, laid down his weapons, and disrobed. Bridger did likewise. They then walked to each other and embraced. Bridger's men ran between the two men and the Crow. Bridger shouted he would trade Little Gun for Meek. Although the Crow were furious, The Bold agreed to trade Meek for Little Gun, saying he would not give up a chief for a White dog's scalp.[12]

This 1832 portrait made at Fort Union depicts Hó-ra-tó-a, a Crow man, with a spear in hand, arrows at the ready, and bow strung. PAINTING BY GEORGE CATLIN, COURTESY OF THE SMITHSONIAN AMERICAN ART MUSEUM, 1985.66.165.

Bridger invited The Bold and forty warriors into camp to parley. The Bold said they were at war with the Whites, but he made peace with Bridger for three months since they were at war with their common enemy, the Blackfeet. As a goodwill gesture, The Bold returned Meek's mule, gun, and beaver pelts.[13]

The weather continued favorably for beaver hunting until mid-November when the small trapping parties returned to the Clark's Fork encampment. The brigade remained there until Christmas, then traveled to the Yellowstone River where they established their winter camp at the base of a high hill near modern-day Park City, Montana. They built a small observation post on the hilltop and stationed one or two men there with a telescope. Each day, Bridger climbed the hill with his telescope to survey the countryside, looking for "squalls." An abundance of cottonwood trees grew downriver. The men stripped bark from the trees to feed the horses and mules. Plenty of buffalo roamed the area. Everyone was warm living in buffalo hide lodges. Osborne Russell wrote, "The long winter evenings were passed away by collecting in some of the most spacious lodges and entering into debates arguments or spinning long yarns until midnight in perfect good humor. . . ." They called it "The Rocky Mountain College."[14]

On January 28, 1837, Osborne Russell, Isaac Rose, Joe Meek, and four other trappers left on an extended buffalo hunt up the Clark's Fork. The following day, they were riding toward Rock Creek, within fifteen feet of a ravine, when eighty naked Blackfeet warriors popped up, fired a volley, and charged.[15]

Rose, who was in the lead, was the main target. One ball went through his cap, another grazed his chest, and a third injured his wrist. A fourth ball hit his right arm from behind and below the elbow and exited the forearm, causing him to drop his rifle. A Blackfeet grabbed it, took aim at Meek, and fired, the ball passing through Meek's cap. Another warrior attempted to grab Rose's horse's bridle, but Rose struck him in the face with his riding whip, and his horse raced to join the others fleeing the attack. Meek's obstinate mule would not budge until warriors ran at him, and then he took off, quickly outdistancing the other animals.[16]

After a thirty-mile ride, they made it back to the brigade encampment. Rose had lost a lot of blood. Bridger and an Indian healer examined his wound. They believed he had been hit by a poisoned ball. His arm swelled to enormous size, peeling his skin to the shoulder. Everyone feared he would die. For days, any movement or loud noises would send him into near convulsions. Rose's messmates cared for him, and after a week his arm began to heal.[17]

Several days later, a twenty-man Blackfeet party was spied six miles downriver crossing the plain to the Yellowstone. Bridger, leading twenty mountaineers, Delaware, and Flathead, mounted their horses and rode toward the Blackfeet, who saw them coming and began to reinforce an old structure in the timber. Bridger's men surrounded the Blackfeet. The fight lasted until darkness and frigid temperatures convinced the trappers to return to their encampment. During the fight, one trapper received a hip wound and a poisoned ball hit Manhead, a Delaware. The ball entered the calf of his leg, traveling upward and lodging under his kneecap. Manhead's leg swelled, and he would die in agony four days later.[18]

The next morning, the trappers returned to the Blackfeet fort, but the warriors were gone. The trappers killed several Blackfeet during the fight, and their companions placed their bodies in the river under the ice. Evidence suggested up to seven wounded had been removed by travois.[19]

On February 22, 1837, Bridger climbed the hill to the observation post for his daily scan of the countryside. At about 1 P.M., he returned to camp, "appearing somewhat alarmed." A large force of Blackfeet were gathered in the timber ten miles downriver.[20]

Bridger had everyone—men and women—begin building a 6-to-8-foot-high, 250-foot-square palisade around the camp as well as a blockhouse in the center of the fort. When the Blackfeet attacked, the women, children, and wounded would enter the blockhouse. It would be their last defense if the Blackfeet breached the wall. Kit Carson said, "Our fort was strongly built and nothing but artillery could do any damage to it."[21]

They herded the livestock inside the wall. Bridger had between 150 and 200 guns for trade. He distributed these to everyone so that after they fired their personal weapons they could pick up a trade gun and fire another round.[22]

Bridger doubled the night guard. It was quiet but bitterly cold. Russell, who was on guard duty from 9 P.M. to midnight, wrote:

> ". . . the weather was clear the stars shone with an unusual lustre [*sic*] and the trees cracked like pistols about 10 oclk [*sic*] the northern lights commenced streaming up darting flashing rushing to and fro like the movements of an army at length the shooting and flashing died away and gradually turned to a deep blood red spreading over one half of the sky. This awful and sublime phenomenon . . . lasted near two hours. . . ."[23]

By noon on February 23, the fort was complete. Bridger, leading six men, rode downriver to reconnoiter the Blackfeet encampment. They found them along the river two miles below the fort and estimated the war party to be between 1,100 and 1,600 men, many of whom were on foot. Bridger's people heard the Blackfeet singing during the night. A Delaware crept close to the Blackfeet encampment and saw them holding a war dance. Many mixed and applied paints, preparing for battle.[24]

Early on the morning of February 24, Bridger's cook, a black man named Jim, was gathering firewood outside the walls. A Blackfeet hidden in the trees took a 200-yard shot at him. Fortunately, Jim was not hurt, and the Blackfeet ran off.[25]

Maselino, a Mexican, climbed the hill to the observation post to stand watch. Unknown to Bridger's men, two Blackfeet warriors occupied the post. When Maselino was within fifty yards of the post, the warriors shot at him. One ball hit him in the heel. As the warriors rushed toward him, he made a leap then rolled himself into a ball, rolling and sliding on the snow to the bottom. Some trappers took care of Maselino as others climbed the hill and chased the Blackfeet out of the observation post.[26]

The Delaware and Flathead prepared themselves for the coming fight, applying red and black paint. A half hour after the observation post incident, Bridger's people spotted the Blackfeet. Two columns advanced on the river ice to within 400 yards of the fort, then turned onto the plain and came to a halt.[27]

The Delaware and Flathead left the fort and advanced toward the oncoming Blackfeet. They took positions behind bushes and trees, shouting to the Blackfeet that they were ready to greet them with their rifles as soon as they came within range.[28]

The Blackfeet remained in place for a half hour. The leaders were most likely conferring on their course of action. A chief, wearing a white blanket, advanced toward the fort then signaled they would not fight but return to their villages. The large assembly moved off in the direction of Three Forks. Bridger's people speculated the Blackfeet leaders might have called off the attack when they saw the strength of the fort. They might have believed the astronomical display two nights before was an unfavorable sign, or perhaps it was a combination of both reasons.[29]

On February 28, 1837, Bridger led the brigade from its winter quarters to the Bighorn River. Six inches of snow covering the ground slowed their travel, and they reached the Bighorn eight days later at Bovy Fork where they encamped. Buffalo herds grazed in the vicinity, so the trappers and their families had plenty of meat. They relaxed, played ball, wrestled, and ran foot races.[30]

On March 14, a large Crow village was spotted moving down the Bighorn toward the encampment. Some brigade members began fortifying the camp while others rode to the Crow to parley. The mountaineers who had ridden out soon returned with Crow leaders and an American Fur Company trader. They were led by Long Hair, an eighty-year-old man whose hair was over eleven feet long and tied in an eighteen-inch queue. Bridger smoked with the leaders and let them explore the encampment. The next morning, Long Hair moved his village to within 300 yards of Bridger's brigade. The village consisted of 200 lodges and about the same number of warriors. Long Hair's village stayed with the brigade until March 25 then moved six miles downriver.[31]

During this time, an incident occurred involving Joe Meek and Umentucken, Mountain Lamb. She had become his wife after Milton Sublette left the mountains. Crow were in camp, trading furs and hides for merchandise. According to Meek, one Crow "was promenading about camp inspecting whatever came in his way." The man struck Mountain Lamb with his whip. Outraged, Meek shot him dead. The Crow believed the mountaineers were attacking and began to fight. Before Bridger could stop it, two or three Crow had been shot and one mountaineer killed. After the Crow left camp, still upset, Bridger confronted Meek.

"Well, you raised a hell of a row in camp," Bridger said.

"Very sorry Bridger, but couldn't help it," Meek responded. "No devil of an Indian shall strike Meek's wife."

"But you got a man killed."

"Sorry for the man; couldn't help it, though, Bridger."

Concerned the Crow might seek additional revenge beyond the death of the mountaineer, Bridger moved the camp away from the vicinity of the Crow village.[32]

On April 1, the brigade began its spring beaver hunt, traveling westward up Bovy Fork. Bridger sent small parties to hunt beaver in the Clark's Fork and Rock Creek watersheds. They had to be constantly on guard. The Blackfeet stalked them, trying to kill them or steal traps and horses. On May 5, they trapped on the Bighorn River tributaries; on May 15, they traveled into the Bighorn Mountains; on May 24, the brigade reached the north fork of the Popo Agie River, where they encamped several days. The Blackfeet continued to harass them. Then they traveled west, trapping along the way. On June 10, they reached the Green River twelve miles below Horse Creek where other hunting parties and tribes were gathering for the 1837 rendezvous.[33]

As William Stewart's commissioned painter, Alfred Jacob Miller witnessed firsthand the setting, scope, and activities of the fur trade rendezvous. Wearing a suit of armor, Jim Bridger sits on a dark horse on the bluff to the left. PAINTING BY ALFRED JACOB MILLER, COURTESY OF THE WALTERS ART MUSEUM, 37.1940.159.

During the first days of the rendezvous, people were in good spirits, visiting and exchanging news. Men gambled at cards and the Indian hand game. People raced and bet on horses.[34]

On June 15, things changed. A sixty-lodge Bannock village arrived, camping three miles from Bridger's brigade. Back in April, these Bannock had stolen horses and traps from a party of French Canadians on the Bear River. They had the audacity to come to the rendezvous with the stolen horses and traps. When asked to return them to their rightful owners, they refused.[35]

Four or five Whites and two Nez Percé from Bridger's brigade visited the Bannock village to recover the stolen horses. Discovering that the Bannock men were away on a buffalo hunt, Bridger's men brought the stolen horses back to camp.[36]

At about 3 P.M., thirty armed Bannock riders entered Bridger's camp at full gallop. Reining to a halt, they demanded the Nez Percé return the horses. If not, they would fight them. The Bannock did not want to fight the Whites. There were six Nez Percé in Bridger's brigade, and they had given the horses to the Whites for their own protection. Bridger held the bridle of one of the recovered horses.[37]

Realizing the Whites had possession of the horses, some Bannock began to leave. Osborne Russell knew the Bannock language, and one Bannock said to him that he did not come to fight Whites. But a fierce-looking warrior shouted, "We came to get horses or blood and let us do it." Russell warned Bridger's men they could be attacked.[38]

The Bannock leader rushed through the crowd at Bridger, who still held a recovered horse by the bridle. Grabbing the bridle, the leader started to jerk the horse from Bridger. Two rifle balls slammed into the Bannock's body, and he fell dead. Bridger's cook, Jim, fired one of those shots.[39]

A general melee ensued. An arrow struck Mountain Lamb, Joe Meek's wife, in her chest, killing her. Twelve Bannock were shot from their horses as they raced away.[40]

Bridger's men mounted their horses and chased after them. The Bannock retreated to an island in the river where they put up a defense as the trappers plundered their village. After three days, the Bannock asked for an end to the fighting. The trappers agreed after the Bannock promised to be friendly in the future.[41]

The rendezvousers returned to their pastimes, waiting for the trade caravan. Indian bands and trapper parties continued to arrive through the rest of June and into July. Andrew Drips' brigade rode in from their hunt along the Snake River. On June 28, John McLeod arrived with a Hudson's Bay Company brigade as well as the lay missionary, William Gray, and a small contingent of Flathead. Gray was returning from Oregon to the States to request that the American Board of Commissioners for Foreign Missions send a mission to the Spokane Indians.[42]

Hunters constantly rode out and returned with buffalo meat. Some men, both mountaineers and Indians, bought, sold, and gambled for anything, including women. Twenty-five Delaware performed their scalp dance, and days later the Shoshone put on their scalp dance. Black Harris rode in from the caravan, informing the rendezvousers it would arrive by mid-July. On July 12, Nathaniel Wyeth's second in command, Captain Joseph Thing, and his men arrived. A large party of Crow rode in, supporting a delegation of three Crow leaders and a White man named Meldrum. They came with a medicine pipe to make peace with the Whites, Flathead, Nez Percé, and Shoshone. They wanted to be on friendly terms, to trade, and to join with the Flathead in their war with the Blackfeet.[43]

Anyone wanting to head to the States traveled with the returning caravan. Gray was anxious to leave earlier than the caravan would be departing and enquired about that possibility with Drips and Harris.[44]

On Tuesday, July 18, the caravan, consisting of forty-five men and twenty mule-driven carts, arrived. Tom Fitzpatrick was the leader with Etienne Provost second in command. Lucien Fontenelle was with them, as was William Stewart and his party of nine, including artist Alfred Miller.[45]

Twenty-seven-year-old Miller was born in Baltimore, Maryland, and had studied portraiture under Baltimore artists. Family and friends provided funds for him to study in Europe, and in 1837, he established a studio in New Orleans. Stewart visited Miller's studio, was impressed with his artwork, and hired him to sketch scenery and incidents on his western excursion. Miller would draw more than 200 sketches during the trip.[46]

With the arrival of the caravan, "Joy now beamed in every countenance," Russell wrote. Mountaineers were eager for letters from home, newspapers, and to hear about events back in the States. Trade was brisk. Pelts brought $4 to $5 a pound, but the cost of goods was high. Coffee and sugar were $2 a pint, tobacco $2 a pound, and alcohol $4 a pint. Many mountaineers spent their money on drunken sprees.[47]

Stewart presented Bridger a full set of armor similar to that worn by Great Britain's Life Guards, a royal cavalry regiment. Of course, he had to try it on, and whenever he wore it riding around the rendezvous, he created a sensation.[48]

The day after the caravan arrived, the Shoshone paraded through the camps. Some 250 men galloped on their best horses. Some were dressed in their finest, while others were naked. They sang, yelled, and fired their guns. On the return to their camp, they stopped at the Delaware camp to smoke.[49]

That evening, Stewart held a buffalo dinner in his large tent. David Brown, a guest who had arrived with the caravan, described the scene. Stewart invited thirty "noted characters in the mountains," including Jim Bridger, Bill Williams, and Joe Meek. He had brought "choice old liquors" that freely flowed for the men's enjoyment.[50]

Brown learned that Bridger, squatting at Stewart's right, was familiar with the mountain regions all the way to the West Coast. His bravery was unquestioned, as was his horsemanship. He was an expert marksman, once killing twenty buffalo with twenty shots. He had no book learning and could not read or write. He was knowledgeable of and admired Indian cultures and beliefs, and he became offended if someone disrespected them.[51]

Bridger was over six feet tall, athletic, and well-built, without an ounce of fat. Brown wrote, "His cheekbones were high, his nose hooked or aquiline, the expression of his eyes mild and thoughtful, and that of his face grave, almost to solemnity. . . ." However, he had developed a goiter, an enlarged thyroid, making his neck as thick as his head.[52]

Still anxious to head east before the caravan's return, William Gray persuaded two young Whites and five young Indians to go with him. One was Nez Percé, one Iroquois, and three were Flathead, two of whom were the sons of a chief, Grand Visage, who entrusted Gray with their care. Mountaineers tried to convince Gray to wait for the caravan, saying it was too dangerous for a small party. Gray made light of their concern based on his positive experience the previous year. Bridger tried to talk some sense into Gray. Brown, who heard the exchange, said Gray replied with "foolish and fantastic dogma." Bridger slapped his rifle breech with his right hand saying, "Sir, the grace of God won't carry a man through these prairies! It takes powder and ball." Paying no heed, Gray and his men left at 8 A.M., July 25.[53]

Alfred Miller estimated 3,000 Indians attended the rendezvous. Tribes held large open-air council meetings. Each tribe performed dances and held archery contests. A form of field hockey was a popular sport. The merriment continued with horse racing. Indians were especially fond of betting on the races, and some would bet all they had. Company men and Hudson's Bay men raced their horses to see who owned the fastest.[54]

Before the rendezvous ended, word arrived concerning Gray's party. Miller heard that "a hostile tribe encountered them and killed nearly all his [Gray's] escort,—suffering himself to go free, on the strength of his being a 'medicine man' . . . ."[55]

Sioux warriors had attacked Gray's party on August 7 at Ash Hollow in present-day Nebraska. According to Gray, Joseph Papair, a French trader with the Sioux, told Gray the Sioux would not hurt him and the other Whites, but they planned to kill the foreign Indians. Gray was negotiating with Papair for the lives of his Indians when the Sioux slaughtered them all. Many mountaineers and Flathead believed Gray had traded the lives of the Indians for his own life.[56]

The 1837 rendezvous ended in mid-August. Andrew Drips led the caravan east, and Stewart's party accompanied it. Trapping parties set out to hunt beaver south of the Colorado River and west toward Salt Lake. Fontenelle led a 110-man brigade with Bridger as pilot. They rode north to the Yellowstone, Blackfeet country. The brigade hunted all that fall then established their winter camp on the Powder River. They had no problems with the Blackfeet and could not understand why. A Crow village arrived, encamping nearby. The Crow informed them smallpox had broken out among the Blackfeet, and they had headed north to escape it.[57]

Smallpox is very contagious, spread by coughing, sneezing, talking, and infected items. After a seven- to sixteen-day incubation period, fever, chills, body aches, and vomiting commence. Red spots covering the skin grow into pus-filled blisters. There is no cure, and three out of ten people infected die. The best way to combat smallpox is through vaccination and quarantine. At the time of the Blackfeet infection, vaccines were available in the States but not on the frontier.[58]

In 1837, the Company's steamboat, *St. Peters,* left St. Louis bound for Fort Union. Unbeknownst to the passengers, smallpox-infected clothing had been brought onboard. Several Indian women passengers contracted the disease. The steamboat stopped at Fort Clark, where the Mandan, Hidatsa, and Arikara became infected. By the time the *St. Peters* reached Fort Union on June 24, several crewmembers had died. Charles Larpenteur, the fort manager, warned Indians to stay away. Some listened, others did not. Larpenteur tried to inoculate people, but his efforts failed. The disease spread.[59]

Alexander Harvey had his voyageurs quickly load his keelboat with cargo from the *St. Peters.* He was transporting goods the Blackfeet were expecting at Fort McKenzie on the Missouri River, thirteen miles downriver from present-day Fort Benton, Montana. Harvey raced to leave Fort Union before his crew and passengers contracted smallpox. However, by the time they reached the mouth of the Judith River, a Blackfeet man and two other passengers had smallpox. Harvey sent an express to Alexander Culbertson, the Fort McKenzie manager, informing him he would wait at the Judith until the smallpox ran its course.[60]

A 500-lodge village of Peigan and Blood Blackfeet was encamped at the fort, waiting for the goods. Culbertson told them about the smallpox, but they insisted the keelboat be brought to the fort. If not, they threatened to burn down the fort and kill Culbertson's men. He sent for the keelboat and a brisk trade ensued. As the Blackfeet rode north to hunt buffalo, the smallpox-infected keelboat passengers died. Ten days later, smallpox broke out among the Blackfeet. Thousands would die before the epidemic would run its course.[61]

Fontenelle and Bridger's brigade remained encamped on the Powder River during the winter of 1836 to 1837. Beaver and other furbearing animals were scarce.[62]

Upriver from the brigade's encampment sat the Portuguese Houses, a trading post eleven miles east of present-day Kaycee, Wyoming. Portuguese trader Antonio Montaro, who had been leading a Bonneville brigade in Crow country since 1834, built the trading post.[63]

Osborne Russell and three others had left Fontenelle and Bridger's brigade July 30, 1837, to trap the headwaters of the Yellowstone, Missouri, and Bighorn Rivers. Fontenelle told them to meet the brigade at Howell's grave at the Clark's Fork on October 15. If the brigade was not there, they would leave a message as to their whereabouts. When Russell's party arrived in mid-October, there was no brigade and no message. They waited until October 27, then left, thinking they would pass the winter on a Wind River tributary. On November 1, they were along the Bighorn River when a band of Crow stole their horses and some belongings. Russell's party cached their furs and burned their tack and saddles, planning to walk to Fort Laramie. Twenty-five Crow warriors led by the thieves' chief, Little Soldier, galloped up to Russell and his companions. Little Soldier asked to smoke, saying he was sorry for his men's actions. If Russell's party came to their village, they would give back their horses and possessions. They could stay with his village until the Blanket Chief, Jim Bridger, came to visit. The mountaineers believed it was a trick. Little Soldier was sad when they said no. He asked what he should do with their horses and possessions. They said give them to the Blanket Chief. With that, they shouldered their rifles and marched off for Fort Laramie.[64]

Fontenelle and Bridger learned Little Soldier's men had robbed Russell's party. Fontenelle visited Little Soldier's village and recovered all identifiable property belonging to Russell's party except for their beaver pelts. The Crow had traded those to Antonio Montaro. Fontenelle and some men rode to the Portuguese Houses where he confronted Montaro, who denied he possessed the stolen beaver pelts. Fontenelle's clerk searched the storehouse and discovered pelts marked with Osborne and the others' names. Fontenelle took them to the brigade's camp. There had already been bad blood between American Fur Company men and Bonneville men. Brigade members and Crow raiders harassed Montaro's men throughout the winter.[65]

That December, Fontenelle and twenty-five men rode south to Fort Laramie to acquire supplies for the brigade. Doc Newell, leading five men, one woman, and a child, arrived at Bridger's camp January 5, 1838. They had been trading with the Crow. With the addition of Newell's party there were eighty men, all in good spirits and health.[66]

The temperatures were frigid and the snow deep. The men peeled cottonwood bark to feed their animals. Buffalo were so plentiful, the horse herders had trouble keeping them from mixing with the livestock to eat the peeled bark. The mountaineers had to build large fires to keep the buffalo out of camp.[67]

On February 7, 1838, Fontenelle's party returned from Fort Laramie with supplies. Fontenelle had remained at the fort while Osborne Russell, who had walked to the fort, joined them.[68]

A trader named Orrick arrived in the Powder River country to trade with the Crow and hired away some of Bridger's men. Newell wrote that the Crow "much annoyed" Orrick, and warriors rode past Bridger's encampment making hostile threats.[69]

By March 25, spring weather arrived. The buffalo scattered over the prairie as the mountaineers prepared for the spring beaver hunt. On March 29, the brigade traveled down the Powder River, then cut cross country, reaching the Little Bighorn River on April 18. From there they traveled west, searching for beaver. Finding very few, the mountaineers believed the Crow had over-trapped the steams.[70]

As the brigade followed the Yellowstone upriver, they found plenty of buffalo, elk, deer, and bighorn sheep. By May 6, they were on Rock Creek, and by May 27, the brigade was on the Gallatin River. From there, they proceeded to the Madison. On June 2, they were riding upriver when they discovered a Blackfeet village trail three to four days old. Following the trail along the river, they came upon a single lodge. Inside were eight smallpox-ravaged bodies.[71]

The next day, Bridger led the brigade away from the Madison into mountainous country to avoid the Blackfeet village. The mountaineers protested Bridger's actions so strongly he relented and led them back toward the Madison. The following morning, as the brigade topped a ridge, they saw the Blackfeet village three miles in the distance. Bridger called a halt, found a defensive position, and prepared for any Blackfeet attack. He made no plans to attack the village, disappointing some of the men. Russell wrote, "Our leader was no military commander."[72]

Fifteen mountaineers took matters into their own hands and rode to the village. They dismounted and crept to the top of a ridge overlooking the village where they fired several rounds before the Blackfeet could mount a counterattack. The mountaineers ran to their horses and raced back toward the brigade's position. Five times their number of Blackfeet pursued them.[73]

A warrior galloped alongside Joe Meek, nocked an arrow, and was about to shoot him when the arrow slipped from the bow. Doc Newell saw another warrior lying on the ground and, believing him dead, dismounted to take his scalp. As Newell grabbed the man's hair, he sprang to his feet, knife in hand. It was a fight to the death that Newell won.[74]

Cotton Mansfield's horse fell, pinning him under it. As six warriors surrounded him, he shouted, "Tell Old Gabe that Old Cotton is gone." Kit Carson rode nearby, dismounted from his horse, and fired, killing one warrior. The others left off their attack on Mansfield. Carson's shot spooked his horse, which broke away and raced alongside the other horses and riders. Mansfield's horse regained its feet, and he remounted and rode away. Carson called to a mountaineer named White, who rode to him, and they rode double back to the brigade.[75]

Meek noticed one Blackfeet pursuer was a woman. Her horse was shot, and she was afoot. Meek advanced to take her prisoner, but two warriors came between them as a third rode to her. She grabbed the rider's horse's tail and ran behind and out of danger.[76]

The retreating mountaineers made it back to the brigade. The Blackfeet took a rocky, elevated position 300 yards away. More warriors arrived, their number increasing to about 150. After two hours of shooting at the brigade without inflicting any damage, the Blackfeet ceased firing. One shouted in Flathead that the mountaineers were not men to attack their village and then run away and hide in the rocks.[77]

An old Iroquois took offense at the Blackfeet remarks and told the nearest mountaineers they needed to put an end to the Blackfeet talk. Stripping naked, he performed a war dance and song. Twenty mountaineers mounted their horses and followed him as he led a charge up the slope to the rocks. The Blackfeet shot at them, but no one was hit. It was an intense fight, but the mountaineers drove the Blackfeet from the rocks. The warriors descended the slope to their horses and slowly rode back to the village, taking their wounded and most of their dead. Newell wrote that the mountaineers killed seven Blackfeet and wounded fifteen, and the Blackfeet wounded several mountaineers.[78]

Bridger led the brigade upriver to within a quarter mile of the Blackfeet village then established camp for the night. The next morning, they discovered the Blackfeet village had moved three miles farther upriver.[79]

Bridger broke camp, planning to proceed upriver and bypass the Blackfeet using a high bench running above the village. As they rode upriver, they saw mounted Blackfeet warriors blocking their advance, forming a line from the river up onto the bench and into thick pines on the mountainside.[80]

The old Iroquois led thirty mounted men to a ravine where they advanced close to the left of the Blackfeet line without being seen. The old man gave a "horrid yell," and the mountaineers charged the Blackfeet, who wheeled their horses and raced back to their village. The Iroquois and his men stopped 300 yards from the village and stood guard while the brigade passed by, continuing upriver. Once they were safely past, the Iroquois and his men rejoined the brigade.[81]

On June 6, the brigade left the Madison River heading south to Henry's Lake. They camped at the lake, then proceeded along the shoreline to the southeast where they saw fifteen Blackfeet lodges in the distance. They made camp, planning to attack the following day. The next morning, as the brigade rode toward the village, a delegation of six unarmed Peigan Blackfeet met them two miles from their camp. Bridger rode ahead to meet with them. They acted friendly. Little Robe, their chief, told Bridger that smallpox had devastated their people. They invited the mountaineers to their village to smoke and trade. The brigade members felt ashamed and relented of their desire to attack. They entered the village and spent several hours trading with the Blackfeet, leaving on friendly terms. The brigade proceeded on its way and camped for the night along the trail. The next morning, unaware of Bridger's brigade, a Blackfeet husband and wife with their daughter rode into camp. The brigade allowed them to leave unharmed.[82]

From June 11 to 14, the brigade trapped along the Snake River. They rode to Pierre's Hole where they met ten of their trappers who had been out on their own. Blackfeet raiders had stolen most of their horses, and one of their men had been shot in the thigh. Two men deserted, stealing Company horses. Newell speculated they left for the Hudson's Bay Company.[83]

On June 18, the brigade crossed the mountains into Jackson Hole where they continued trapping. From there, they rode toward Horse Creek on the Green River where the Company would hold the rendezvous. Doc Newell rode out from the brigade to try to locate the trade caravan. He ran into riders from the caravan sent out to inform the brigade that the Company had moved the rendezvous east to the confluence of the Popo Agie and Wind Rivers. Newell returned to the brigade to inform them of the change.[84]

Andrew Drips led the 1838 caravan. The Company's twenty horse-drawn carts loaded with merchandise arrived at the rendezvous on June 22. Black Harris and Lucien Fontenelle rode with the caravan, as did William Stewart with his entourage and several tourists, including two sons of William Clark. People bound for the West Coast traveled with the caravan, including a Swiss named John Sutter. A decade later, in 1848, Sutter's fort in California would be the site of the discovery of gold and the start of the California gold rush. Nine Oregon-bound missionaries journeyed with the caravan, one of whom was William Gray, who had recently married and brought along his bride, Mary Dix.[85]

Word spread among the mountaineers and tribes that back on August 7, 1837, Gray had allowed Sioux warriors to kill the Indians entrusted to him to save his own life and those of two other Whites. Flathead Chief Grand Visage, who lost two sons, held Gray responsible. The Flathead wanted revenge, but mountaineer friends talked them out of it. On the night of the Fourth of July, however, four drunken mountaineers went to Gray's tent to punish him. Fellow missionary Cushing Eells was able to turn them away.[86]

At 10 P.M. on July 5, Jim Bridger's brigade arrived. The 100 men, 60 women, and their children rode directly to Drips' camp where both groups raised a great shout, played drums, and fired guns. Fifteen to twenty Delaware, Shawnee, and mountaineers painted their faces and went to the missionary encampment, performing a war dance as they sang, pounded on drums, and fired their guns. One of them waved a Blackfeet scalp. Myra Eells wrote, ". . . they looked like the emissaries of the devil, worshiping their own master."[87]

William Stewart brought another suit of armor that a drunken Joe Meek wore around the rendezvous. He had married a Nez Percé woman, and they had a baby girl together. His wife disapproved of his drunken antics.[88]

Jim Bridger paid his respects to the missionary party, and they invited him to dinner several times.[89]

Mountaineers had fewer pelts due to increased trapping pressure on beaver populations. Not only were American and Indian trappers competing for beaver, but the Hudson's Bay Company continued its policy of decimating beaver populations, creating a "fur desert" to lessen American influence in Oregon Country.[90]

Andrew Drips brought bad news. Beaver prices were down. Fashions were changing. Silk was in vogue, and the fur of nutria, a South American rodent, was less expensive to use in making felt hats. The Panic of 1837, an economic depression, still held down fur prices; people did not have money to spend.[91]

The Company reduced beaver pelt values from $5 to $3, and many trappers became alarmed. A rumor spread that the Company planned to end bringing supplies to the rendezvous and discontinue its Rocky Mountains operations. Dissatisfied mountaineers left. Some stole horses, traps, and other valuable items.[92]

On July 8, Francis Ermatinger, chief trader for Hudson's Bay Company at Fort Hall, arrived with two employees and Reverend Jason Lee and others bound for the States. Trappers asked Ermatinger for employment, but he refused. Ermatinger agreed to escort Gray's missionaries westward, and they left on

July 12. Disgusted with Joe Meek's drunken behavior and homesick for her people, Meek's wife took their daughter and went with them.[93]

Jim Bridger needed to take care of his finances. On July 13, someone wrote a letter on behalf of Bridger for Bill Sublette giving Sublette power of attorney to collect Bridger's money in payment for his services to Pratte, Chouteau, & Company and to invest it for him. The second general letter stated Sublette had power of attorney for Bridger and authorized Sublette to collect $3,317.13 for Bridger's two years of employment with Pratte, Chouteau, & Company and invest it for him. Bridger signed both letters with his X. Accompanying the letters was a written acknowledgement from Andrew Drips, Agent for the Company, that the Company owed Bridger that amount of money.[94]

The rendezvous ended July 20, and Lucien Fontenelle led the caravan east. It's not known if Stewart's party went along, but he returned to St. Louis by September 28. Kit Carson and seven men left for Brown's Hole in present-day northwest Colorado.[95]

Andrew Drips led a brigade on the fall beaver hunt with Bridger acting as pilot. Osborne Russell guided an advance party of thirty mountaineers up the Wind River. The brigade would follow shortly, comprised of sixty men, their families, and a few Flathead and Nez Percé bands. Russell's party trapped streams in the Wind River and Jackson's Hole region, rendezvousing with the brigade near Jackson's Hole on July 29.[96]

On August 4, the brigade crossed the mountains to Pierre's Hole. Small parties rode out from the brigade to trap. Doc Newell decided to leave the brigade and rode to Fort Hall, taking his wife and two little boys with him. By August 11, the brigade came to Bechler Meadows in Falls River Basin. Osborne Russell and several companions left, ending their employment with the Company. That September, Newell returned to the brigade again at Pierre's Hole and went back to work for the Company. He had worked for Hudson's Bay for a month. He said times were hard, beaver pelts scarce, and provisions low.[97]

Joe Meek had failed to convince his wife to return to him. He was with the Flathead and Nez Percé at a place he called Missouri Lake. They held a massive buffalo hunt, killing 2,000 to 3,000 buffalo for their winter food supply. Drips and Bridger's brigade was there and traded the hunters for 1,500 buffalo tongues to help feed the brigade.[98]

The brigade may have trapped in the Missouri River's Three Forks region through the fall. Meek said he trapped on his own and acquired a large amount of beaver pelts. He knew the brigade was going to travel through his location and planned to play a joke on them. He wrote on a buffalo skull the number of beaver pelts he had collected and that he was selling them to the Hudson's Bay Company. When Drips and Bridger found Meek's note, they were angry and sent riders to stop him, but they didn't find him. Weeks later, the brigade returned to Pierre's Hole where Meek rode into camp. Bridger and Drips demanded to know why he had sold the pelts to Hudson's Bay. He laughed, neither confirming nor denying he had sold them to their competitor. Drips threatened Meek, who laughed even more. Bridger suspected Meek was tricking them. Meek finally showed them a certificate signed by Company employee Joe Walker stating Meek had turned over the furs to him.[99]

In December, the brigade rode to the Green River then to the Wind River to winter. Nothing is known of their activities during the winter and spring, but they must have conducted their spring beaver hunt in that area.[100]

The 1839 rendezvous was held at Horse Creek on the Green River. It's not certain when Drips and Bridger's brigade arrived, but it was before the caravan. The lodges of over 1,000 Shoshone, Flathead, and Nez Percé lined the Green River for a mile. Interspersed among them were White trappers, some working for small independent companies, others free trappers on their own.[101]

On July 5, Black Harris, leading the Company's caravan, arrived with four two-wheeled mule-drawn carts, each loaded with 800 to 900 pounds of supplies managed by eight Company employees. Altogether twenty-seven people made up the party, which included a missionary group, two married couples and a bachelor. Some were headed to Oregon, others to California. Francis Ermatinger arrived with a dozen Hudson's Bay men. Beaver pelts were $4 a pound, but the price of goods was greatly inflated. Beavers had become scarce and with the rise in the price of goods, many mountaineers had to tone down their carousing and gambling.[102]

Harris brought bad news. The Rocky Mountain Outfit had lost money every year since 1836. Therefore, the Company was disbanding the outfit; it would not support any more brigades. It was sobering news for the mountaineers. Some such as Joe Meek planned to stay in the mountains, continuing to trap and trade. Others planned to head to Santa Fe or California.[103]

Jim Bridger was out of a job. He needed to make new arrangements to continue in the fur trade. He would travel to St. Louis to explore business ventures with the top businessmen. He arranged with the Flathead to care for Cora and their three-year-old daughter, Mary Ann. They most likely left on July 10 with several hundred Flathead returning to their country along with the Hudson's Bay men and the travelers who had arrived with Harris.[104]

Jim Bridger and Andrew Drips joined the caravan on its journey back to St. Louis. It had been seventeen years since Bridger had left that city.[105]

---

1 Russell, Haines, ed., *Journal,* 41–42. Hafen, ed., *Mountain Men,* 245. Enzler, *Bridger,* 96. DeVoto, *Missouri,* 258, 270. Morgan, Harris, eds., *Anderson,* 295, 310. Gray, *Oregon,* 130. Johnson, ed. *Wyeth,* 105 n47.

2 Russell, Haines, ed., *Journal,* 41–42, 44.

3 Ibid, 44.

4 Ibid, 44–47, 163 n90.

5 Utley, *Life,* 87.

6 Russell, Haines, ed., *Journal,* 47–49, 163 n91. Marsh, *Rose,* 127–128.

7 Russell, Haines, ed., *Journal,* 49. Marsh, *Rose,* 121–122.

8 Russell, Haines, ed., *Journal,* 49. Marsh, *Rose,* 123–126.

9 Russell, Haines, ed., *Journal,* 50. Marsh, *Rose,* 126–127.

10 Victor, Blevins, ed., *River,* 128–129.

11 Ibid, 130–131.

12 Ibid, 131–132.

13 Ibid.

14 Russell, Haines, ed., *Journal,* 51–53, 164 n100. Marsh, *Rose,* 133.

15 Russell, Haines, ed., *Journal,* 51–52. Marsh, *Rose,* 138–139.

16 Marsh, *Rose,* 140–141. Victor, Blevins, ed., *River,* 113.

17 Marsh, *Rose,* 142–143.

18 Russell, Haines, ed., *Journal.* Marsh, *Rose,* 136–137.

19 Russell, Haines, ed., *Journal,* 52.

20 Ibid, 52–53.

21 Russell, Haines, ed., *Journal,* 53. Marsh, *Rose,* 144–146. Quaife, ed., *Carson,* 58.

22 Marsh, *Rose,* 145. Victor, Blevins, ed., *River,* 134.

23 Russell, Haines, ed., *Journal,* 53.

24 Russell, Haines, ed., *Journal,* 53–54. Marsh, *Rose,* 143–145. Quaife, ed., *Carson,* 58. Victor, Blevins, ed., *River,* 134.

25 Russell, Haines, ed., *Journal,* 54. Victor, Blevins, ed., *River,* 135.

26 Russell, Haines, ed., *Journal,* 54. Marsh, *Rose,* 143–144.

27 Russell, Haines, ed., *Journal,* 54. Marsh, *Rose,* 146.

28 Marsh, *Rose,* 147.

29 Marsh, *Rose,* 147. Russell, Haines, ed., *Journal,* 54.

30 Russell, Haines, ed., *Journal,* 54–55.

31 Ibid, 55.

32 Victor, Blevins, ed., *River,* 115–116, 119, 134.

33 Russell, Haines, ed., *Journal,* 55–58.

34 Ibid, 58.

35 Ibid, 58–59.

36 Ibid, 59.

37 Ibid.

38 Ibid.

39 Russell, Haines, ed., *Journal,* 59–60. Victor, Blevins, ed., *River,* 135.

40 Russell, Haines, ed., *Journal,* 60. Victor, Blevins, ed., *River,* 135.

[41] Russell, Haines, ed., *Journal,* 60. Victor, Blevins, ed., *River,* 135–136.
[42] William Gray, "The Unpublished Journal of William H. Gray; from December 1836 to October 1837," *Whitman College Quarterly* (Walla Walla, WA: Whitman College, 1913), 53. Morgan, Harris, eds., *Anderson,* 295. DeVoto, *Missouri,* 327–329.
[43] Gray, "Unpublished Journal," 56–58. Brown, *Rocky Mountains,* 19.
[44] Gray, "Unpublished Journal," 55–56.
[45] Miller, Ross, ed., *Miller,* xix, 49, 76, 197. Gray, "Unpublished Journal," 60. Russell, Haines, ed., *Journal,* 60.
[46] Miller, Ross, ed., *Miller,* xiii–xvii, xix, xxxv–xxxvi.
[47] Russell, Haines, ed., *Journal,* 60. Brown, *Rocky Mountains,* 31–33.
[48] Miller, Ross, ed., *Miller,* 159.
[49] Gray, "Unpublished Journal," 61.
[50] Brown, *Rocky Mountains,* 20–22, 24–25.
[51] Ibid, 22–24.
[52] Ibid, 23–24.
[53] Brown, *Rocky Mountains,* 44. Victor, Blevins, ed., *River,* 167. Gray, "Unpublished Journal," 62–63, 69.
[54] Brown, *Rocky Mountains,* 40. Miller, Ross, ed., *Miller,* 127, 175, 189.
[55] Miller, Ross, ed., *Miller,* 185.
[56] Gray, "Unpublished Journal," 67–70. Victor, Blevins, ed., *River,* 167–168.
[57] Miller, Ross, ed., *Miller,* 199. Marsh, *Rose,* 107. DeVoto, *Missouri,* 335. Morgan, Harris, eds., *Anderson,* 311. Russell, Haines, ed., *Journal,* 60. Quaife, ed., *Carson,* 47–48.
[58] "Smallpox," *The World Book Encyclopedia,* S–Sn, Vol. 17 (Chicago, IL: Field Enterprise Educational Corporation, 1976), 423.
[59] John Ewers, *The Blackfeet: Raiders of the Northwestern Plains* (Norman, OK: University of Oklahoma Press, 1958), 65. Robertson, *Struggle,* 233. Barbour, *Fort Union,* 136. Larpenteur, Coues, ed., *Trader,* 132–133.
[60] Ewers, *Blackfeet,* 65. Robertson, *Struggle,* 171–172.
[61] Ewers, *Blackfeet,* 65–66. Robertson, *Struggle,* 172.
[62] Newell, Johansen, ed., *Memoranda,* 35–36.
[63] Russell, Haines, ed., *Journal,* 167–168 n130. Morgan, Harris, eds., *Anderson,* 256–257. Robertson, *Struggle,* 176.
[64] Russell, Haines, ed., *Journal,* 61–62, 69–72.
[65] Russell, Haines, ed., *Journal,* 80–81. Victor, Blevins, ed., *River,* 158–159.
[66] Russell, Haines, ed., *Journal,* 81. Newell, Johansen, ed., *Memoranda,* 34–36.
[67] Russell, Haines, ed., *Journal,* 81. Newell, Johansen, ed., *Memoranda,* 36. Quaife, ed., *Carson,* 49.
[68] Russell, Haines, ed., *Journal,* 81.
[69] Newell, Johansen, ed., *Memoranda,* 36.
[70] Russell, Haines, ed., *Journal,* 81–82.
[71] Russell, Haines, ed., *Journal,* 84–86. Newell, Johansen, ed., *Memoranda,* 36.
[72] Russell, Haines, ed., *Journal,* 86.
[73] Ibid, 86–87.
[74] Victor, Blevins, ed., *River,* 164–165.
[75] Victor, Blevins, ed., *River,* 165. Quaife, ed., *Carson,* 51.
[76] Victor, Blevins, ed., *River,* 165.
[77] Russell, Haines, ed., *Journal,* 87.
[78] Russell, Haines, ed., *Journal,* 88. Quaife, ed., *Carson,* 51. Newell, Johansen, ed., *Memoranda,* 36.
[79] Russell, Haines, ed., *Journal,* 88.
[80] Ibid.
[81] Ibid, 88–89.
[82] Russell, Haines, ed., *Journal,* 89. Newell, Johansen, ed., *Memoranda,* 37. Victor, Blevins, ed., *River,* 166–167.
[83] Russell, Haines, ed., *Journal,* 89. Newell, Johansen, ed., *Memoranda,* 37.
[84] Russell, Haines, ed., *Journal,* 90. Newell, Johansen, ed., *Memoranda,* 37, 46 n39.
[85] Russell, Haines, ed., *Journal,* 90. Morgan, Harris, eds., *Anderson,* 295, 311. DeVoto, *Missouri,* 343–344, 350–351. Alter, *Jim Bridger,* 180. Gray, *Oregon,* 177.
[86] Gray, *Oregon,* 174. DeVoto, *Missouri,* 245. Victor, Blevins, ed., *River,* 168.
[87] Newell, Johansen, ed., *Memoranda,* 46 n38. Morgan, Harris, eds., *Anderson,* 264. Alter, *Jim Bridger,* 180.
[88] Victor, Blevins, ed., *River,* 171.
[89] Alter, *Bridger,* 180. DeVoto, *Missouri,* 353.
[90] Donlin, *Fur,* 282–284.
[91] Ibid, 281, 283.

[92] Newell, Johansen, ed., *Memoranda,* 37, 46–47 n40. Russell, Haines, ed., *Journal,* 91.

[93] Newell, Johansen, ed., *Memoranda,* 46–47 n40. Russell, Haines, ed., *Journal,* 90. Alter, *Bridger,* 180. DeVoto, *Missouri,* 354, 358. Victor, Blevins, ed., *River,* 171.

[94] Alter, *Bridger,* 181–182.

[95] DeVoto, *Missouri,* 358. Russell, Haines, ed., *Journal,* 90. Morgan, Harris, eds., *Anderson,* 311. Quaife, ed., *Carson,* 54.

[96] Russell, Haines, ed., *Journal,* 90–91.

[97] Russell, Haines, ed., *Journal,* 91–92, 170 n148. Newell, Johansen, ed., *Memoranda,* 37.

[98] Victor, Blevins, ed., *River,* 179–180.

[99] Ibid, 182–183.

[100] Newell, Johansen, ed., *Memoranda,* 38. Morgan, Harris, eds., *Anderson,* 264–265.

[101] F. A. Wislizenus, *A Journey to the Rocky Mountains in the Year 1839* (St. Louis, MO: Missouri Historical Society, 1912), 84, 86–88.

[102] Wislizenus, *Journey,* 28–29, 55, 85, 87–88, 92. Newell, Johansen, ed., *Memoranda,* 38.

[103] Hafen, ed., *Mountain Men,* 48. Victor, Blevins, ed., *River,* 185–186.

[104] Caesar, *King,* 184. Wislizenus, *Journey,* 92.

[105] Morgan, Harris, eds., *Anderson,* 265.

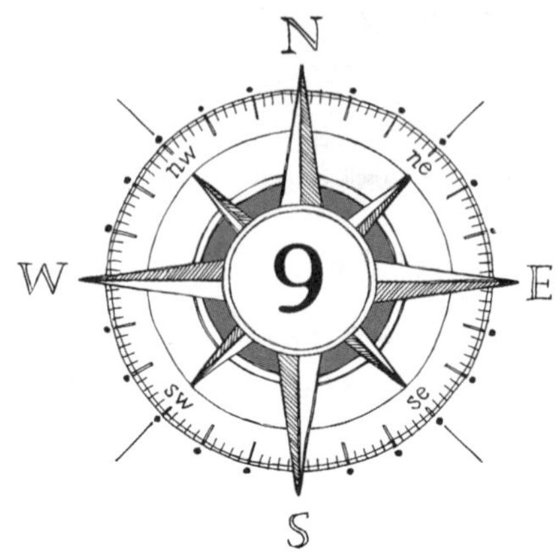

Fraeb & Bridger

1839–1842

By September 1839, St. Louis had drastically changed since Jim Bridger left in 1822. With a population of 16,000 people, the city was prosperous and expanding. The 1838 *City Directory* stated, "Vast numbers of new buildings had caused a significant spread in business locations, thereby changing the complexion of former residential neighborhoods." The city paved its streets and expanded the wharf. It bustled with steamboats coming and going, loading and unloading people and goods.[1]

Upon his return, Bridger got right down to business. Pratte, Chouteau, & Company had reorganized to Pierre Chouteau Jr. & Company. People still referred to it as the Company. Its account books record a $408 payment to Bridger on September 17, 1839. He visited old friends Bill Sublette and Robert Campbell, business partners since 1833. Under the name Sublette & Campbell, they continued to invest in the fur trade.[2]

Bridger stayed at the Union Hotel. He ate prepared food, later claiming to Captain William Raynolds that he had gone seventeen years without eating bread.[3] He crossed the Mississippi River to visit his old haunts at American Bottom, but it was a depressing trip. Returning to St. Louis, he developed a fever. He told H. J. Clayton, who he met at the Union Hotel he was ready to head back to the mountains. "Go with me now," Bridger invited Clayton. "You will have no need of money there."[4]

Bridger met with his old partner, Henry Fraeb. Since the sale of the Rocky Mountain Fur Company, Fraeb had been involved in several trapping and trading ventures. He had recently hit rock bottom. Fraeb and his partner, Edmund Christy, had failed to repay a debt to Sublette & Campbell, who took them to court. When Fraeb failed to appear, the court ruled against him and stated it could not find any of his assets.[5]

Bridger wanted to establish his own trapping and trading business and take merchandise to the 1840 rendezvous, but he had a problem. He could not read or write and needed a trustworthy partner who could keep the books and handle the paperwork. Bridger found that partner in Henry Fraeb.[6]

On March 14, 1840, the new partnership of Fraeb & Bridger bought merchandise from the Company, $65 of which was on credit. They acquired horses and mules to transport the goods and hired thirty men to manage the caravan and work in the trapping brigade. They left St. Louis in April 1840, bound for Horse Creek on the Green River.[7]

Bridger and Fraeb's caravan soon arrived at Westport on the western border of Missouri. The Company was also sending a small caravan led by Andrew Drips, and Black Harris rode along. The two caravans planned to travel together for mutual protection.[8]

Like Bridger, Father Pierre-Jean De Smet roamed widely throughout the Great Plains, Rocky Mountains, and Pacific Northwest. BRADY-HANDY COLLECTION, COURTESY OF THE LIBRARY OF CONGRESS, LC-DIG-CWPBH-03561.

Several small parties accompanied the combined caravans. Three Protestant missionaries and their wives managed two loaded wagons. Joel and Mary Walker hauled their four children and supplies in two wagons. Walker, who was mountaineer Joe Walker's older brother, had been a Santa Fe trader. He planned to settle in California. Another traveler was Pierre-Jean De Smet.[9]

De Smet was a Catholic missionary who planned to establish a mission with the Flathead in Oregon.

Originally from Belgium, thirty-nine-year-old Father De Smet had been in the United States since 1821 and had been working with Indian tribes since 1823. They gave him the name Black Robe. He was a likeable person with a great sense of humor.[10]

Bridger and De Smet hit it off, becoming lifelong friends. They must have enjoyed each other's stories. De Smet learned that Bridger had been hit by two arrows and wrote, "Being asked if the wounds had been long suppurating [festering], he answered humorously, 'in the mountains meat never spoils.'"[11]

On April 30, 1840, the caravan left for the Green River rendezvous. On June 4, they stopped at a forty-lodge Cheyenne village on the North Platte River. De Smet was introduced to the Cheyenne leaders as a minister of the Great Spirit. They invited him to smoke and eat with them then listened to his gospel message.[12]

Men prepare for a ceremony at a Cheyenne encampment. PHOTOGRAPH BY EDWARD S. CURTIS, COURTESY OF THE LIBRARY OF CONGRESS, LC-USZ62-120089.

Jim Baker's life (1818–1898) as a trapper, hunter, and army scout paralleled much of Jim Bridger's. "Old Gabe" and "Honest Jim" were friends. PHOTOGRAPH FROM *TWENTY YEARS AMONG OUR SAVAGE INDIANS*, BY JAMES LEE HUMFREVILLE, HARTFORD PUBLISHING, 1897.

The caravan encountered large Indian bands along the way. Jim Baker, a caravan member, was impressed with Bridger's knowledge and negotiation skills with the tribes. "Thanks be to Jim Bridger for our safety," he said.[13]

On June 30, 1840, the caravan reached the rendezvous at Horse Creek on the Green River. Trappers and a great number of Indians from a variety of tribes greeted them. The most numerous were the Shoshone. Everyone was eager to trade. Unfortunately, beaver pelts were few. Doc Newell wrote, ". . . times were certainly hard . . . everything dull. . . ."[14]

Jim Bridger must have been happy to be back in the mountains, reuniting with his wife and daughter and greeting old friends.

On Sunday, July 5, De Smet held mass in French and English as interpreters translated his remarks into Flathead and Shoshone. Afterwards, thirty Shoshone chiefs met with him to learn more about Christianity. When he was done explaining, they conferred among themselves, then gave him an invitation to come teach them. On Monday, July 6, the rendezvous began to break up. De Smet left with a Flathead escort and twelve French Canadians.[15]

The Protestant missionary party had agreed to hire Black Harris to pilot them to Fort Hall. Harris' price was high. When Doc Newell heard about it, he told the missionaries he would guide them at a lower price, to which they agreed. Harris was furious. Newell was riding horseback seventy to eighty yards away from Harris when Harris fired his rifle at him. It was a close miss. Newell chased after Harris who hid in a thicket. Harris' action angered everyone. Andrew Drips told Harris if he had shot Newell, he would have hanged him.[16]

Drips led the Company caravan back to St. Louis. Jim Bridger and Henry Fraeb did not return east. Joe Walker, Fraeb, and Bridger led a nine-man trapping and trading party to California.[17] Unfortunately, no one wrote about their travels. The only records are documents in California with Fraeb and Walker's names; there is no mention of Bridger, possibly because he couldn't write his name.

Joe Walker had obtained a visa from the Mexican chargé d'affaires in Washington, D.C., allowing him to remain in California for two months to purchase horses. The Fraeb, Walker, and Bridger party traveled downriver along the Green until they reached the Spanish Trail heading southwest toward southern California. By February 10, 1841, they reached Los Angeles. There, they met with the prefect who recorded that Walker and two other Americans, most likely Bridger and Fraeb, led nine Americans who bought horses.[18]

They brought beaver packs, totaling 417 pounds. Los Angeles businessman Abel Stearns bought them at three pesos per pound, amounting to $1,147 in U.S. dollars. With those funds, they purchased 100 mares, 2 stallions, and 17 mules. They also bought goods—coffee, tobacco, sugar, beans, soap, and liquor. The Americans' last recorded transaction was on April 7, 1841.[19]

By midsummer, Jim Bridger, Henry Fraeb, and their men were back in the Rockies, building a trading post, Fort Bridger, on the Green River's west bank, several miles below Big Sandy. There was no rendezvous this year, but bands of Shoshone and Flathead came to trade.[20]

On July 23, 1841, Fraeb with twenty men and their families rode from the fort to hunt buffalo to make meat for the winter. They hadn't gone far when they encountered the old Iroquois mountaineer John Grey, who was out ahead scouting for the John Bidwell and John Bartleson party piloted by Tom Fitzpatrick.[21]

Seventy-seven people comprised the Bidwell-Bartleson party, many bound for California or Oregon. They were a motley crew: families, missionaries, sportsmen, would-be mountaineers, and old mountaineers. Father De Smet was with them, having traveled back to St. Louis by way of the Missouri River and now returning to Oregon, leading six Catholic missionaries.[22]

Bartleson brought whiskey to trade with the mountaineers. The two parties camped together for three days, visiting and trading. Methodist missionary Charles Williams wrote that the mountaineers were a "wicked, swearing company of men." He had a low opinion of Fitzpatrick, "a wicked worldly man," as well as his traveling companions, who were "an ignorant hard-hearted people."[23]

They encamped close enough to Fort Bridger that Jim Bridger and others would have come to visit. Bridger would have spent time with his old partner, Fitzpatrick, and friend, Father De Smet.

Goods and merchandise were available for purchase, but prices were high. Williams wrote that "sugar sold for $1.50 per pound; powder and lead from $1.50 to $2.50 per pound." De Smet performed a marriage ceremony for two travelers, "Mr. Richard Fillan and a Mrs. Gray, who had left her husband in Missouri," Williams wrote.[24]

Jim and Cora Bridger decided their six-year-old daughter, Mary Ann, should be educated at the Whitman Mission in Oregon. They probably sent her with the Bidwell-Bartleson party. There were other children in the party, and Bridger's friends, Fitzpatrick and Father De Smet, could keep an eye on her.[25]

After parting company with the Bidwell-Bartleson party, Henry Fraeb led his buffalo hunters, their families, and several Shoshone east. Reaching the confluence of the Little Snake River and Battle Creek, they built a trading cabin and a corral.[26]

Several differing stories tell what happened next. This is how it might have happened. Fraeb's hunters encountered a Sioux, Cheyenne, and Arapaho buffalo-hunting party. Fraeb exchanged whiskey for the hunters' jerked meat. After consuming the alcohol, the hunters believed Fraeb's men had cheated them. In addition, the Shoshone hunters were enemies.[27]

Fraeb and most of the men were away hunting buffalo when a 500-man Sioux, Cheyenne, and Arapaho raiding party attacked the encampment, killing two women, a White man, and a Shoshone man, and driving off 160 horses. Fraeb sent a messenger to inform Bridger of the attack. Bridger sent three men with a message to Fraeb warning him to leave immediately and rejoin him at Fort Bridger. But Fraeb wanted to finish the buffalo hunt. Ten days after the initial attack, around August 8, they were preparing to leave when a raiding party struck. Fraeb had his men take defensive positions at the trading cabin and corral. The attack lasted from dawn to dusk. Fraeb's men claimed they shot roughly forty attackers, but Fraeb and eight of his men were killed. After the raiders left with their captured horses, Fraeb's survivors returned to Fort Bridger. Jim Bridger was now without a partner.[28]

Bridger and his men finished the construction of Fort Bridger, their base of operations through the fall of 1841 and into the winter and spring of 1842. In December 1841, the Bridger family grew with the birth of a son, Felix Francis.[29]

Jim Bridger needed to find a new business partner, one who could read and write.

---

[1] "St. Louis, Missouri Population History 1840–2021," *Biggest US Cities,* accessed January 26, 2024. St. Louis, Missouri Population History | 1840–2022 (biggestuscities.com). "Physical Growth of the City of Saint Louis," *St. Louis City Plan Commission-1969,* accessed January 26, 2024, https://www.museum.state.il.us/RiverWeb/landings/Ambot/Archives/History69/index.html#boom.

[2] Morgan, Harris, eds., *Anderson,* 265. Robertson, *Struggle,* xvii. Caesar, *King,* 185. Sunder, *Sublette,* 116, 118, 157.

[3] William Raynolds, *Report of the Expedition of the Yellowstone River* (Washington, D.C.: Government Printing Office, 1868), 77.

[4] Enzler, *Bridger,* 114–116.

[5] Sunder, *Sublette,* 158.

[6] Morgan, Harris, eds., *Anderson,* 265, 315.

[7] Ibid, 30–31, 265, 315.

[8] Ibid, 30, 328.

[9] Will Bagley, *So Rugged and Mountainous: Blazing the Trails to Oregon and California, 1812–1848* (Norman, OK: University of Oklahoma Press, 2010), 82.

[10] Ibid.

[11] Hiram Chittenden and Alfred Richardson, *Life, Letters and Travels of Father Pierre-Jean De Smet, S. J. 1801–1873,* Vols. 3, 4 (New York, NY: Frances P. Harper, 1905), 1012, 1483–1484.

[12] Pierre-Jean De Smet, *Letters and Sketches: With a Narrative of a Year's Residence Among the Indian Tribes of the Rocky Mountains* (Philadelphia, PA: M. Fithian, 1843), 13–14, 32–33.

[13] Vestal, *Bridger,* 134.

[14] De Smet, *Letters,* 14–15, 34. Morgan, Harris, eds., *Anderson,* 30–31. Newell, Johansen, ed., *Memoranda,* 39.

[15] De Smet, *Letters,* 14–16.

[16] Morgan, Harris, eds., *Anderson,* 328. Newell, Johansen, ed., *Memoranda,* 39.

[17] Morgan, Harris, eds., *Anderson,* 265, 295.

[18] Morgan, Harris, eds., *Anderson,* 381.

[19] Morgan, Harris, eds., *Anderson,* 315, 381. Enzler, *Bridger,* 119.

[20] Joseph Williams, *Narrative of a Tour from the State of Indiana to the Oregon Territory in the Years 1841–2* (New York, NY: Edward Ebersadt, 1921), 42. Morgan, Harris, eds., *Anderson,* 266.

[21] Morgan, Harris, eds., *Anderson,* 315. Williams, *Narrative,* 42.

[22] Bagley, *Rugged,* 84–85, 88.

[23] Bagley, *Rugged,* 88. Morgan, Harris, eds., *Anderson,* 315. Williams, *Narrative,* 34, 42.

[24] Williams, *Narrative,* 42.

[25] Enzler, *Bridger,* 121–122.

[26] Vestal, *Bridger,* 133. Enzler, *Bridger,* 121. Alter, *Bridger,* 197–198.

[27] Vestal, *Bridger,* 138–139.

[28] Enzler, *Bridger,* 121. Alter, *Bridger,* 197.

[29] Enzler, *Bridger,* 122.

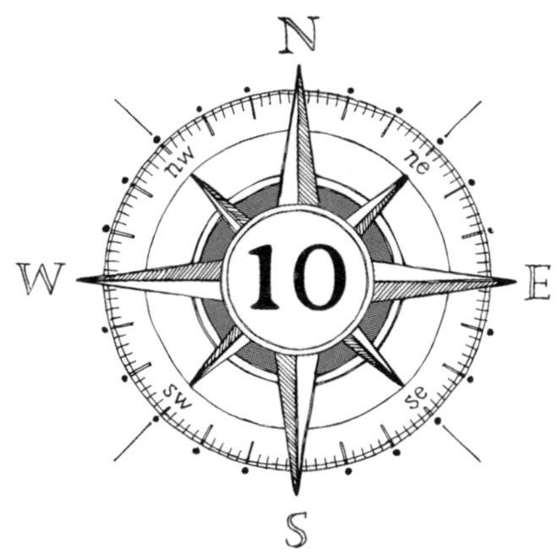

Fort Bridger

1842–1847

During the spring of 1842, Bridger's men trapped and traded while the Hudson's Bay Company expanded its efforts. Richard Grant was Hudson's Bay's new manager at Fort Hall. His boss, George Simpson, considered him unscrupulous, unsteady, and a drunkard. Grant viewed Bridger as his main competitor and worked to undermine him, spreading false information that Bridger's men had stolen Hudson's Bay horses. When one of Bridger's brigade leaders, Thomas "Pegleg" Smith, disputed with Bridger over wages, he betrayed Bridger, selling his beaver packs to Grant and going to work for him.[1]

Bridger needed to transport thirty beaver packs to St. Louis. But Sioux, Cheyenne, and Gros Ventre war parties were harassing travelers along the caravan route now known as the Oregon Trail. Bridger and twenty of his men joined Tom Fitzpatrick and other mountaineers for mutual protection as they rode east. Bridger guided them over a little-known route that bypassed the war parties, arriving at Fort Laramie on July 3, 1842.[2]

West of the fort, they had met Elijah White, Indian agent for Oregon, and twenty-two-year-old attorney Lansford Hastings, together leading a 112-person wagon train bound for Oregon. White hired Fitzpatrick as a guide to Fort Hall.[3]

On July 8, Bridger's party was riding along the North Platte, where they met a government expedition under the leadership of Lieutenant John Charles Frémont and guided by Kit Carson. The expedition was conducting a topographic survey of the Oregon Trail from Missouri's western border to South Pass. At the time, Frémont and several men were away, exploring the South Platte River. Bridger warned expedition members about the war parties. The expedition was only twenty-five men strong, and Bridger's report alarmed them. He offered to guide them to the Sweetwater River, but only the absent Frémont could make that decision.[4]

Reaching St. Louis, Bridger sold the beaver packs and paid his men. On September 3, he reimbursed Pierre Chouteau Jr. & Company $65, paying in full Fraeb & Bridger's loan.[5]

Bridger then partnered with an old acquaintance, Louis Vasquez, who had been trapping and trading in the Rocky Mountains since 1822. Vasquez had gone into debt in his latest venture. Pierre Chouteau Jr. & Company lent goods and money to the new outfit, Bridger & Vasquez. On August 20, 1842, Vasquez wrote his brother, "I am leaving to make money or die."[6]

The two partners led thirty to forty men hauling merchandise to Bridger's fort, arriving on November 1, 1842. Deciding not to use the fort, they rode fifty-four miles west to Blacks Fork, a tributary of the Green River. There, they built a new Fort Bridger. It was a good location, situated on a north–south Indian trade route as well as on the Oregon Trail and located in friendly Shoshone country, though claimed by Mexico. Bridger and Vasquez sent out trapping and trading brigades but had trouble acquiring furs as the Hudson's Bay Company worked to outcompete them.[7]

In the spring of 1843, they constructed a new fort on lowlands closer to Blacks Fork. A wooden stockade enclosed log cabins, including a combination blacksmith shop and trading room. A corral held livestock. According to Grenville Dodge, "the land on which Fort Bridger is located was obtained by Bridger from the Mexican government." In early July, Vasquez, leading twenty to thirty men, took their furs to Fort Laramie while Bridger remained at the fort.[8]

One day in late July, Bridger and two employees were inside the fort, and most of the men from the nearby Shoshone village were on a buffalo hunt when a seventy-five-man Cheyenne raiding party struck. They captured one of Bridger's hunters, forcing him to reveal information about the fort. They split into two groups, one to steal the fort's horses and the other to steal horses from the Shoshone and mountaineers camped nearby. The party raiding the fort's

In 1843, Bridger and Vasquez built a more permanent Fort Bridger just east of Blacks Fork in the southwest corner of present-day Wyoming. LITHOGRAPH BY ACKERMAN LITHOGRAPHY, COURTESY OF THE BEINECKE RARE BOOK AND MANUSCRIPT LIBRARY, YALE UNIVERSITY, ZC58 852UO.

horse herd killed and scalped a Flathead horse guard, speared a woman and boy, kidnapped a girl, and stole 70 horses. The party raiding the Shoshone and mountaineer herds raced through the village, spearing people and stealing 200 horses. About eight people were killed in both raids. Returning from the buffalo hunt, Shoshone and mountaineers chased after the raiders and recovered most of the horses.[9]

The Company sent Bridger & Vasquez poor-quality merchandise, and the new men Bridger had to work with he called "greenhorns." That August, he led thirty greenhorns to trap the Wind and Milk Rivers while Vasquez remained at the fort. Bridger discovered that reports of abundant beaver along the Milk River were exaggerated—his trappers acquired only three packs. In late November, he led the brigade down the Missouri River to Fort Union, encamping a half-mile away to pass the winter.[10]

On December 10, 1843, Edward Denig, Fort Union's clerk, wrote a letter on Bridger's behalf to Pierre Chouteau outlining Bridger's business plans.

Emigrant traffic was increasing. Travelers had money and needed to replace horses, buy supplies, and repair equipment. Bridger said, ". . . should I receive the goods hereby ordered, will do a considerable business in that way with them." He planned a spring beaver hunt, then after the arrival of his merchandise, he would lead a brigade to California, returning with furs, horses, and valuable shells. Yet he was concerned about Vasquez' poor conduct when he had visited Fort Laramie. William Laidlaw, in charge of Fort Union, wrote that Vasquez had neglected business "by drinking and frolicking." Bridger ended his letter by mentioning finances and requesting a California passport.[11]

A few days before Christmas, a Sioux raiding party wounded a guard and stole six horses from Fort Union's herd. Bridger, leading his men in pursuit of the raiders, was joined by Ellingsworth, a bookkeeper, and Gardepie, an old man, part White, part Creek, from Fort Mortimer, the Union Fur Company's nearby post. The raiders halted on a hilltop as more warriors joined them, while the pursuers stopped at the hill's base. The Sioux made signs to the trappers to come fight. Bridger could not get his men to attack. Gardepie whipped his horse, shouting to them to follow him up the hill. Only Ellingsworth joined him. As they galloped toward the hilltop, warriors concealed in a ravine fired a volley, killing Gardepie. The Sioux shouted again for Bridger's men to come fight, but they returned to camp. Bridger was embarrassed for his men's cowardly actions. He remained dissatisfied with them, and many left.[12]

Afterward, William Laidlaw wrote Chouteau, "He [Bridger] is not a man calculated to manage men, and in my opinion will never succeed in making profitable returns." On January 4, 1844, Company representative Honoré Picotte wrote to Chouteau, saying that neither Bridger nor Laidlaw, who was also in debt to the Company, should be sent more merchandise, stating "their order is too heavy!"[13]

In April 1844, Bridger led thirteen men to the Great Salt Lake, hunting beaver and gathering salt. Indians attacked, killing two men and wounding another.[14]

That summer, more than 1,500 emigrants traveled the Oregon Trail. Some took the newly opened Sublette Cutoff to Fort Hall that diverged from the trail east of Fort Bridger. It was fifty miles shorter, but there was no water for forty of those miles.[15]

Travelers on the Oregon Trail could make repairs and replenish livestock at Fort Bridger on Blacks Fork. ILLUSTRATION COURTESY OF THE NATIONAL PARK SERVICE.

Fort Bridger was a welcome relief to weary travelers. They could buy goods, replace livestock, and make repairs in the blacksmith shop. There was excellent pasturage for livestock and good-quality water.[16]

In late August, mountaineers gathered near Fort Bridger, enjoying card games, shooting matches, and other pastimes. Bridger prepared for the California trip, selecting supplies and trade goods and hiring thirty mountaineers.[17]

On August 30, 1844, the day Bridger was leaving, emigrant John Minto wanted to trade a small double-barreled shotgun missing a hammer for three deerskins to make a buckskin suit. Bridger examined the gun saying, "Young man, I can't do it; we get few deerskins here. I'll give you ten goat [antelope] skins; that's the best I can do." Minto took Bridger's offer.[18]

Bridger led his brigade from the fort, bound for California. He may have ridden south to the Spanish Trail or taken the Oregon Trail heading northwest. He later referred to places he visited: southern California, the Sacramento River, and Oregon Country.[19]

In late summer 1845, Bridger's brigade returned to Fort Bridger. Vasquez led ten men on a hunt, and Bridger and his men took what they had acquired in California as well as what Vasquez had on hand to Fort Laramie: 840 beaver pelts and castoreum, 675 dressed deerskins, 25 mules, 24 horses, and 1,400

California shells. They arrived at Fort Laramie on September 2, 1845, where the Company representative estimated the value of everything at $5,000, excluding the shells. The Company would determine their value later.[20]

Traveling the Oregon Trail west of Fort Laramie was dangerous. Sioux and Cheyenne war parties attacked Whites they considered friends of the Shoshone. Bridger and two of his French-Canadian trappers planned to use his little-known trail through the Wind River Mountains to bypass the war parties and return to Fort Bridger. He invited along a ten-man party led by Lansford Hastings.[21]

Hastings had published *The Emigrants' Guide to Oregon and California* describing routes west and providing advice. On pages 138 and 139, he proposed a new route diverging from the Oregon Trail 200 miles east of Fort Hall and "thence bearing west southwest, to the Salt Lake; and thence continuing down to the bay of St. Francisco. . . ." He made no mention of deserts, rough terrain, and mountains the traveler would cross. Hastings' divergence from the Oregon Trail was near Fort Bridger; however he did not mention it.[22]

Bridger's mountain trail was rough and hazardous, taking twenty days, but they arrived safely at Fort Bridger. Hastings' party pushed on, following the Oregon Trail to Fort Hall, not taking his proposed route. They would take the California Trail from Fort Hall, safely crossing the Sierra Nevada and reaching Sutter's Fort on Christmas Day, 1845.[23]

During the winter of 1845 to 1846, Jim and Cora Bridger welcomed a new member to the family, Mary Josephine. Soon after the baby's birth, Cora died. Bridger later married a Ute woman, Chipeta or White Singing Bird.[24]

He led a brigade on a spring hunt to Jackson Hole and Yellowstone Lake. Later rendezvousing with Vasquez at Fort Bridger, they took their furs to Fort Laramie, arriving May 7, 1846, and reporting everything peaceful. During this visit, Vasquez married Narcissa Ashcroft, who had two children from a previous marriage.[25]

On June 7, Lansford Hastings, leading a small eastbound party that included mountaineer James Clyman, stopped at Fort Bridger, which was abandoned at the time because Bridger and Vasquez were at Fort Laramie. Hastings' party had ridden mules over his proposed route from California, which became known as the Hastings Cutoff. Hastings traveled east to South Pass where he informed emigrants of his cutoff. Clyman did not like it, believing the established wagon road was better.[26]

On June 15, 1846, the United States and Great Britain signed the Oregon Treaty, establishing the U.S.-Canadian border at the 49th parallel. Even though Fort Hall was south of the border, the Hudson's Bay Company continued its operation there.[27]

By July 17, 1846, Bridger and Vasquez had reoccupied their fort and were open for business. Taos traders encamped in the meadows offered merchandise to emigrants, while 500 Shoshone engaged in trading. Edwin Bryant wrote:

> Circles of white-tented wagons may now be seen in every direction, and the smoke from the campfires is curling upwards, morning, noon, and evening. An immense number of oxen and horses are scattered over the entire valley grazing upon the green grass. Parties of Indians, hunters and emigrants are galloping to and fro and the scene is almost one of holiday liveliness.[28]

A reconstruction of Fort Bridger gives a sense of the stockade's interior appearance. PHOTOGRAPH BY CAROL HIGHSMITH, COURTESY OF THE LIBRARY OF CONGRESS, LC-DIG-HIGHSM-38397.

Hastings, returning to Fort Bridger, had convinced four parties to take his cutoff. On July 20, James Hudspeth left, leading eleven men, including Bryant, followed by the Harlan-Young party of 200 people and forty wagons. Hastings accompanied this party. Six days later, the twenty-wagon Hoppe's Company followed.[29]

The last group was the Donner-Reed party, totaling eighty-seven people and twenty-three wagons. They reached Fort Bridger on July 27, remaining until July 31 to rest their animals. James Reed, one of the leaders, was determined to take the Hastings Cutoff even though his friend, James Clyman, whom he had met earlier along the trail, warned him not to deviate from the Oregon Trail. Clyman later said, "[I] told him about the great desert and the roughness of the Sierras, and that a straight route might be impractical."[30]

Reed wrote to James Keyes that Bridger and Vasquez had 200 head of cattle and lots of horses and mules for trade or sale. He bought livestock from them, writing, "they can be relied on for doing business honorably and fairly." He added they were "the only fair traders in these parts." Bridger said most of Hastings Cutoff was level but warned of a forty-mile stretch without water. He told Reed where he could harvest hay for their livestock. Reed hoped Hastings would send back a message informing them of an alternate route with water and avoiding the desert. The Donner-Reed party took the Hastings Cutoff on July 31.[31]

In August, Bridger led a brigade up the Green River to Jackson Hole, then to Yellowstone Lake. They wintered on the Yellowstone at the Bighorn River, trading with the Crow, who knew Bridger as Blanket Chief, and the Lakota, who knew him as Big Throat. In 1847, Bridger's brigade most likely went on a spring beaver hunt before returning to Fort Bridger.[32]

The 1846 to 1847 winter was harsh. Lots of livestock died at Fort Hall and Fort Bridger. The Shoshone lost an estimated 6,000 horses. Richard Grant wrote, "my opponents, Bridger & Vasquez, will have to give up this year." More bad news arrived. Due to poor decisions, hostile Indians, and bad weather, the Donner-Reed party had become snowbound in the Sierra Nevada. Provisions ran out, people died, and before it was over some resorted to cannibalism.[33]

In 1871, Reed published an account of the Donner-Reed party, shifting blame for taking the Hastings Cutoff to Vasquez. He stated that friends on

Hudspeth's packtrain had left with Vasquez letters for Reed telling him not to take the Hastings Cutoff, but "Vasquez being interested in having the new route traveled, kept these letters."[34] It does not make sense, however, that Vasquez would have purposely withheld Reed's letters. Emigrants would still stop at the fort whether they stayed on the Oregon Trail or took the Hastings Cutoff. James Clyman had advised Reed not to take Hastings Cutoff, but he did.

---

1 Bagley, *Rugged,* 185. Enzler, *Bridger,* 122–123.

2 John Charles Frémont, *Report of the Exploring Expedition to the Rocky Mountains in the Year 1842.* (Washington, D.C.: Gales and Seaton, Printers, 1845). Enzler, *Bridger,* 123–125. Alter, *Bridger,* 203.

3 Bagley, *Rugged,* 180, 182.

4 Frémont, *Expedition,* 3–9, 37.

5 Enzler, *Bridger,* 126.

6 Morgan, Harris, eds., *Anderson,* 373, 375.

7 Morgan, Harris, eds., *Anderson,* 267, 375. Enzler, *Bridger,* 126–127. Alter, *Bridger,* 205. Bagley, *Rugged,* 340–341.

8 Morgan, Harris, eds., *Anderson,* 375. Enzler, *Bridger,* 127. Dodge, *Bridger,* 16. Alter, *Bridger,* 206.

9 Matthew Field, Kate Gregg, ed., John McDermott, ed., *Prairie and Mountain Sketches.* (Norman, OK: University of Oklahoma Press, 1957), 126, 138–139. Enzler, *Bridger,* 130.

10 Enzler, *Bridger,* 131. Alter, *Bridger,* 209. Larpenteur, Coues, ed. *Trader,* 211.

11 Enzler, *Bridger,* 131–132. Alter, *Bridger,* 208–211.

12 Larpenteur, Coues, ed. *Trader,* 212–215.

13 Larpenteur, Coues, ed. *Trader,* 213. Alter, *Bridger,* 210–213.

14 Enzler, *Bridger,* 133–134.

15 Enzler, *Bridger,* 134. Bagley, *Rugged,* 99, 342.

16 Bagley, *Rugged,* 343.

17 John Minto, "Reminisces of Experiences on the Oregon Trail in 1844." *Oregon Historical Quarterly,* Vol. 2, No. 2, (June 1901), 164. Hasselstrom, *Clyman,* 111.

18 Minto, "Reminisces," 166. Hasselstrom, *Clyman,* 111.

19 Alter, *Bridger,* 214–215, 217.

20 Ibid, 216–217.

21 Dale Morgan, ed., *Overland in 1846: Diaries and Letters of the California-Oregon Trail,* Vol. 1 (Lincoln, NE: University of Nebraska Press, 1963), 30–31.

22 Lansford Hastings, *The Emigrants' Guide to Oregon and California* (Cincinnati, OH: George Conklin, 1845), 138–139.

23 Morgan, ed., *Overland,* 31–33.

24 Alter, *Bridger,* 218. Enzler, *Bridger,* 150.

25 Alter, *Bridger,* 218. Enzler, *Bridger,* 140. Morgan, ed., *Overland,* 588–589, 757 n90. Morgan, Harris, eds., *Anderson,* 367.

26 Enzler, *Bridger,* 140. Bagley, *Rugged,* 306–307. Hasselstrom, *Clyman,* 246–247, 255.

27 Bernard DeVoto, *The Year of Decision, 1846* (Boston, MA: Little, Brown & Company, 1943), 226. Justin Smith, "Clearing up confusion about Fort Hall history," *Idaho State Journal,* May 14, 2021, accessed May 7, 2024. https://www.idahostatejournal.com/freeaccess/clearing-up-confusion-about-fort-hall-history/article_7f0f387b-5187-56f7-8b64-6190e90bd3a2.html.

28 Edwin Bryant, *What I Saw in California* (New York, NY: D. Appleton & Co., 1849), 142, 144–145.

29 Morgan, ed., *Overland,* 279. Bagley, *Rugged,* 311.

30 Morgan, ed., *Overland,* 261. Bagley, *Rugged,* 312. Hasselstrom, *Clyman,* 268.

31 Morgan, ed., *Overland,* 279–280.

32 Enzler, *Bridger,* 98, 146, 164,

33 Bagley, *Rugged,* 323. Alter, *Bridger,* 227.

34 Kristin Johnson, ed. *"Unfortunate Emigrants": Narratives of the Donner Party* (Logan, UT: Utah State University Press, 1996), 186. Bryant, *California,* 142.

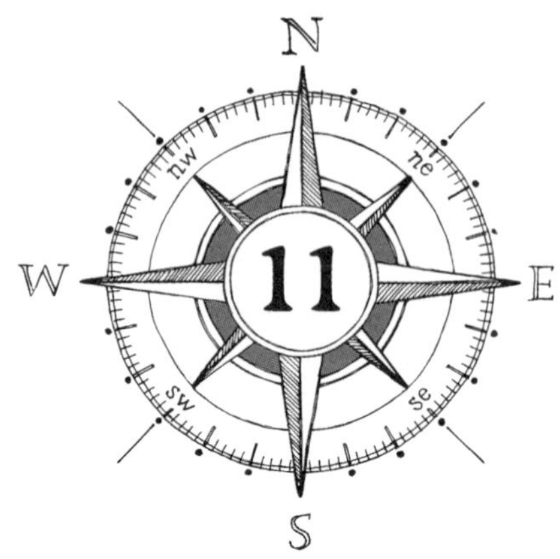

Saints, Sinners, Soldiers, and Indians

1847–1853

Jim Bridger and two employees left Fort Bridger in June 1847, hauling furs to Fort Laramie. He also needed to talk with Company representatives about contractual fulfillments. On June 28, near the confluence of the Little Sandy and Big Sandy Rivers, they encountered a 143-member party of Mormons led by their president, Brigham Young.[1]

Joseph Smith, founder of the Church of Jesus Christ of Latter-day Saints, whose members were known as Mormons, had tasked Brigham Young to find a Mormon home where they could establish a theocracy far from Americans. After Smith was killed in a gunbattle in Carthage, Illinois, on June 27, 1844, Young became the Mormons' leader and later selected the Salt Lake Valley as the site to build their community.[2]

Young wanted to talk with Bridger and invited him and his men to dinner. Young told Bridger he planned to settle the Mormons in the Salt Lake Valley and asked what they could expect. Bridger considered it his paradise and was willing to settle there with them. He did not think they could grow crops there, however, due to a short frost-free season, saying, "I would give a thousand dollars if I knew that an ear of corn could be ripened in these mountains." He warned Young not to bring many people until they determined if they could grow crops, and to be careful of Indians living around Utah Lake. After breakfasting together the next morning, Bridger encouraged

Mormon leader Brigham Young, here circa 1855, initially sought Jim Bridger's advice but later soured on the mountain man. ILLUSTRATION COURTESY OF THE BEINECKE RARE BOOK AND MANUSCRIPT LIBRARY, YALE UNIVERSITY, ZC10 +855PI.

Young to visit his fort. Fire had destroyed the blacksmith shop, but the anvil was good, and they were welcome to use it. Mormons operated a ferry on the Little Sandy River, and Young wrote Bridger a pass to use it. Bridger told one of his employees, Samuel Rogers, "I am sorry for the women and children; they will get into that valley and starve to death."[3]

After conducting his business at Fort Laramie, Bridger returned to his fort where he and Vasquez continued to provide livestock, supplies, and services to emigrants as well as the tribes. They employed roughly twenty men, mostly French-Canadians, many married to Indian wives. In July, Narcissa Vasquez gave birth to a baby boy. Later that month, Loren Hastings (no known relation to Lansford Hastings) arrived with a wagon train. The night of their arrival, the men and their wives, along with a fiddle player, held a dance at the fort until 2 A.M. Hastings showed Chipeta Bridger and the other women of the fort "how to dance US dances," and "There was some wild romance in this."[4]

There is no information on Jim Bridger from the fall of 1847 to the first months of 1848. The winter was severe, so he may have hunkered down at the fort with his family.

Two years earlier, tensions between the United States and Mexico over the border, Texas, and California had erupted into the Mexican-American War. Finally, on February 2, 1848, the two countries signed the Treaty of Guadalupe Hidalgo in which Mexico ceded to the United States 1.2 million square miles of what is now most of the western portion of the country roughly between the 42nd parallel and today's border with Mexico. Fort Bridger and the Mormon settlements were now under U.S. jurisdiction.[5]

On April 9, 1848, Joe Meek stopped at Fort Bridger on his way to Washington, D.C., to report to President James Polk on the latest Oregon news. He brought bad news about Bridger's daughter Mary Ann, who had been very sick after being released from a month's captivity by the Cayuse.[6] In the fall of 1847, measles-infected emigrants had arrived in Oregon. The disease spread, killing many Indians. Dr. Marcus Whitman cared for the Cayuse at his mission, but more than half died. Some thought Whitman was poisoning them. On November 19, Cayuse men killed Whitman, his wife Narcissa, and twelve others. They took forty-seven people captive, including Mary Ann Bridger and Meek's daughter, Helen Mar, who died of measles while in captivity. Meek represented settlers who wanted the federal government to organize Oregon into a territory and seek retribution. Mary Ann Bridger had died from her illness in March 1848.[7]

With the advent of the summer of 1848, emigrants bound for Oregon, California, and the Great Salt Lake continued to arrive at Fort Bridger. Even though travelers could take the Sublette and other cutoffs, there was still plenty of traffic.[8]

Virginia Bridger was born July 4, 1848.[9] Unfortunately, Chipeta died nine days later. Bridger had two young children and an infant to care for, and he remarried shortly after Chipeta's death. His third wife was a Shoshone woman named Little Fawn whom he called Mary.[10]

Indians attacked Mormon settlers, and Brigham Young accused Bridger of encouraging them. On July 16, 1848, Bridger had a letter written to Young stating he would never instigate attacks on Mormons, and he remained their friend, promising, ". . . should you want a favor at my hands at any time I shall always think myself happy in doing it for you. From your friend and well-wisher James Bridger." Pressed by White emigrants and settlers, the Ute became hostile. In October, Bridger visited the Uintah band, but their attitude and actions alarmed him, and he returned to Fort Bridger.[11]

Bridger led a brigade to the Yellowstone River where they spent the winter of 1848 to 1849. He suffered an illness but, gathering medicinal roots, he doctored himself. He took the men on a spring beaver hunt to the Musselshell River, Snowy Mountains, Judith River, and Big Belt Mountains. Reaching the Missouri River's Great Falls in April, they discovered a nearby Blackfeet village with an estimated 400 warriors. Bridger doubled the guard, taking a turn himself at midnight. The next morning, the Blackfeet attacked and the brigade repelled them. During the second attack, a warrior holding a warclub in one hand and knife in the other grappled with Bridger. The warrior swung his club, but Bridger blocked it with his rifle barrel. The warrior tried to knife Bridger, but he blocked the thrust with his rifle, then used it to bash the warrior's forehead. After the brigade repelled them a third time, the Blackfeet left. Later that spring, Bridger's brigade returned to Fort Bridger where they learned the price of beaver had plummeted to seventy-five cents per pelt.[12]

In April and May 1849, Vasquez sent two letters to Young, warning of possible Indian attacks on Mormon settlers. Young read the May letter to his council, saying, "I believe I know that Old Bridger is death on us, and if he knew 400,000 Indians were coming against us, and any man were to let us know, he would cut his throat." Young believed unsavory rumors about Bridger but was favorable to Vasquez, allowing him to open a store in Salt Lake City.

A wagon train of Mormon settlers crosses open range on the approach to Fort Bridger. PAINTING BY WILLIAM HENRY JACKSON, COURTESY OF THE NATIONAL PARK SERVICE.

Young believed Bridger spied on the Mormons and reported on them to Senator Thomas Hart Benton in Washington, D.C. He also believed Bridger and other mountaineers were stirring up the Indians against the Mormons. A former disgruntled Bridger employee, Pegleg Smith, didn't help matters when he wrote to Young that Bridger and Vasquez might be causing the hostilities because they were jealous of Mormon traders. Nevertheless, 1,500 Mormon emigrants traveled by Fort Bridger that year, and Bridger was always hospitable to them.[13]

Back on January 24, 1848, James Marshall was building a sawmill for John Sutter on the South Fork of the American River in California when he discovered gold. Four months later, news of California gold reached the States. People were skeptical until President Polk announced its discovery in December. The rush was on. One principal route to California was the Oregon Trail passing Fort Bridger.[14]

The Forty-Niners bound for California goldfields joined those already heading there for a new beginning as well as emigrants journeying to Oregon and the Great Salt Lake Basin, their numbers reaching 25,000.[15]

Vasquez was traveling to Fort Laramie in the spring of 1849 when he met the first Forty-Niners. They bought every horse and ox he could spare. He sent a man back to Fort Bridger to bring 130 head of livestock. Both Bridger and Vasquez operated ferries across the Green River, charging emigrants to cross. Vasquez also brought merchandise to South Pass, selling to travelers and telling those bound for Oregon they should stay on the original trail and not take the Sublette Cutoff. Bridger remained at the fort, trading, selling goods, overseeing the blacksmith shop, and offering free advice. Bridger's reputation for honesty increased.[16]

On August 11, 1849, an Army Corps of Topographical Engineers expedition arrived at Fort Bridger. Accompanying them on his way to California was H. J. Clayton, whom Bridger had met years ago in St. Louis. Bridger invited Clayton to eat with him, and Clayton was impressed with Bridger's children and his wife, Mary, who he said was a "great beauty." Clayton raved about the meal she prepared of "fresh trout and delicious venison, with hard bread obtained from California immigrants, and excellent tea."[17]

Captain Howard Stansbury led the sixteen-man expedition, with Lieutenant John Gunnison second in command. The army's mission had expanded to protect emigrants along the Oregon Trail, building Fort Kearny at Grand Island on the Platte River and buying Fort Laramie. Stansbury was to scout locations for a third fort, find a more direct route between Fort Bridger and Salt Lake City, survey the Great Salt Lake Basin, and look for potential transcontinental railroad routes. Bridger was hospitable and helpful.[18]

Stansbury and Gunnison believed Fort Bridger would make an excellent site for a military post and Indian agency. Gunnison wrote that Bridger would be the best choice for an Indian agent since he had many personal connections with them. He described Bridger as "one of the hardy race of mountain trappers" who had made enough money to retire East but who preferred to live in the mountains. "With a buffalo skin and piece of charcoal, he will map out any portion of this immense region, and delineate mountains, streams, and the circular valleys called 'holes' with wonderful accuracy." Gunnison believed Bridger would make an excellent guide for any expedition.[19]

Stansbury and Gunnison discussed with Bridger potential cutoffs that could shorten the trails from Fort Bridger to Salt Lake City and to Fort Hall. Bridger had crossed the Wasatch Mountains using various routes and agreed to guide them. Gunnison led the expedition on the road to Salt Lake City while Stansbury, Bridger, and three men left Fort Bridger on August 20. Several times, Bridger told Stansbury the easiest route to travel, but Stansbury went his own way, only to learn Bridger was right. On August 27, Bridger brought them out of the mountains into Ogden's Hole; from there it was an easy journey to Salt Lake City. Stansbury was satisfied they had found the route for a good wagon road from Fort Bridger to the head of the Salt Lake. On Bridger's return home, he ran into H. J. Clayton and said he was disgusted guiding Stansbury and wouldn't be doing that again.[20]

There's no further information on Jim Bridger until the summer of 1850. Emigrant Charles Ferguson stopped at Fort Bridger and said Bridger was very helpful, and he was proud to have his children read to Ferguson. The register at Fort Laramie recorded 39,000 people heading west. A good portion of them would have taken the trail to Fort Bridger. Bridger and Vasquez had plenty of merchandise and livestock for sale.[21]

On September 5, 1850, Stansbury's expedition returned to Fort Bridger after mapping and taking scientific observations in the Great Salt Lake Basin. Bridger had told Stansbury about a more direct route from Fort Bridger to Fort Laramie with a pass easier than South Pass that might make a good railroad route. Stansbury wanted to investigate it and Bridger "with great spirit" offered to guide the expedition. He must have forgiven Stansbury's stubbornness.[22]

The expedition left on September 10. Two days later, Bridger led them eastward toward Pilot Butte, away from the northeast-running Oregon Trail. As they were breaking camp the following morning, a twenty-man war party charged down on them. The expedition members took defensive positions as Bridger and Stansbury rode toward the warriors. They were Shoshone. When they saw Bridger and Stansbury, they became friendly. They were in pursuit of a band of Ute and had mistaken the expedition for their enemies. Later that day, the expedition crossed the Green River. Stansbury believed that, with a little improvement, Bridger's route would make a good road.[23]

On September 20, Bridger led Stansbury's expedition over a gradual pass roughly twenty-two miles long. When Stansbury and his men realized they had crossed the continental divide, they gave "One universal shout" of joy. Stansbury was impressed, believing it "a most excellent route, whether for a wagon or railroad," and named it Bridger's Pass.[24]

They continued eastward reaching the Laramie Plains on September 26. The next day, scouts alerted the expedition they had spotted Indians. They proceeded on as the number of Indians on the ridgelines increased. By noon, they reached the Laramie River as warriors rode toward them from all directions. Stansbury had the men establish a defensive position in a cottonwood grove, then displayed the United States flag.[25]

Bridger shouldered his rifle and walked out toward the mounted warriors. A group rode up to him, and they conversed in sign language. They were Oglala Lakota, and when they recognized Bridger and saw the men were White and not a Crow war party, they raced into camp to shake everyone's hands. Stansbury gave them presents of flour, sugar, coffee, and tobacco, and shared a meal with them. The Oglala said several hundred people were in their band and sent a message for the village to move close to where Stansbury encamped.[26]

After the meal, the Oglala principal men, Stansbury, and Bridger sat in a circle around a fire and smoked the pipe of peace. Many Oglala leaders knew Bridger personally and those who didn't knew his reputation. Bridger communicated with them using sign language. For over an hour he talked with his hands, keeping the Oglala entertained. At times they exclaimed in surprise, other times they broke out in hearty laughter.[27]

Bridger remained with the expedition at least as far as Chimney Rock on the North Platte below Fort Laramie. He said Chimney Rock had been much higher and speculated lightning or some other natural cause had led to its reduction.[28]

Stansbury believed Bridger had shown him a practical route through the Rocky Mountains from Fort Bridger to Fort Laramie, calculating it was sixty-one miles shorter than that stretch of the Oregon Trail. Stansbury reported, ". . . the unhesitating conclusion that, in point of diminished distance, easy grades, freedom from serious obstacles, and convenience and abundant supply of materials for construction, the line of this reconnaissance presents a trace for a road that is not only perfectly feasible, but decidedly preferable to the other." Six years later, the army surveyed Bridger's route and built a road called the

Overland Trail. The transcontinental railroad later roughly followed this route, and today so does Interstate 80.[29]

Congress established Utah Territory on September 9, 1850, and President Millard Fillmore appointed Brigham Young governor and superintendent of Indian Affairs. Fort Bridger, which is today in southwest Wyoming, was part of Utah Territory. The 1850 Census, taken between April 1 and July 1851, listed Bridger and his family and Vasquez and his family as living at Fort Bridger.[30]

In 1851, a bitter winter and heavy, long-lasting spring rains reduced emigrant traffic bound for California to only 1,100 and Oregon to 3,600 people. Continued emigrant traffic had reduced the buffalo herds and other game along the Oregon Trail. Emigrants chopped down trees for firewood, and their livestock overgrazed the grass. Tribes wanted compensation for their losses. Emigrants considered Indian demands and actions as begging and stealing; they wanted the army's protection.[31]

Back in 1846, the government had appointed Tom Fitzpatrick as an Indian agent. He believed the government needed to compensate the tribes for loss of game and natural resources. He also wanted to end tribal warfare by establishing tribal boundaries. Fitzpatrick presented his ideas to a variety of tribes and suggested they meet at a grand council. Many agreed. Fitzpatrick convinced Colonel David Mitchell, Superintendent of Western Indians, and they presented the idea to the Commissioner of Indian Affairs and Secretary of War. They both agreed, but the plan needed congressional approval. By 1851, Congress approved $100,000 to hold the council and provide gifts to the tribes. Fitzpatrick and Mitchell selected Fort Laramie for the council site and the date as September 1, 1851.[32]

Tribes began to arrive, as did a company of dragoons to augment two companies garrisoning Fort Laramie. There was not enough grass for all the horses, so Fitzpatrick and Mitchell moved the council site thirty-five miles downriver on the North Platte to Horse Creek. Sioux, Cheyenne, Arapaho, Gros Ventre, Mandan, Arikara, Hidatsa, Assiniboine, Crow, Blackfeet, and Shoshone leaders and their bands came to the council meeting. Robert Campbell and Father De Smet were part of the U.S. commission.[33]

Washakie, chief of the Shoshone, arrived with sixty warriors and his friend Jim Bridger to interpret. They were not in a good mood. Along their route, Cheyenne warriors had killed and scalped two of their men.[34]

Bridger rode ahead to learn where the Shoshone should camp. Fitzpatrick told him there were no gifts for the Shoshone because they were under Brigham Young's jurisdiction and not his. Bridger argued their case, saying they had just as much right to be there and receive gifts as the other tribes since emigrants were affecting their lands, as well. Fitzpatrick finally agreed to allow them to participate. Since many tribes considered the Shoshone enemies, Fitzpatrick told Bridger they could camp with the dragoons' camp between them and the other tribes. As the Shoshone rode near the Sioux encampment, Sioux warriors made ready to defend themselves. One Sioux warrior jumped on his horse, nocked an arrow in his bow, and raced toward Washakie. Warriors on both sides shouted. Washakie raised his rifle to shoot. A French-Canadian interpreter raced after the Sioux warrior, caught him, and dragged him from the saddle before he could shoot. The Shoshone proceeded to their campsite. It was later learned Washakie had killed the man's father.[35]

David Mitchell invited Bridger to work with him and the other commissioners. Bridger joined with Fitzpatrick and De Smet to set and map tribal boundaries. In addition, De Smet made a map of the Yellowstone geothermal region based on Bridger's information.[36]

Editor B. Gratz Brown, reporting for the *Missouri Republican,* wrote about Bridger:

> He is not an educated man, but seems to have an intuitive knowledge of the topography of the country, the courses of streams, the direction of mountains, and is never lost wherever he may be. . . . Every thing Bridger has seen, he recollects with entire precision, and in his wild life . . . he has traversed the whole country in many directions.[37]

On September 17, 1851, tribal leaders signed the Horse Creek Treaty. It created tribal territory boundaries and bound the signers to be peaceful with one another. It gave the federal government permission to build roads and forts in tribal territories. The tribes would make restitution if emigrants were harmed. The government would protect the tribes from Americans and provide $50,000 in goods each year. At the conclusion of the council, a caravan arrived with $50,000 worth of goods. The tribes didn't understand most of the treaty or the concept of boundaries. Bands of tribes that did not sign did not abide by the treaty. Most tribes continued in conflict with their traditional enemies. When Congress ratified the treaty in 1852, it unilaterally reduced the number of years of annuities from fifty to fifteen.[38]

Jim Bridger would have returned to his fort with his Shoshone friends and spent the winter of 1851 to 1852 there.[39]

On April 29, 1852, Jacob Holeman, the Utah Territory Indian agent stationed in Salt Lake City, wrote to Luke Lea, U.S. Commissioner of Indian Affairs, concerning the Ute and Mormons. Jim Bridger told him the Ute were upset about Mormons settling on their lands and wanted to know if they had the right to prevent it. Holeman then met with Ute leaders and listened to their complaints. They pledged their friendship and asked him to send them traders. Holeman sent traders from Fort Bridger "whom they treated with great kindness and respect," and a party of Mormon traders from Salt Lake City whom the Utes expressed hostility toward. Holeman added the Shoshone were equally upset with Mormon settlement on their lands.[40]

Up to this time, Bridger had spent most of his life unfettered by laws and regulations, but the territorial government in Salt Lake City was now creating them. Green River County was established in 1852, and Fort Bridger was within its boundaries. The legislature passed a livestock ownership law. When ownership transferred, the animal's brand needed to be reversed. If a person was found with an animal with its brand not reversed, the animal could be considered stolen. That same year, four California-bound emigrants bought horses at Fort Bridger. The brands were not reversed, and when the men reached Salt Lake City, authorities confiscated their horses. The men sued Bridger & Vasquez, and a court awarded them $904.[41]

In the late summer of 1852, Louis Vasquez decided to relocate his family to Westport, Missouri. He took with him two of Bridger's children, Felix and Mary Josephine, to be enrolled in Catholic schools at St. Charles. Father De Smet would assist in their enrollment and Robert Campbell, who managed Bridger's money, would pay for their schooling, room, and board. Bridger was doing well financially. On August 28, he bought five houses for $400 on Blacks Fork about a mile from the fort.[42]

On October 19, Benjamin and Elizabeth Ferris, on their way to Salt Lake City, stopped at Fort Bridger. President Fillmore had appointed Ferris secretary for Utah Territory. Bridger invited them to his cabin and introduced them to his wife, who was generous and pleasant, and children, who were "keen and bright-eyed." Elizabeth wrote, "This man [Bridger] strongly attracted my attention; there was more than civility about him—there was native politeness . . . his language is very graphic and descriptive, and he is evidently a man of great shrewdness." He urged the Ferrises to stay with them for the winter. Heavy snow could fall any day, and they might have a hard time reaching Salt Lake City. However, they proceeded on the next day.[43] The Ferrises were fortunate, arriving in Salt Lake City before significant winter storms, but Ferris was appalled by the attitudes and tenets of Mormonism, and he resigned his territorial appointment after only six months.[44]

In April 1853, travelers from Salt Lake City to Fort Bridger had to negotiate deep snow, became lost, consumed their supplies, and ended up crawling into the fort. A party of Mexicans had a similar experience, losing several members.[45] Bridger had been right. It was a rough winter.

---

1 Alter, *Bridger,* 223–224.

2 David Bigler, Will Bagley, *The Mormon Rebellion: America's First Civil War, 1857–1858* (Norman, OK: University of Oklahoma Press, 2011), 7–8. Crutchfield, Moulton, Del Bene, eds, *Settlement,* Vol. 2, 441.

3 Alter, *Bridger,* 224–226. Enzler, *Bridger,* 149.

4 Bagley, *Rugged,* 363. Enzler, *Bridger,* 150.

5 Crutchfield, Moulton, Del Bene, eds, *Settlement,* Vol. 1, 244–245.

6 Alter, *Bridger,* 228. Enzler, *Bridger,* 157–158.

7 Alter, *Bridger,* 228. Enzler, *Bridger,* 156–158.

8 Alter, *Bridger,* 228–229.

9 1848 is the date used. Depending on the source it could have been 1847, 1849, or 1850.

10 Enzler, *Bridger,* 158.

11 Ibid, 151–152.

12 Enzler, *Bridger,* 160. Alter, *Bridger,* 230.

13 Enzler, *Bridger,* 152–153. Alter, *Bridger,* 236–237.

14 Bagley, *Rugged,* 373, 400.

15 Enzler, *Bridger,* 162.

16 Enzler, *Bridger,* 160–162. Alter, *Bridger,* 232–233.

17 Enzler, *Bridger,* 163.

18 Howard Stansbury, *Explorations of the Valley of the Great Salt Lake of Utah* (Washington, DC: Robert Armstrong Public Printer, 1853), 74. Crutchfield, Moulton, Del Bene, eds., *Settlement,* Vol. 1 and Vol. 2, 199, 201, 448. Enzler, *Bridger,* 164.

19 John Gunnison, *The Mormons, or the Latter Day Saints* (Philadelphia, PA: Lippincott, Grambo & Co., 1852), 150–152. Stansbury, *Explorations,* 228.

20 Stansbury, *Explorations,* 76, 79, 81, 84. Enzler, *Bridger,* 168.

21 Enzler, *Bridger,* 170–171.

22 Stansbury, *Explorations,* 228–229.

23 Ibid, 229, 231–233.

24 Ibid, 241–243, 300.

25 Ibid, 250–252.

26 Ibid, 252–253.

[27] Ibid, 254.

[28] Ibid, 51.

[29] Stansbury, *Explorations,* 262. Enzler, *Bridger,* 176.

[30] Billington, *Westward Expansion,* 547. Bigler, Bagley, *Mormon Rebellion,* 39, 42. "Brigham Young," Wikipedia, accessed May 14, 2024, https://en.wikipedia.org/wiki/Brigham_Young. "The Seventh Census of The United States: Utah and Slavery," *Utah Historical Society,* accessed May 14, 2024. The Seventh Census of the United States: Utah and Slaver (Spring 2017) | Utah Historical Society. 1850 US Census, Ancestry.com.

[31] Will Bagley, *With Golden Visions Bright Before Them: Trails to the Mining West, 1849–1852* (Norman, OK: University of Oklahoma Press, 2012), 299–300, 327–329.

[32] McChristian, *Fort Laramie,* 51–52.

[33] Ibid, 53, 55–57.

[34] Ibid, 55.

[35] McChristian, *Fort Laramie,* 55. Enzler, *Bridger,* 178–179.

[36] Enzler, *Bridger,* 181–182.

[37] Alter, *Bridger,* 244–245.

[38] Crutchfield, Moulton, Del Bene, eds., *Settlement,* Vol. 1, 259–260. McChristian, *Fort Laramie,* 59–61.

[39] Alter, *Bridger,* 246.

[40] Ibid, 250–251.

[41] Enzler, *Bridger,* 184–185.

[42] Enzler, *Bridger,* 185–186. Alter, *Bridger,* 251.

[43] Mrs. B. G. Ferris, *The Mormons at Home* (New York, NY: Dix & Edwards, 1856), 83–85.

[44] Burns, Thomas W., *Initial Ithacans* (Ithaca, NY: Press of the Ithaca Journal, 1904), 49–52.

[45] Ferris, *Mormons,* 207.

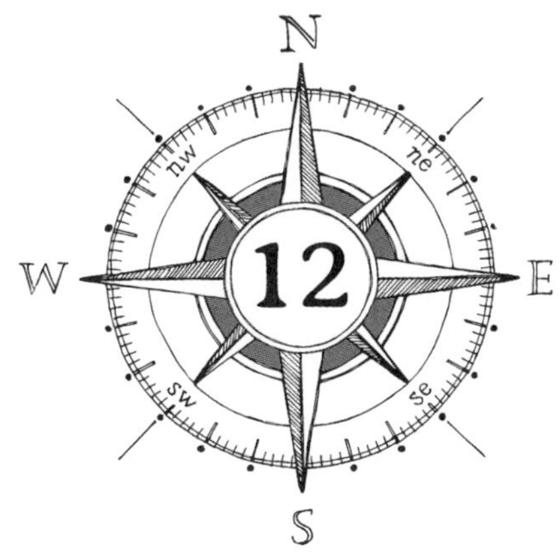

Trouble in Paradise

1853–1858

Jim Bridger, Louis Vasquez, and other mountaineers had been operating ferries on the Green River since 1849 with approval from the Shoshone. On January 16, 1852, the Utah Legislature gave Green River ferry rights to Thomas Moor for one year. Anyone else operating a ferry would be fined $1,000. The mountaineers ignored it. On January 7, 1853, the legislature gave the ferry rights to Mormon Church leader Daniel Wells, who sold his rights to the Mormon company Hawley, Thompson, and McDonald. The mountaineers continued to operate ferries, causing conflict with Utah Territory authorities.[1]

Confrontations also erupted between the Ute and Mormons. Young revoked all Indian trading licenses and liquor licenses for Fort Bridger and Green River. The Mormons believed Bridger incited the Ute to attack them. On August 17, 1853, Judge Leonidas Shaver issued a writ to arrest Jim Bridger, charging that, on August 1, 1853, he "unlawfully aided and abetted the Ute Indians, and supplied them with arms and ammunition for the purpose of committing depredation upon and making war on the citizens of the United States."[2]

Brigham Young planned the "Ft Bridger and Green River Expedition." Attorney General James Ferguson, who was also a sheriff and territorial militia major, was appointed to lead the posse to arrest Bridger. On August 20, Young instructed Ferguson to take fifty men and, when they reached Fort Bridger, to arrest Bridger as well as confiscate all guns and ammunition and "spill upon the ground any and all spiritous liquors."[3]

James Ferguson led the posse to arrest Jim Bridger on trumped-up charges. PHOTOGRAPH COURTESY OF THE CHURCH OF JESUS CHRIST, LATTER-DAY SAINTS ARCHIVES.

Before leaving Salt Lake City, Ferguson's posse swelled to 150 men. Bridger learned a posse was on its way to arrest him and hid in nearby timber. On August 25, Ferguson's men took possession of Fort Bridger and all of Bridger's goods and livestock. They found no ammunition, but they did find liquor, which they drank. Mary helped Bridger elude the posse while he kept an eye on his fort using a spyglass. Posse members rode to the Green River ferries where they killed several mountaineers and confiscated their property, including livestock and whiskey.[4]

Bridger was in no hurry to leave, and he employed government surveyor John Hockaday to survey his Fort Bridger property. When Hockaday completed the survey of Bridger's property boundaries on November 6, 1853, he determined its area was "three thousand eight hundred and ninety-eight acres, two rods." Bridger filed a copy with the General Land Office in Washington, D.C., on March 9, 1854.[5]

He took his family to Fort Laramie, then to Westport, which is now part of Kansas City, Missouri, where he left them. He planned to travel to Washington, D.C., to plead his case that he was innocent and to have his fort and possessions restored to him. On December 17, he met Robert Campbell and Tom Fitzpatrick in Campbell's St. Louis office. Fitzpatrick was traveling to Washington, D.C., to present for approval treaties with the Comanche, Kiowa, and Plains Apache. Bridger and Fitzpatrick traveled together, leaving St. Louis on Christmas Day.[6]

They arrived in Washington on January 4, 1854. Bridger and his lawyer asked Secretary of War Jefferson Davis to submit Bridger's claim to President Franklin Pierce. Davis sent it instead to Attorney General Caleb Cushing.[7]

While Bridger waited for a response, Fitzpatrick traveled to New York City on business. When he returned, he contracted pneumonia. Campbell, in Philadelphia on business, was notified and rushed to Washington. Fitzpatrick's old friends Bridger and Campbell were at his bedside when he died on February 7, 1854.[8] He was about fifty-five years old.

On February 25, while Bridger lobbied in Washington, the Mormons inventoried everything at his fort, valuing the items at $2,736. Someone forged Bridger's name, falsifying his agreement with the value.[9]

Congress was working on a Nebraska Territory bill. One proposal set Utah's eastern boundary at the Bear River and Wasatch Mountains. Fort Bridger would be in the new Nebraska Territory. Bridger was in favor of that and told every senator who would listen. News of Bridger's efforts reached Brigham Young, who wrote to his friend Senator Stephen Douglas on April 29 stating Bridger didn't know what he was talking about and adding, "The perfect folly for any one to listen to Bridger's statements on any subject, even to Indian trade, and trapping, is so obvious, to any one possessed of the least discernment. . . ." The same day, Young wrote a letter to Utah's delegate to Congress, John Bernhisel, to tell Congress, ". . . keep your pet Bridger there, if you wish to preserve him, for if the [Utah] legal officers get hold of him, & just laws of your own making are enforced, he may be strung up between the heavens & earth." Congress did not change the boundary and Fort Bridger remained in Utah Territory.[10]

On June 26, 1854, Davis wrote Bridger, telling him the president had no authority to consider his case. Bridger had not waited for Davis' answer. He was back in St. Louis before May 1. There he met St. George Gore.[11]

Gore was a rich Irish nobleman. An avid hunter, he planned a two-year hunting trip around the West. He hired forty men and acquired fourteen hunting dogs, 112 horses, and twelve yoke of oxen to pull twenty-one carts and six wagons filled with supplies, guns, three tons of ammunition, tents, chairs, and a bathtub. Gore hired Bridger as his guide and Henri Chatillon as his hunter.[12]

Bridger attended to family and business matters. Mary Josephine and Felix were at school in St. Charles. Mary and Bridger decided to send Virginia, now age six, and John, age four, to school there as well. Baby Mary Elizabeth would remain with her mother. Bridger was well off financially. Robert Campbell invested over $9,000 for him. Vasquez bought property for their partnership in New Santa Fe, Missouri, along the Santa Fe Trail. They partnered with Josiah Watts, opening a store there with Watts acting as manager.[13]

Gore's passport allowed him to hunt on Indian lands starting May 24, 1854. Bridger led the expedition through Kansas and Nebraska Territories. When they reached Fort Laramie that autumn, a letter from Campbell to Gore was there. Bridger's son John had died of bilious dysentery. Bridger needed to head home but told Gore he would return in the spring. Gore planned to establish a winter camp ninety miles west of Fort Laramie.[14]

On March 22, 1855, Bridger bought 287 acres of farmland and woods nine miles south of Westport and hired Josiah Watts to construct a two-story house. In April, Bridger boarded a steamboat to visit his children in St. Charles and to conduct business for Gore with Robert Campbell in St. Louis. Bridger developed pneumonia and disembarked at Sibley, Missouri. He was so ill, people thought he would die, but he recovered and proceeded to visit his children and Campbell.[15]

Brigham Young ranted against those he considered opponents to the Mormon Church, saying they should welcome having their heads chopped off for their sins and "if any scoundrels come here, cut their throats."[16] With that in mind and with Bridger's arrest warrant still in force, some believe Bridger returned to Fort Bridger and sold it.

On July 31, 1855, Lewis Robison, the Mormon Church's purchasing agent, arrived at Fort Supply near Fort Bridger. Within the week, he wrote to Daniel Wells, Mormon Church leader, to share information from Bill Hickman, the Green River County sheriff, prosecuting attorney, and tax assessor and collector, who had been a member of the posse sent to capture Bridger. Hickman claimed he had met with Bridger to learn if he would sell his fort. Hickman reported to Robison that Bridger was careless and indifferent about selling.[17] Why didn't Hickman arrest Bridger?

Notwithstanding many official titles, including sheriff, William "Wild Bill" Hickman was unsavory and prone to violence. PHOTOGRAPH COURTESY OF THE CHURCH OF JESUS CHRIST, LATTER-DAY SAINTS ARCHIVES.

Robison claimed that, after negotiating with Bridger, he offered to buy the fort, lock, stock, and barrel, for $8,000. An agreement, dated August 3, 1855, stated Robison would send Bridger half the money upfront with the balance due fifteen months later.[18]

The agreement was signed:

his
Jas x Bridger
mark

H. F. Morrell, Agent, signed for Louis Vasquez. Almerin Grow and William H. Hickman signed for the Mormon Church. Of course, anyone could make an X for Bridger with or without his permission. According to the agreement, Robison was to manage the property for the Church. But Bridger never mentioned returning to Fort Bridger or receiving a payment. The document was not recorded in Salt Lake City until October 21, 1858, three years after its supposed signing. At the bottom of the document is the following: "The above is an exact copy of the Contract given to me by Bridger & Vasques [*sic*]. Lewis Robison." Under that is written, "A copy of Agreement from Bridger & Vasques [*sic*] to Lewis Robison." Dated August 3, 1855, Robison wrote a document stating that he paid Bridger $4,000, part of which included "nine hundred and sixty dollars of a gold money marked twenty dollars United States Assay Office of Gold San Francisco California." Almerin Grow was the lone witness.[19]

Another Fort Bridger sales document was signed on October 18, 1858, three days before the 1855 sales document was recorded. Vasquez signed this one and may have received $4,000. Brigham Young gave Lewis Robison a deed to Fort Bridger in 1858. Only the Mormon Church recognized the deed; it was never filed in Salt Lake City, and the U.S. Army did not recognize it when Robison tried to claim Fort Bridger in July 1861.[20]

What types of characters were these Mormon men who signed the alleged Fort Bridger sales documents?

Bill Hickman, who signed the Fort Bridger purchase document dated August 3, 1855, was the first sheriff, tax collector, tax assessor, assistant federal marshal, and legislator for Green River County. Despite being conferred with so much public trust, he was mean spirited and prone to violence, including murder. Of several homicides he boasted about, one was that of his non-Mormon friend Richard Yates, a mountaineer who made a living along the Green River selling supplies to emigrants. Brigham Young resented Yates' competition with his Mormons. In October 1857, Mormon militia arrested Yates, claiming he was a spy for the U.S. Army.

Hickman and his party were escorting Yates to Salt Lake City when instructions from Brigham Young arrived to have Yates "used up." At night, Hickman and two others approached the sleeping Yates, "upon which his brains were knocked out with an ax," and then buried him in an unmarked grave. Hickman presented Brigham Young $900 he had taken from Yates.[21] Years later, on June 12, 1868, the Mormon Church excommunicated Hickman for a variety of reasons.[22]

Lewis Robison, cited in the August 3 Fort Bridger purchase document as the buyer of the fort, was the Mormon Church's purchasing agent as well as the Utah militia's quartermaster general. Robison led a party of men to the charred remains of federal government wagons that Mormon militia had previously burned to recover iron hardware from them. On their return to Fort Bridger on October 24, 1857, they stopped at Yates' cabin and stole forty-eight horses, thirty-six blankets, and various other items.[23]

Almerin Grow, who signed the August 3 Fort Bridger purchase document, was a Salt Lake City attorney. Before Grow left on a Mormon mission to Great Britain on August 5, 1856, federal judges suspended Grow and Andrew Stewart from practicing law in Utah Territory "for base and dishonorable conduct in their profession."[24] In October 1856, Grow married Mary Ann Donnelly in Liverpool, returned to the United States on March 28, 1857, and arrived in Utah on September 26, 1857.[25] He was soon in trouble again. On January 1,

1858, Brigham Young ordered Grow expelled from Utah and his children taken from him. Fellow missionary and later church historian A. Milton Musser wrote about Grow, "Though naturally smart, he has become immeasurably insane . . . wearing his wife's clothing, etc."[26] On September 9, 1858, Grow wrote to Brigham Young, requesting help in regaining his priesthood and the custody of his children in exchange for moving to Fillmore, Utah, as Young had asked him.[27] As late as September 22, 1860, Grow was still in Salt Lake City practicing law. He never regained custody of his children.[28]

These were the men who claimed Jim Bridger had sold his fort.

In 1857, Bridger told army captain Randolph Marcy that the Mormons had become greedy for his fort and came after him with "a force of 'avenging angels.'" He escaped "leaving all his cattle and other property in possession of the Mormons."[29]

William Drown, the First Dragoons' bugler, met Bridger and wrote in his journal on November 3, 1857, ". . . the Mormons . . . came to him and gave him his choice—to receive from them $8,000 for his place here [Fort Bridger], leaving all his cattle and everything as it was, or be forced to leave without any remuneration. He chose to leave. . . ."[30]

In 1873, Bridger was still trying to be compensated for his fort. He had a letter drafted for him to Senator Benjamin Butler that stated in part, "I was robbed and threatened with death by the Mormons, by the direction of Brigham Young, of all my merchandise, livestock, in fact everything I possessed."[31] Jim Bridger believed he never sold his fort to the Mormons.

On June 19, 1855, John Smith recorded meeting Bridger near Fort Kearny "on his way to the mountains." Bridger led Gore's expedition north from Fort Laramie when the grass was high enough for grazing. They were west of the Black Hills near Inyan Kara Mountain in present-day Wyoming when Sioux raiders stole some of Gore's horses. Bridger led the hunting expedition westward to Pumpkin Buttes, then downstream along the Powder River to the Yellowstone and on to the Tongue River. Gore set men to building cabins for the 1855 to 1856 winter. Bridger left the expedition, returning to his family. In the spring of 1856, he arrived at Gore's camp to continue his guiding services. He led them to Rosebud Creek, visited a Crow village, and returned to the Tongue River.[32]

Gore often invited Bridger to dinner. Afterwards, sharing his wine with Bridger, he read from his books and then asked Bridger to comment. Bridger thought Shakespeare was too "highfalutin" and Baron Munchausen was a "durn'd liar."[33]

By June, Gore finished his hunt. In three years, he shot 40 grizzly bears, 2,500 buffalo, and numerous elk, deer, pronghorn, and small game. The Sioux complained that Gore killed vast numbers of animals "purely for sport." Bridger was not known for excessive hunting; there is no record of what he thought about Gore's slaughter.[34]

Bridger's services ended on June 10, 1856, and Gore would credit Bridger's account with Robert Campbell at $1,350. As Gore's men built two flatboats to haul his gear and trophies down the Yellowstone, Bridger and several others left, arriving at Fort Union on June 30.[35]

Gouverneur K. Warren, then a lieutenant with the Corps of Topographical Engineers, led a thirty-four-man expedition to survey the Yellowstone River. One member was geologist Ferdinand Hayden. They arrived at Fort Union the same time as Bridger and hired him to guide them up the Yellowstone.[36]

Leaving on July 25, they needed to return to Fort Union in one month. They surveyed the land, took scientific observations, and collected rocks and fossils. Bridger led them as far as the Powder River; from there, they had to turn back. Bridger told them about the Yellowstone geothermal wonders, whetting the interest of Warren and Hayden. James Stevenson, Hayden's assistant naturalist, was enthralled with Bridger, writing, "[Bridger's] memory was an encyclopedia. He had vivid, and evidently, accurate recollection of the details of events connected with his life and ventures and would, while sitting by the camp fire at night, recite hundreds of events."[37]

Bridger was asked to build an elongated bull boat, which he directed the men in constructing. When finished, they loaded the collections on it. Some of the soldiers poled while Bridger steered it downriver. Upon reaching Fort Union, they readied the expedition's mackinaw boat and left on September 1. Bridger was invited to join them as they continued scientific observations down the Missouri. Reaching Sioux City, Iowa, on November 15, they boarded a steamboat bound for St. Louis, and Bridger left them at Westport.[38]

Bridger remained with his family during the 1856 to 1857 winter. In March, he traveled to St. Charles to visit his children and then to St. Louis, where, on March 25, he met an old mountaineer friend, Samuel Tulloch, in Robert Campbell's office. They responded to a letter from Warren stating that Bridger was the first White man to reach the Great Salt Lake.[39]

When the federal government organized the Utah Territory on September 9, 1850, it appointed Brigham Young governor and Indian superintendent. Using the Mormon militia known as Danites, Young enforced his will, but he was accused of spending federal funds on church projects and intimidating non-Mormon government officials. By March 1857, President James Buchanan concluded that the Mormons were in a state of rebellion. He replaced Brigham Young as governor with a non-Mormon, Alfred Cumming, and appointed non-Mormons to territorial positions. Young refused to step down. Buchanan ordered 2,500 troops under the command of Colonel Albert Sidney Johnston to escort the officials to Salt Lake City and ensure they took their positions.[40]

In mid-July, the army began sending units from Fort Leavenworth to forts along the Oregon Trail. Jim Bridger was at Fort Laramie on July 16 when the army hired him as scout and interpreter at $5 per day. It took time for what was called the Army of Utah to organize. On September 3, Bridger led Colonel Edmund Alexander and his Tenth Infantry along the trail toward Salt Lake City.[41]

Several events occurred affecting Bridger's life that he would not learn about until later. His daughter Mary Josephine died and was buried in St. Charles on September 7. His wife, Mary, gave birth to a boy, naming him William. She was sick most of September and so was Felix, who had finished school and was now home.[42]

General William Harney had sent Captain Stewart Van Vliet to find forage and supplies for the army along its route to Salt Lake City and to inform Brigham Young that the army would be establishing a fort near Salt Lake City. On September 14, Van Vliet left Salt Lake City after Young told him he would prevent the Army of Utah from entering Utah Territory. The following day, Young declared martial law, ordering Utah's territorial militia to repel any invasion; "no person shall be allowed to pass or repass into or through or from the Territory without a permit."[43]

On September 17, 1857, Colonel Johnston, leading six companies of the Second Dragoons, left Fort Leavenworth escorting Governor Cumming and other officials bound for Salt Lake City.[44]

Jim Bridger was guiding Colonel Alexander's Tenth Infantry along the Sweetwater River west of Devils Gate on September 21 when they encountered Captain Van Vliet riding east. Van Vliet informed Alexander of Young's rebellion before proceeding on to report to Colonel Johnston. On September 27, the Tenth Infantry reached the Green River, where Chief Washakie and his Shoshone warriors waited to join the fight against the Mormons. Alexander told Washakie to stay out of it. On September 30, the Tenth reached Ham's Fork where the Mormon militia had burned the meadows to reduce forage for the army's livestock. On October 2, Lewis Robison set fire to Fort Bridger as other Mormons torched Fort Supply. That same day, Mormon militia attacked three supply trains, burning the wagons and contents and absconding with the livestock.[45]

Bridger left Alexander at Ham's Fork and rode back along the Oregon Trail to find Colonel Johnston, passing supply trains and troops on the march to join Alexander.[46]

In early October, Garland Hurt, Utah Indian agent, joined federal troops on the Sweetwater River. Ute Indians had informed him that a California-bound wagon train had passed through Salt Lake City and days later encamped at Mountain Meadows on the Spanish Trail, where, on September 11, a force of Mormons and Ute massacred the men, women, and children. Mormon leaders learned Hurt knew of the massacre and raised 300 men to arrest him. With the aid of Ute friends, Hurt escaped and reached the troops on the Oregon Trail.[47]

Bridger found Colonel Johnston east of South Pass where snowstorms were brewing. Major Fitz John Porter wrote, "Bridger, the faithful and experienced guide, ever on the alert, would point in time to the 'snow-boats,' which, like balloons, sailing from the snowcapped mountains, warned us of storms, and would hasten to a good and early camp in time for shelter before the tempest broke upon us."[48]

They reached South Pass on October 15. Porter wrote, "a cold and driving snowstorm barred progress for a few days." On November 3, Johnston joined Alexander on Ham's Fork. That evening, First Dragoons' bugler William Drown wrote about Bridger, "Our old guide has received a regular appointment this evening from Colonel Johnston, as principal guide through Utah; and is to rank as Major."[49]

The Army of Utah began its march to Fort Bridger, thirty miles to the west, on November 6. Temperatures dropped, fierce winds blew, and snow fell as the men trudged forward and 3,000 horses, mules, and cattle died. Twelve days later, they reached Fort Bridger.[50]

The loss of supply trains and livestock, the Mormons burning the meadows and Fort Bridger, and heavy snowfall in the mountain passes leading to Salt Lake City convinced Johnston to wait until spring to advance. The army would endure a miserable winter in makeshift huts and tents at Fort Bridger.[51]

On November 18, 1857, Bridger and Assistant Quartermaster John Dickerson signed a ten-year agreement that the army would lease the Fort Bridger property according to Hockaday's survey, paying Bridger & Vasquez $600 per year after they established the title. In his lease transmittal, Dickerson wrote, "[Bridger] bases his claim to the land on some Mexican or Spanish law . . . I think it exceedingly doubtful whether his title is good."[52]

The next day, Lieutenant Colonel Phillip St. Cooke's Second Dragoons, escorting Utah Territory's governor Alfred Cumming and other officials, arrived at Fort Bridger. Bridger climbed to a high point to scan the countryside. Captain John Phelps saw Bridger standing alone, looking pensive. "He was a perfect monarch of all he surveyed," Phelps wrote, "and never dreamed that his kingdom would ever be disturbed by emigration in his day—so remote was it from the United States. . . . But the Mormons came. Mr. Bridger's reign was ended. They seized upon this point and ejected its ancient owner."[53]

During the winter, Bridger informed travelers on the safest trails. He advised Colonel Johnston on the pros and cons of various routes the army could take to Salt Lake City, and he entertained soldiers with his adventures and tall tales.[54]

President Buchanan sent Colonel Thomas Kane to negotiate with Brigham Young. Kane traveled back and forth between Fort Bridger and Salt Lake City. Eventually, Governor Cumming and Young came to an agreement that Young and the Mormons would be pardoned, and U.S. troops would not attack if the Mormons accepted Cumming as governor and allowed the establishment of a military post forty miles southwest of Salt Lake City. Governor Cumming and Young formalized the agreement, and on June 26, 1858, Colonel Johnston and his troops peacefully marched through Salt Lake City. Johnston led the troops to the site of their new post, naming it Camp Floyd after the secretary of war.

Bridger continued guiding detachments until July 20 when he was discharged and started homeward.[55]

Solomon Hale was in the Salt Lake City office of Captain William Hooper, Secretary of Utah Territory, when Bridger entered to discuss land issues. Hale said about Bridger, "One was impressed with the sincerity and honesty of the man. He was a man of character, embodying great courage and leadership."[56]

---

1 Enzler, *Bridger,* 161, 188–189.
2 Ibid, 189–190.
3 Ibid, 189–191.
4 William Hickman, *Brigham's Destroying Angel: The Life, Confession, and Disclosures of Bill Hickman* (New York, NY: Geo A. Crofutt, Publisher, 1872), 91–93. Randoph Marcy, *Thirty Years of Army Life on the Border* (New York, NY: Harper & Brothers, Publishers, 1866), 401. Enzler, *Bridger,* 190–192. Alter, *Bridger,* 251–252.
5 Alter, *Bridger,* 253–254.
6 Enzler, *Bridger,* 192–193.
7 Ibid, 193.
8 Ibid.
9 Ibid, 191.
10 "1854 April 29 Letter to Stephen A. Douglas," The Brigham Young Center, accessed May 17, 2024. https://brighamyoungcenter.org/s/byp/item/4668#?c=&m=&s=&cv=. Enzler, *Bridger,* 194–195.
11 Enzler, *Bridger,* 195, 202.
12 Enzler, *Bridger,* 197. Alter, *Bridger,* 260.
13 Enzler, *Bridger,* 196.
14 Ibid, 197–199.
15 Ibid, 199–200.
16 Ibid, 200.
17 Fred Gowans and Eugene Campbell, *Fort Bridger: Island in the Wilderness* (Provo, UT: Brigham Young University Press, 1975), 49, 63, 66, 176.
18 Ibid, 70, 162.
19 Alter, *Bridger,* 273–275. Gowans, Campbell, *Fort Bridger,* 72, 74.
20 Alter, *Bridger,* 275–277. Gowans, Campbell, *Fort Bridger,* 162–163.
21 Bigler, Bagley, *Mormon Rebellion,* 220–221.
22 Lynn Hilton and Hope Hilton, "Hickman, William Adams," Utah History Encyclopedia, accessed February 1, 2025, https://www.uen.org/utah_history_encyclopedia/h/HICKMAN_WILLIAM.shtml. Hickman, *Brigham's Destroying Angel,* 122–127.
23 Bigler, Bagley, *Mormon Rebellion,* 210, 221.
24 "Interesting Letter from Judge Drummond—Interference of the Mormons with the Courts of Law," *New York Times,* Tuesday, May 26, 1857, page 1, Newspapers.com, accessed February 1, 2025, https://www.newspapers.com/image/20335357/?match=1&terms=%22Almerin%20Grow%22.
25 "Almerin M Grow," Church History Biographical Database, The Church of Jesus Christ of Latter-Day Saints. accessed February 1, 2025. https://history.churchofjesuschrist.org/chd/individual/almerin-m-grow-1816?lang=eng.
26 "Jan 1, 1858 - Almerin Grow expelled from Utah for Gender Non-Conforming [Part 17]," Time.graphics, accessed February 1, 2025. https://time.graphics/event/6997415.
27 "Almerin Grow letter to Brigham Young," BYU Library - Special Collections, accessed February 1, 2025. https://archives.lib.byu.edu/repositories/ltpsc/resources/upb_mss8731.
28 "Probate Court," *The Mountaineer,* Sat, Sep 22, 1860, Page 1. Newspapers.com, accessed February 1, 2025. https://www.newspapers.com/image/1139642263/?match=1&terms=%22Almerin%20Grow%22.
29 Marcy, *Army Life,* 401.
30 Theophilus Rodenbough, *From Everglade to Cañon with the Second Dragoons* (New York, NY: D. Van Nostrand, Publisher, 1875), 194, 214.
31 Gowans, Campbell, *Fort Bridger,* 55.

[32] Clark Spence, "A Celtic Nimrod in the Old West," *Montana: The Magazine of Western History* 9, No. 2, 1959. Gowans, Campbell, *Fort Bridger,* 66. Alter, *Bridger,* 260. Enzler, *Bridger,* 201.
[33] Marcy, *Army Life,* 403.
[34] Marcy, *Army Life,* 402. Alter, *Bridger,* 261.
[35] Enzler, *Bridger,* 202.
[36] Enzler, *Bridger,* 203–204. Crutchfield, Moulton, Del Bene, eds., *Settlement,* Vol. 2, 490–491.
[37] Gouverneur Warren, *Preliminary Report of Explorations in Nebraska and Dakota in the Years 1855-'56-'57* (Washington, DC: Government Printing Office, 1875), 15–16. Enzler, *Bridger,* 206. Alter, *Bridger,* 260.
[38] Enzler, *Bridger,* 207. Warren, *Preliminary Report,* 16.
[39] Enzler, *Bridger,* 208.
[40] George Walton, *Sentinel of the Plains: Fort Leavenworth and the American West* (Englewood Cliffs, NJ: Prentice-Hall, Inc., 1973), 80. Crutchfield, Moulton, Del Bene, eds., *Settlement,* Vol. 2, 479, 513.
[41] Walton, *Sentinel,* 80. Bigler, Bagley, *Mormon Rebellion,* 183. Alter, *Bridger,* 266. Enzler, *Bridger,* 210.
[42] Enzler, *Bridger,* 211.
[43] Bigler, Bagley, *Mormon Rebellion,* 144, 147–149.
[44] Walton, *Sentinel,* 80–81.
[45] William Preston Johnston, *The Life of General Albert Sidney Johnston* (New York, NY: D. Appleton and Co., 1878), 211. Bigler, Bagley, *Mormon Rebellion,* 180, 207. Alter, *Bridger,* 266. Gowans, Campbell, *Fort Bridger,* 99.
[46] Enzler, *Bridger,* 211.
[47] Bigler, Bagley, *Mormon Rebellion,* 150, 152–154.
[48] Johnston, *Johnston,* 211.
[49] Rodenbough, *Dragoons,* 214. Johnston, *Johnston,* 211. Bigler, Bagley, *Mormon Rebellion,* 225.
[50] Bigler, Bagley, *Mormon Rebellion,* 225, 229.
[51] Bigler, Bagley, *Mormon Rebellion,* 83–84. Crutchfield, Moulton, Del Bene, eds, *Settlement,* Vol. 2, 480.
[52] Alter, *Bridger,* 268–269.
[53] Bigler, Bagley, *Mormon Rebellion,* 229. Alter, *Bridger,* 215–216.
[54] Alter, *Bridger,* 269–271.
[55] Page Smith, *The Nation Comes of Age: A People's History of the Ante-Bellum Years* (New York, NY: McGraw-Hill Book Company, 1981), 565. Crutchfield, Moulton, Del Bene, eds., *Settlement,* Vol. 2, 480. Bigler, Bagley, *Mormon Rebellion,* 326. Alter, *Bridger,* 272.
[56] Enzler, *Bridger,* 219.

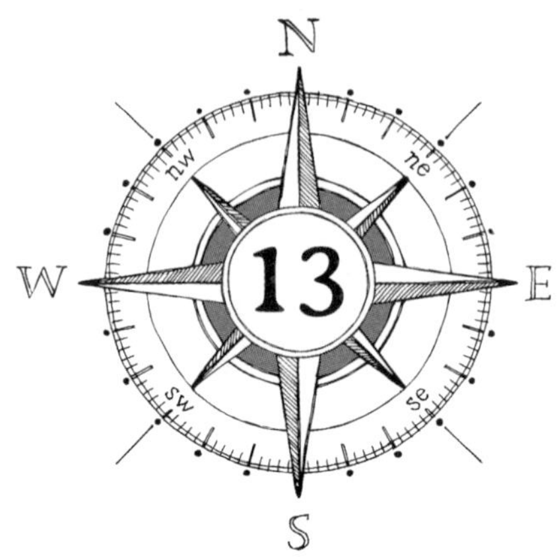

Army Guide

1859–1865

In the spring of 1859, the U.S. Army hired Jim Bridger to guide a fourteen-man expedition conducting an eighteen-month topographic survey of the Yellowstone and Missouri River headwaters. Chief topographer Captain William Raynolds led the expedition, which included geologist Ferdinand Hayden.[1]

Two Missouri River steamboats transporting expedition members, and annuities for the Sioux, picked up Bridger at Kansas City, along with a thirty-one-man infantry escort at Fort Randall. By June 18, they were unloading wagons, equipment, and supplies at Fort Pierre. Lakota leaders confronted Raynolds, stating that General William Harney had told them no Whites would travel through their country. If the Lakota did not let the expedition pass, Raynolds threatened to withhold their annuities. They granted permission.[2]

On June 28, the expedition left Fort Pierre, traveling west through rough terrain. Reaching the Cheyenne River, they remained in camp on Sunday, July 3. That night, a bright light appeared on the prairie to the north. Bridger said Indians were signaling their movements. Each night, distant fires would appear. On July 11, the expedition camped near Bear Butte at the northeast edge of the Black Hills. From there, they headed northwest, skirting the Black Hills, and by July 22 reached the Powder River.[3]

Bridger told tales of the Yellowstone geothermal country. He supplemented their food supply by hunting buffalo, elk, and bear. James Stevenson wrote,

"[Bridger's] many wanderings among the mountains and over the plains had invested him with many of the instincts of the animals of that region, and he frequently exhibited them in the highest degree."[4]

On August 4, they crossed the divide between the Powder River and the Tongue River. Raynolds wanted to travel down the Tongue to the Yellowstone, then follow it upriver. Bridger cautioned against that due to the Yellowstone's steep bluffs. Raynolds wrote, "I shall accept his advice out of deference to his remarkable knowledge of the country."[5]

Bridger led the expedition westward over the divide separating the Tongue River and Rosebud Creek. Raynolds wrote, "The ravines upon each side of us were impassable, and the selection of the road proved Bridger's excellence as a guide." They reached Rosebud Creek on August 10 and the Yellowstone on August 15. There they encamped, waiting to be resupplied by steamboats heading upriver to Fort Sarpy. After receiving the supplies, the expedition continued up the Yellowstone River on August 29.[6]

On September 2, they reached the Bighorn River, and on September 8 Bridger guided them to the mouth of Bighorn Canyon. Raynolds wrote, ". . . we reached the impassable wall of perpendicular rock . . . Bridger claims to have descended the lower cañon of the Big Horn . . . upon a raft . . . and his descriptions of the grandeur of the scenery along its banks are glowing and remarkable."[7]

A steamboat laden with supplies navigates the Missouri River. 1833 PAINTING BY KARL BODMER, COURTESY OF THE LIBRARY OF CONGRESS, LC-USZ62-12869.

It was time to head south for winter quarters along the Oregon Trail. They followed the Bighorn to its confluence with the Little Bighorn, then followed that river upstream to the south. Leaving the Little Bighorn headwaters,

Bridger led them southward along the Bighorn Mountains' eastern slopes. They crossed the Tongue River on September 14, passed Lake De Smet on September 19, then reached the Powder River, where they encamped from September 26 until October 1, while Bridger scouted to the south for a trail the wagons could navigate.[8]

On October 10, 1859, Bridger led them to Red Buttes on the North Platte River and the Oregon Trail. They traveled eastward, and Bridger left them at the Deer Creek Indian agency, their winter camp 100 miles west of Fort Laramie, agreeing to return in the spring.[9]

When Bridger arrived at Fort Laramie, he received a letter someone read to him; his wife, Mary, had died. Leaving Fort Laramie on October 29, he spent the winter in Westport, caring for his children and attending to business.[10]

In the spring of 1860, Bridger rejoined Raynolds' expedition at Deer Creek. The escort this time was a thirty-man detachment of the Second Dragoons commanded by Lieutenant John Mullins. On May 10, they headed west, transporting their equipment and supplies by pack mule. Raynolds planned to explore the Wind River headwaters, find a wagon route to the Yellowstone headwaters, then travel to Three Forks, ending at Fort Benton on the Missouri.[11]

They were along the Wind River on the morning of May 26. Bridger felt ill and reluctant to leave camp, but when a bear was spotted across the river, he perked up and shot it, then later that morning he shot an elk. The expedition had plenty of fresh meat.[12]

Entering the Wind River headwaters, Bridger told Raynolds they needed to cross to the Columbia headwaters then back to the Yellowstone headwaters, but Raynolds would not listen. Bridger wanted him to take a western pass Raynolds would later name Union Pass, but Raynolds insisted on heading straight north until on May 30, facing a massive rock wall stretching thousands of feet above them, Raynolds conceded that "the old man of the mountains" was right. Bridger said, "I told you you could not go through. A bird can't fly over that without taking a supply of grub along."[13]

The men and animals endured a hard slog through deep snow crossing Union Pass to the Gros Ventre River. Over the next few days, Raynolds would not listen to Bridger, wasting time and effort and insisting on going his own way. Reaching Jackson Hole on June 12, they needed to cross the flooded Snake

River. Bridger suggested building a bull boat. Raynolds gave him a few men to help but insisted on finding a ford. Lance Corporal Bradley, in attempting to cross the river, drowned. They never found his body. Raynolds then instructed the men to build a raft. The next day, they attempted to cross with the raft and a guide rope, but the current was too swift, and it was "pronounced a complete failure." Raynolds conceded to Bridger and assigned more men to finish the bull boat. It worked, with a three-man crew hauling supplies, equipment, and men. They coaxed the horses and mules to swim across. Over the course of three days and ten trips, they made the crossing.[14]

On June 18, Bridger led the expedition over Teton Pass to Pierre's Hole. From there they crossed over a pass to the north later named Raynolds Pass. On June 29, they camped at Three Forks; on July 12, they reached Great Falls; and on July 14, they arrived at Fort Benton.[15]

Raynolds split his command. He waited while a boat was being built for further exploration of the Missouri downriver to its confluence with the Yellowstone, while Lieutenant Mullins would lead twenty men overland on the south side of the Missouri to the Yellowstone's confluence. Mullins left on July 20 with Jim Bridger as his guide.[16]

On July 24, Mullins' detachment encountered a friendly band of Blackfeet who invited them to their village. Mullins estimated there were between 150 to 200 people. He was surprised to see "The Star Spangled Banner" flying from the top of the chief's lodge. The chief invited him to smoke, eat, and talk. Several Flathead were with them, so it was easy for the chief and Mullins to talk, with Bridger and the Flathead interpreting. Mullins presented the Blackfeet with some gifts, and they gave him a large amount of buffalo meat.[17]

On August 3, twelve fast-riding warriors approached the camp. Mullins' men hobbled the horses and mules, then took defensive positions while Bridger rode out to meet the riders. They parleyed, then rode into camp with Bridger. After Bridger told Mullins they were friendly Crow, three of them fired their rifles in the air. Bridger asked them what was going on. They replied "their hearts were bad" and they planned to take revenge on White men. Suddenly, 250 mounted warriors charged the camp, yelling and firing shots, trying to stampede the livestock. Bridger calmed down the Crow enough to translate for Mullins and talk with their leader, Great Bear, who said, "Our hearts are bad.

The white man is no longer a friend to the Crow Indian. The Great Father has deceived us." He related how the government gave the Sioux their annuities but delivered Crow annuities to Sioux country, where the Sioux would not allow them to get their goods. The Sioux took Fort Sarpy from them, and they were killing their men and stealing their horses. He ended by saying, "and now our hearts being black, we have come out to fight *you*." Mullins said it was not his fault, and he would have it investigated. Great Bear calmed down enough not to attack but warned Mullins not to come near their village, because there were warriors whose hearts were black, and he would not be able to control them. Throughout the incident, Stevenson was impressed with Bridger's "tact and coolness."[18]

On August 11, Mullins' detachment reached Fort Union, where Raynolds and the rest of the expedition waited. At the end of Mullins' report to Raynolds, he wrote, "I cannot conclude, sir, without expressing my appreciation of the services of the gentlemen assigned to my command as civil assistants; of Bridger, the guide, it is unnecessary to say anything, as his reputation is not confined to our own country."[19]

Some expedition members left Fort Union on August 15, heading downriver in two mackinaw boats, one named *Jim Bridger,* hauling collections, equipment, and supplies, while the rest of the expedition, including Bridger as guide, traveled overland, reaching Fort Pierre on September 7. From there they continued along the river, reaching Omaha, Nebraska, on October 4. There the expedition disbanded, and Bridger returned home.[20]

That winter, Raynolds sent Bridger a letter asking his help in mapmaking. On April 12, 1861, Hugh Campbell replied to Raynolds that Bridger was willing to help. If he wanted to send sketches and questions, Bridger would look at them, or if Raynolds paid his way, he would travel to Washington. Unfortunately, the Civil War erupted and the maps were put on hold. Jim Bridger remained loyal to the Union and, when called upon, continued to work for the U.S. Army.[21]

The Central Overland California and Pikes Peak (C.O.C. & C.P.P.) Express Company was the mail carrier between the East and West Coasts. The company was interested in a direct route through the Rocky Mountains' Snowy Range between Denver and Salt Lake City, so they hired Jim Bridger to work with engineer Edward Berthoud and several other mountaineers to search for a route. On May 10, 1861, the ten-member party rode west from Denver into the Rocky Mountains. Berthoud discovered a pass that would be named after him. They followed trails Bridger had traveled in the past to Hot Sulphur Springs, then on to the Yampa River, following that to the Little Snake River and then to the White River. Crossing the Green River, they followed the Uinta River, crossed the Wasatch Range, then followed the Provo River to Provo and on to Salt Lake City. They retraced their route with two survey teams. It was 427 miles, 200 miles less than the current Overland route. Berthoud estimated the cost to build the road would be $100,000. It was not built; the C.O.C. & C.P.P. Express Company had no money for the project. Today's U.S. Highway 40 follows much of the original route pioneered by Bridger, Berthoud, and the others.[22]

That September, Bridger left Denver, spending the winter of 1861 to 1862 with his children in Westport. In the spring of 1862, the army hired him to guide troops along the Oregon Trail. The first transcontinental telegraph line had been constructed along the trail and began operation on October 24, 1861. It was an easy target for tribes angered by the government's broken promises.[23]

Colonel William Collins, commanding a battalion of the Sixth Ohio Cavalry, arrived at Fort Laramie on May 30, 1862. Collins was tasked with protecting the telegraph line and travelers on the Oregon and Overland Trails, in addition to building and manning posts. He brought along his seventeen-year-old son, Caspar.[24]

Bridger guided Collins' men west. Each day, he rode ahead to select a campsite for the night. When they reached Deer Creek, a wagon train was waiting for an escort. Collins detailed thirty men to travel with it. On June 15, they were at Independence Rock. High winds, rain, and pelting hail stopped the troops' advance. As the storm continued the next morning, Bridger left to get out of the wind, saying he planned to find a canyon and make a large fire.[25]

On Sunday, June 29, the troops were resting in camp when a messenger galloped in, reporting Indians had attacked the wagon train, killing two men who had lagged behind. Colonel Collins and Bridger at the head of 100 men rode to the circled wagons five miles away. By the time they arrived, the attackers were gone. Bridger examined the scene of the attack and, from the arrows stuck in the mutilated bodies, determined the attackers had been Arapaho and Cheyenne. Checking the chambers of a pistol still in the grip of the younger man, Bridger saw he had shot four times. Examining the surroundings, he found blood and determined the man had shot one attacker. He estimated twenty in the war party; they had ridden toward the Sweetwater and were long gone.[26]

Crossing South Pass, Collins established a permanent camp at Pacific Springs on June 30. In early August, Bridger took Collins and a small detachment on a six-day exploration trip along the Green River and into the Wind River Mountains. Young Caspar was amused as he watched Bridger roast a jackrabbit and a trout on sticks over a fire, then eat them without salt, washing it all down with a quart of strong coffee.[27]

Due to continued Indian harassment, on July 11, the Postmaster General required the C.O.C. & C.P.P. Express Company to move its route from the Oregon Trail to the more southerly Overland Trail through Bridger Pass. Collins was ordered to also protect the Overland Trail. On August 31, leaving most of his men to protect the Oregon Trail, Collins and a small detachment, including Bridger, returned to Fort Laramie.[28]

The Overland Trail had been rerouted, following the South Platte River through Julesburg, Colorado. Two of Collins' detachments, Companies A and D, were constructing Fort Halleck on the Overland Trail east of Bridger Pass. On September 20, Bridger guided Colonel Collins, Caspar, and seven men on a 125-mile trail to Fort Halleck, taking ten days. On their return to Fort Laramie, Bridger led them on a different route, taking seven days and arriving on October 8, reducing the distance by seventeen miles.[29]

During their summer journey to South Pass, Bridger drew a detailed map of the Sweetwater River, North and South Platte Rivers, and the area's mountain ranges for Colonel Collins. Bridger later drew the map again on an animal skin and gave it to the colonel, who had Caspar transfer it to paper.[30]

Bridger left Fort Laramie for Missouri to spend time with his family. It was relatively peaceful along the trails, although sporadic Indian raids continued through the fall of 1862 and into 1863. Prospectors had discovered gold in the Missouri River headwaters in 1862. The news leaked, and 400 miners arrived in the Beaverhead River area of present-day southwest Montana, establishing a

Situated on the north bank of the Laramie River just upstream from its confluence with the North Platte, Fort Laramie in 1837 was a crossroads for trade and travel, and later a base for military operations in the region. CIRCA 1858–1860 PAINTING BY ALFRED JACOB MILLER, COURTESY OF THE WALTERS ART MUSEUM, 37.1940.49.

This 1837 scene by Alfred Jacob Miller provides a glimpse of life inside the walls of Fort Laramie, circa 1858–1860. PAINTING BY ALFRED JACOB MILLER, COURTESY OF THE WALTERS ART MUSEUM, 37.1940.150.

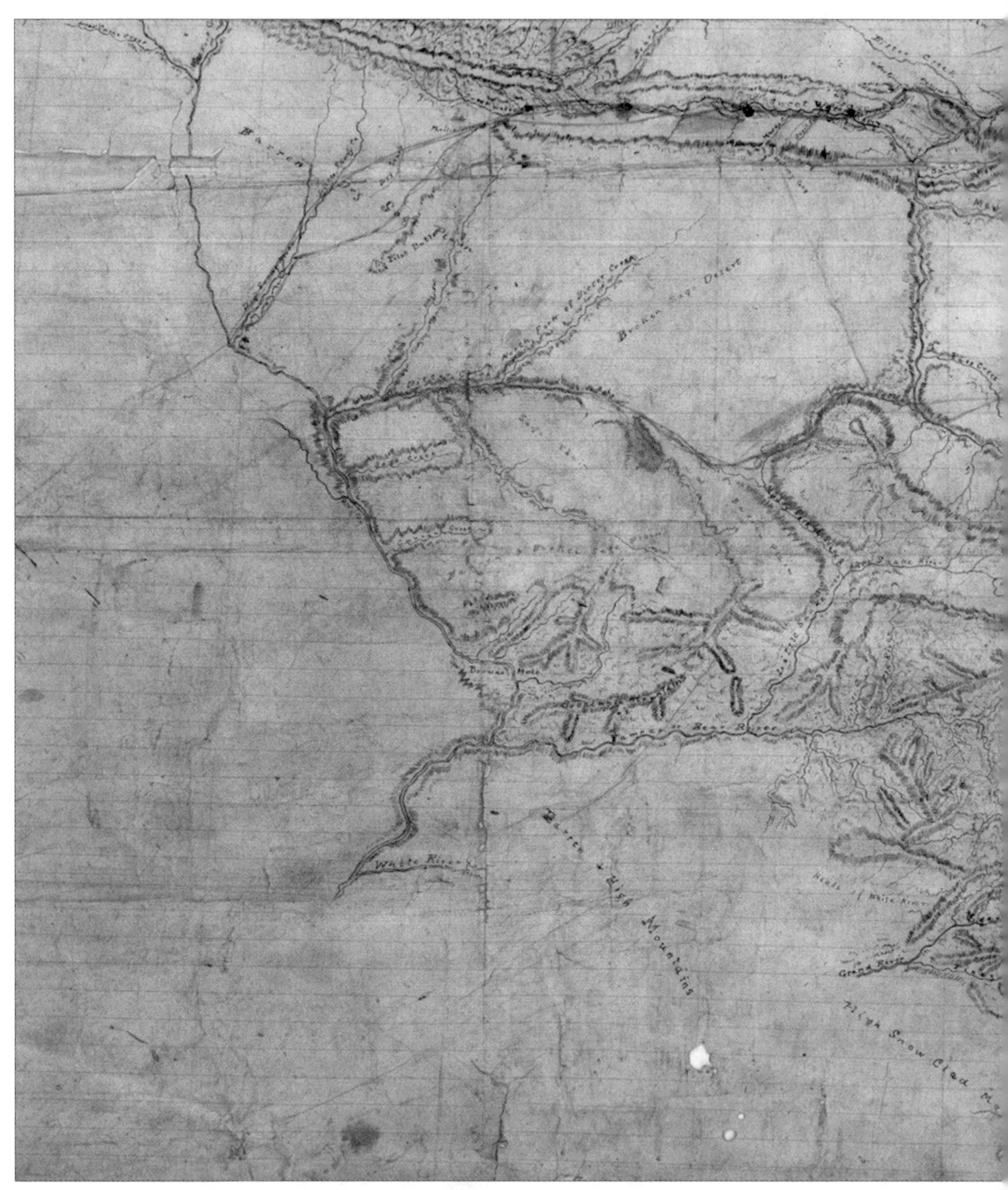

In 1862, Bridger drew a detailed map of the North and South Platte and Sweetwater Rivers, with tributaries and mountain ranges, on animal skin. Colonel William Collins' son Caspar made this copy on paper. MAP BY JIM BRIDGER AND CASPAR COLLINS, COURTESY OF THE AMERICAN HERITAGE CENTER, THE UNIVERSITY OF WYOMING, AH001048.

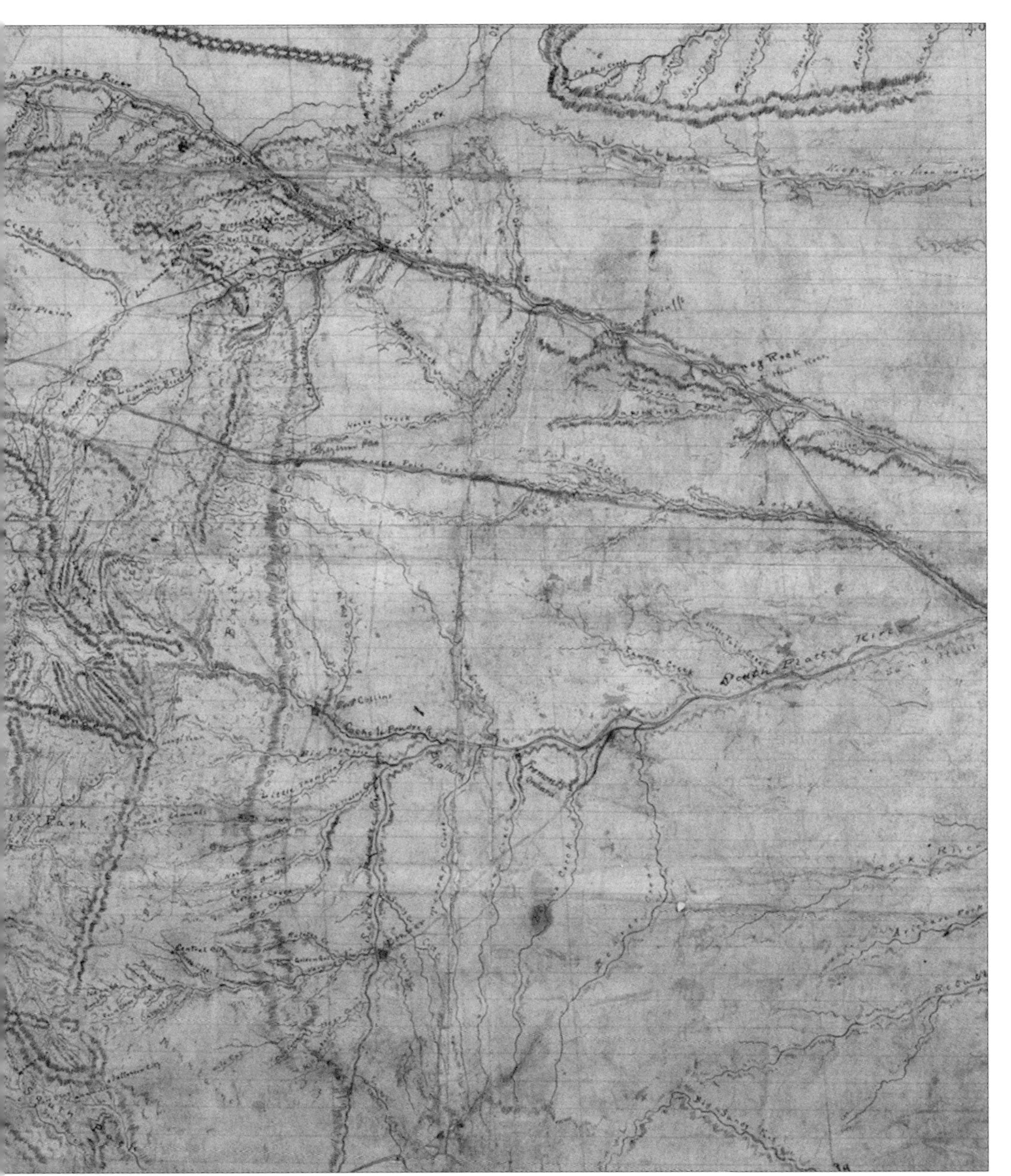

mining camp, Bannack City. In 1863, prospectors found rich gold deposits in Alder Gulch on the east side of the watershed, and nearby Virginia City mushroomed to 4,000 people.[31]

Prospectors traveling to the goldfields from the west used the Mullan Road; from the southeast, the Oregon Trail; and from the east, by Missouri River steamboat to Fort Benton. In the spring of 1863, John Bozeman, John Jacobs, and Jacobs' seven-year-old daughter left Virginia City to find a shorter trail. They pioneered a route down the Yellowstone, cut cross-country southeast to the Bighorn Mountains' eastern slopes, then headed south to the North Platte at Deer Creek on the Oregon Trail. The Bozeman Trail was 400 miles shorter than taking the Oregon Trail. Bozeman and Jacobs offered their services to guide prospectors on their trail to the goldfields. They had to cross Lakota and Crow territories, and neither tribe looked kindly on trespassers.[32]

The army hired Jim Bridger as a guide at Fort Laramie on October 1, 1863, at $5 per day. Captain J. Lee Humfreville wrote that Bridger was a guide for his detachment, which included Arapaho warriors. They left Fort Laramie, riding south along the Rocky Mountain Front Range. At South Park, Colorado, a large unidentified war party attacked them, and the troopers and Arapaho took a defensive hillside position. Hostile warriors entered tall grass and brush leading to the hillside, closing within firing range. Humfreville thought it too dangerous to send men into the grass to flush out the attackers. Bridger wanted to attack. Through sign language, he coerced an Arapaho to go with him. The Arapaho grabbed Bridger's hand and they ran into the brush. Humfreville heard a shot, and Bridger reemerged holding an enemy scalp. The Arapaho never returned. He had either been killed or captured. Humfreville asked the Arapaho to set fire to the grass, but they refused. Using sign language, Bridger convinced them to join him in setting a fire. The grass burned rapidly, forcing out the attackers. They mounted their horses and charged the defenders. Bridger insisted Humfreville's men not leave their position since the warriors outnumbered them three to one. As the warriors rode close, Bridger shot the foremost, and the troopers shot a few more until the attackers retreated. After a few hours of long-distance shots, the attackers left.[33]

That winter, Humfreville and Bridger shared quarters at Fort Laramie. Bridger, a great storyteller, entertained everyone with his tales. Humfreville noted that Bridger never did anything until he wanted to do it. If he was tired, he would sleep no matter the time. When he was hungry, he started a fire and cooked meat while singing Indian songs. Humfreville read Henry Wadsworth Longfellow's *The Song of Hiawatha* to Bridger, who declared it all lies. Bridger asked what the greatest book was; Humfreville recommended Shakespeare. Bridger bought a book of Shakespeare's works and hired a boy to read it to him. Bridger then amused listeners by reciting Shakespeare quotations from memory.[34]

During the winter of 1864, Bridger's family dynamics changed. On January 25, Felix joined the federal Second Regiment Missouri Light Artillery, and Virginia married Albert Wachsman on February 24.[35]

Colonel William Collins and Jim Bridger were concerned that increased emigrant traffic through Indian Country could create conflict. Collins wired headquarters, stating that emigrant numbers were increasing and their routes needed to be controlled, but his superiors disagreed. Bridger knew of a route west of the Bighorn Mountains that he believed wagons could travel, bypassing Lakota territory, whereas the Bozeman Trail on the east side of the Bighorns cut through their hunting grounds. Wagon trains on Bridger's Trail would pass through Shoshone and Crow territories. The Shoshone were Bridger's friends, so they should allow them to pass, and the Crow would probably allow Bridger's wagon trains to pass, too.[36]

The army discharged Bridger on April 30, and he began organizing a wagon train. Some 300 people with 100 wagons agreed to pay him $5 per wagon to guide them. On May 20, 1864, they left Fort Laramie, heading west along the Oregon Trail. When they reached Red Buttes, Bridger led them north.[37]

The Lakota knew about Bridger's Trail. In late spring of 1864, a wagon train on the North Platte met a Lakota band. Upon learning the train was bound for the goldfields, the Lakota told the emigrants if they took the Blanket Road, they would not annoy them. "Blanket" was one of the names the Lakotas used for Jim Bridger.[38]

Bridger ensured his wagon train stayed organized. Mounted men rode to the front of the train and others brought up the rear. They traveled until 3 P.M. or 4 P.M., then circled the wagons to create a corral. A strong guard took the livestock out to graze until sunset then herded the animals into the wagon corral. Guards were posted around the camp at night. In the morning, they took the livestock out to graze until 7 A.M., then brought them back, hitched them to the wagons, and the train began that day's journey. Each Sunday, the people and animals rested, and Methodist minister L. B. Stateler would conduct a church service.[39]

One morning before they reached the Bighorn River, they discovered a large Indian encampment within a mile of them. There was concern they might be Lakota. Bridger had the emigrants prepare for possible attack as he led a small, unarmed group toward the encampment to parley. Seeing the approaching party was unarmed, the chief with a small number of unarmed men rode out to meet them. When they got close enough to recognize faces, the Indians began shouting "Bridger! Bridger!" and broke into a gallop toward the White men. They were Bridger's friends Chief Washakie and his Shoshone on a buffalo hunt. Bridger brought them to the wagon train, where the emigrants rejoiced that they were friends. They prepared a feast for the Shoshone and gave them presents.[40]

Eastern Shoshone Chief Washakie (c. 1810–1900) and Bridger were good friends. Lore has it Bridger married Mary, one of Washakie's daughters. PHOTOGRAPH BY WALTER MCCLINTOCK, COURTESY OF THE BEINECKE RARE BOOK AND MANUSCRIPT LIBRARY, YALE UNIVERSITY, WA MSS S-1175.

Other wagon trains that had been following Bridger's were catching up until the number of emigrants in the party swelled to 1,000. When they reached the Bighorn and later the Yellowstone River, they found each too deep to cross with their wagons, so they built rafts to transport the wagons and swam the livestock across. They journeyed through what would later be named the Bridger Mountains, using Bozeman Pass, arriving at the Madison

River on July 8. From there, the emigrants fanned out depending on which mining camp they were heading to. Those traveling to Virginia City remained with Bridger, arriving there July 11.[41]

Bridger's route had plenty of water and firewood. It did not traverse Lakota hunting grounds, so it was safer, and it was shorter than Bozeman's route, but the Bozeman Trail had more available grass and for that reason became more popular.[42]

Bridger stayed in Virginia City long enough to entertain a large crowd with his tales one evening. By August 3, he was back at Fort Laramie, where the army again hired him as a guide. Each evening, he sat on a bench in front of the sutler's store and talked with whomever wanted to talk. On August 16, his mount bucked him off, which caused a painful stricture, landing him in the hospital for a few days.[43]

On September 18, 1864, Bridger led the last wagon train for the year over his trail. Twenty-five men took ten wagons, making improvements to the trail along the way. On November 1, they were at the Shoshone River (likely crossing near present-day Lovell, Wyoming), and when they reached the Yellowstone it was snowing. When they arrived at Bozeman, the snow was so deep they could not take the wagons any farther. Bridger returned to Fort Laramie, then traveled home to Westport, planning to spend the winter there. However, all was not well on the plains.[44]

As civil war raged in the East during 1864, violence erupted in Colorado Territory between settlers and Cheyenne and Arapaho tribes who saw their hunting grounds diminished. Major Edward Wynkoop attempted to broker a peace and led a delegation of Cheyenne Chief Black Kettle and six other tribal leaders to Denver, where they met with Governor John Evans, Colorado Volunteers Colonel John Chivington, and other officials. Wynkoop and the tribal leaders left the meeting believing they had reached a peace agreement. Colorado officials believed there was no deal. Cheyenne and Arapaho bands wanting peace went to Fort Lyon to show their peaceful intentions. The fort's commander told them to move to Sand Creek. Chivington, riding at the head of Colorado cavalry with four mountain howitzers and roughly 700 men, arrived at the peace-seeking villages at dawn on November 29, 1864. Most everyone in the villages was asleep, and many of the men were away on a buffalo hunt.

Some troopers captured the horse herd, while others surrounded the village and set up the howitzers. Black Kettle raised the U.S. flag and a white flag beneath, signaling they were peaceful. It didn't matter. Chivington ordered his men to attack. When it was over, 200 Cheyenne and Arapaho were dead, mostly women and children. That wasn't the end; soldiers mutilated the bodies. After the Sand Creek Massacre, the Cheyenne sent messengers to all plains tribes asking them to join in their war against the Whites. Many did. For the Sioux, it added fuel to an existing fire. They were angry with increased Missouri River steamboat traffic, establishment of military forts in their territory, and military expeditions against them by Generals Henry Sibley and Alfred Sully.[45]

On January 7, 1865, more than 1,000 Cheyenne and Sioux warriors attacked Julesburg and nearby Fort Rankin, killing fourteen soldiers and four civilians and ransacking Julesburg. Over the next few weeks, warriors wreaked havoc along the South Platte, killing fifty people, stealing merchandise and 1,500 head of livestock, burning buildings, and destroying telegraph lines. That month, Major General Grenville Dodge, commander of the Department of the Missouri, hired Jim Bridger to guide the Eleventh Kansas Cavalry from Fort Riley, Kansas, to Fort Laramie.[46]

Dodge appointed General Patrick Connor to command the District of the Plains. Connor had been promoted for attacking Chief Bear Hunter's Shoshone village in January 1863. Bear Hunter's warriors had murdered some Whites and disrupted telegraph and mail service. On April 23, 1865, Connor's order to hang Big Crow, a Cheyenne, was carried out at Fort Laramie. A Mrs. Morton had identified Big Crow as the man who had taken her captive. They left Big Crow's body hanging for weeks; Bridger would have seen the hanging body and disapproved.[47]

Colonel Thomas Moonlight, Fort Laramie's new commander, arrived after the hanging. On May 3, leading 500 cavalry troopers and with Bridger as his guide, he searched for Cheyenne raiders. Moonlight returned to Fort Laramie on May 20, reporting to Connor, "no Indians nearer than the Bighorn and Powder River." However, Indians were there, watching his troops and resuming their raids after the troops left.[48]

On May 15, 1865, Oglala leader Two Face arrived at Fort Laramie with Mrs. Lucinda Eubank and her young son. Cheyenne warriors had captured them the previous August. Two Face and fellow leader Black Foot (not the same man as Black Foot, the Crow leader) had bought them from the Cheyenne and brought them to the fort in hopes of a reward. Colonel Moonlight determined both Two Face and Black Foot had abused Eubank and had Two Face arrested. On May 24, Black Foot was arrested. The next day, Moonlight passed judgment that the two men must die. On May 26, 1865, Black Foot and Two Face were hanged at the same location Big Crow's body still hung. All three bodies remained hanging for weeks. Bridger said the hangings would lead to dreadful consequences.[49]

General Connor arrived at Fort Laramie on June 22, made it his headquarters, and began planning his Powder River Expedition. Three columns of troops would advance north through Dakota Territory toward the Black Hills to attack the Sioux, Cheyenne, and Arapaho. Colonel Nelson Cole led the eastern column, and Colonel Samuel Walker led the center column. Connor would lead the western column and wanted the columns to rendezvous on Rosebud Creek around September 1. Connor ordered Cole and Walker to kill every male Indian over the age of twelve.[50]

On July 6, 1865, the army hired Bridger as chief guide at $10 per day. Knowing Bridger was a friend of the Shoshone, Connor did not trust him.[51]

The eastern column, numbering 1,400 men, left Omaha on July 1. The center column, numbering 600 men, would leave Fort Laramie on August 5. Connor, leading the western column of 800 men, left Fort Laramie on July 30. As chief guide, Bridger directed six assistant guides. Captain Frank North led ninety-five Pawnee and eighty-four Omaha scouts. One hundred and eighty-four wagons hauled supplies. Connor also planned to build a fort on the Powder River. Bridger guided Connor's column west along the Oregon Trail, then, on August 4, northwest to the Bozeman Trail.[52]

Early each morning, Bridger ate jerky, washing it down with coffee. He reported to Connor, explaining the day's route, including distance to the next camp and good water and grazing locations. He rode off to conduct his scout, either alone or taking a few men. When he returned at the end of the day, he reported to Connor his observations, cooked his dinner, then slept alone, away from the others.[53]

They reached the forks of the Powder River on August 11, where Connor planned to build a fort. Bridger suggested a flat area 100 feet above the river as a good defensive location, and Connor ordered the men to begin construction. Remaining in the area for a week, Connor sent patrols that had several encounters with Indians. In one fight, Pawnee scouts killed twenty-seven Cheyenne raiders.[54]

Connor received information about a fight at Platte Bridge on the North Platte River near present-day Casper, Wyoming. Caspar Collins, the son of Colonel William Collins, had joined the 11th Ohio Volunteer Cavalry and was commissioned a lieutenant. On July 26, 1865, 3,000 Cheyenne, Sioux, and Arapaho warriors attacked; Lieutenant Collins, age twenty, was killed in that fight.[55]

Leaving the 6th Michigan Cavalry to man the fort at the forks of the Powder River (named Fort Connor), on August 22, Connor's column followed the Bozeman Trail northwest until intersecting the Tongue River. From there they planned to follow the Tongue downriver.[56]

Officers and enlisted men who wrote about Bridger respected his knowledge and enjoyed his stories. A young soldier, J. E. Spicer, later wrote, "Bridger . . . understood the ways of the Indians very well and seemed to be able to make friends even with the warriors." Connor, however, didn't trust Bridger. When Bridger led the column to a dangerous looking canyon, Connor turned in his saddle to Bridger, saying, "Jim, if you lead me into an ambuscade, by God, you're the first who's going to die," then slapped his hand on his revolver holster.[57]

On August 26, Bridger took Captain Henry Palmer with him on a scout. They were a mile ahead of the column on a ridge dividing the Powder and Tongue River watersheds. Using his hands to shade his eyes, Bridger pointed out columns of smoke. Palmer looked through his field glasses but couldn't see them. They waited for Connor to arrive. Palmer reported to Connor that Bridger had seen smoke columns. Connor, using his field glasses, surveyed the countryside and said he saw nothing. Bridger quietly mounted his horse and rode on. Palmer rode after Bridger and, before reaching him, heard him say "these damn paper-collar soldiers" telling him there was no smoke.[58]

Connor sent North and his Pawnees to investigate Bridger's smoke. On August 28, they returned, reporting they found a 200- to 300-lodge Arapaho village on the Tongue River at the location where Bridger had seen the smoke. That night, Bridger guided Connor, leading 125 troopers and 90 Indian scouts toward the village.[59]

The next morning, Connor led the charge into the village. Arapaho warriors retreated slowly, allowing the women and children to escape. The Pawnee captured the horse herd while Connor directed the troopers to burn the lodges. The Arapaho counterattacked. A. J. Shotwell said, "During the engagement Bridger seemed always to be in the right place at the opportune time." The Arapaho recaptured their horses and harassed Connor's men as they retreated to their encampment. Connor reported thirty-five Arapaho killed and seven of his men wounded.[60]

Wolves had been following the column, and every night they howled. The night of September 1, there was a distinctive, hideous howl. Bridger identified it as a medicine wolf, a supernatural animal that brought trouble. He and two other guides were so alarmed they left camp and slept in the timber a half-mile downstream.[61]

Nothing horrible happened except heavy rain and snow fell that first week of September as Connor marched his men down the Tongue and back searching for Cole and Walker's columns. He sent out scouting parties, but there were no signs of the columns. They encountered James Sawyer's party with an infantry escort, pioneering a road from Sioux City, Iowa, to the Bozeman Trail. Sawyer had no information on the columns, but Cheyenne and Sioux warriors had attacked his party near Pumpkin Buttes.[62]

On September 11, Frank North and the Pawnee scouts reported they had discovered hundreds of dead cavalry horses and burned saddles and tack on the Powder River. Connor sent North and some of his men to find the columns. This time, Bridger went as their guide.[63]

Connor began the column's march back to Fort Connor, where he planned to regroup, then return to the field against the tribes. However, on September 22, he received a dispatch ordering him to cease operations. He was reassigned to his old command, the District of Utah. When Major General John Pope, commander of the Division of the Missouri, learned of Connor's orders to kill every male Indian over the age of twelve, he telegrammed Dodge, "These instructions are atrocious."[64]

Connor reached Fort Connor on September 24, where he found Colonels Cole and Walker's columns. They had arrived on September 20. The two columns had combined on August 18 at the Belle Fourche River north of the

By the 1860s, Fort Laramie had greatly expanded to suit its role as a military post. 1870 PHOTOGRAPH BY WILLIAM HENRY JACKSON, COURTESY OF THE U.S. GEOLOGICAL SURVEY.

Black Hills. Rations were running low when they reached the Powder River on August 28. By September 4, they had lost 225 horses and mules. With no sign of Connor's column, they decided to head to Fort Laramie, marching up the Powder River. On September 5, they encountered a large Sioux, Cheyenne, and Arapaho village and had fights with them the next three days. From the night of September 8 through 10, the temperature dropped as a violent rain, sleet, and snowstorm struck, killing over 500 animals. They continued their march while warriors harassed them. On September 13, Bridger, North, and the Pawnee scouts found them and guided them to Fort Connor.[65]

General Frank Wheaton now commanded the District of the Plains. Wheaton kept Bridger on the payroll as chief guide, changing his designation on October 1, 1865, from "Guide for Indian Expedition" to "Guide for Post Headquarters."[66]

General Grenville Dodge had always been a railroad man before, during, and after the Civil War. Dodge was at Fort Laramie the autumn of 1865, planning to spend a week exploring the Laramie Mountains' eastern slopes for railroad routes. Dodge assembled a small party, including Jim Bridger, who assisted by guiding to locations for the best grades of ascent and descent, distances, and elevations in the vicinity of the Overland Trail. The final railroad route roughly corresponded to Bridger's suggestions. He was discharged on November 30 but remained at Fort Laramie.[67]

Colonel Henry Maynadier was the new commander of the West Nebraska Sub-district and headquartered at Fort Laramie. Secretary of War Edwin Stanton sent a letter to Maynadier requesting his opinion on the best route to the Montana goldfields: a wagon road starting at the Musselshell River on the Missouri, the Bozeman Trail, or the Bridger Trail. Maynadier asked Bridger to help with his response, mentioning in his letter that Bridger was the most reliable source he knew. Bridger went over each route's merits and problems with Maynadier, believing his route was the safest and least expensive. Maynadier dismissed Bridger's route as "no longer a matter of opinion"; most wagon trains were using the Bozeman Trail, and Maynadier believed it was the shortest. Stanton asked about additional fort locations to protect emigrants. Maynadier responded that a fort should be built on the Bighorn River and another at the mouth of the Clark's Fork of the Yellowstone.[68]

At Christmas, Bridger left Fort Laramie for home. He stopped at Fort Kearny, where Legh Freeman, Kearny's *Semi-Weekly Herald* editor, interviewed him for the January 6, 1866, edition. Bridger said sending the cavalry supported by supply wagons to chase after Indians was "simply absurd, since it results only in heavy loss of animals, and unnecessary exposure of troops." He said, ". . . troops unaccustomed to the frontiers, are stampeded by the yell of the Indians." He planned to go to Washington and propose that the government allow him to select and lead men who could follow the Indians on foot and live off the land the way they did. They would be able to catch up and attack the Indians. The government did not take his offer.[69]

---

[1] Raynolds, *Report,* 4, 18. Alter, *Bridger,* 281.
[2] Raynolds, *Report,* 18, 20–21. Enzler, *Bridger,* 221.
[3] Raynolds, *Report,* 23, 25, 27–30, 34.
[4] Raynolds, *Report,* 33, 57. Enzler, *Bridger,* 224–225.
[5] Raynolds, *Report,* 40–41.
[6] Ibid, 43, 45–46, 49, 52.
[7] Ibid, 52–56.
[8] Ibid, 56–57, 59, 62, 65–67.
[9] Raynolds, *Report,* 70–72. Enzler, *Bridger,* 226. Alter, *Bridger,* 286.
[10] Enzler, *Bridger,* 226, 238.
[11] Raynolds, *Report,* 76, 78. Enzler, *Bridger,* 226–227.
[12] Raynolds, *Report,* 84.
[13] Raynolds, *Report,* 86. Enzler, *Bridger,* 229.
[14] Raynolds, *Report,* 93–95. Enzler, *Bridger,* 230.
[15] Raynolds, *Report,* 100, 106, 110. Enzler, *Bridger,* 230.
[16] Raynolds, *Report,* 110, 161.

[17] Ibid, 164.
[18] Raynolds, *Report,* 166–167. Enzler, *Bridger,* 232.
[19] Raynolds, *Report,* 169.
[20] Raynolds, *Report,* 114, 120, 127. Alter, *Bridger,* 294.
[21] Ibid, 236.
[22] Ralph Moody, *Stagecoach West* (New York, NY: Thomas Y. Crowell Company, 1967), 209–211. Enzler, *Bridger,* 237–238.
[23] Spring, *Collins,* 26–27, Enzler, *Bridger,* 238–240.
[24] Spring, *Collins,* 36. McChristian, *Fort Laramie,* 145.
[25] Spring, *Collins,* 38, 116–117. Enzler, *Bridger,* 240.
[26] William Brackett, "Bonneville and Bridger," *Contributions to the Montana Historical Society,* Vol. 3 (Helena, MT: State Publishing Company, 1900), 194–197. Spring, *Collins,* 119.
[27] Spring, *Collins,* 119, 126, 130. McChristian, *Fort Laramie,* 145.
[28] Spring, *Collins,* 40, 42. Moody, *Stagecoach,* 228. McChristian, *Fort Laramie,* 146.
[29] Spring, *Collins,* 42–43, 140, 142–143. McChristian, *Fort Laramie,* 145.
[30] James Lowe, "A Map of the West in his Head: Jim Bridger, Guide to Plains and Mountains," Wyohistory.org, accessed May 31, 2024, https://www.wyohistory.org/encyclopedia/jim-bridger.
[31] Caesar, *King,* 266. Spring, *Collins,* 46. McChristian, *Fort Laramie,* 152. Billington, *Westward Expansion,* 628–629.
[32] Dorothy Johnson, *The Bloody Bozeman: The Perilous Trail to Montana's Gold* (Missoula, MT: Mountain Press Publishing Company, 1983), 3, 27, 50, 54. McChristian, *Fort Laramie,* 155–156. Billington, *Westward Expansion,* 628–629.
[33] J. Lee Humfreville, *Twenty Years Among Our Hostile Indians* (New York, NY: Hunter & Co., 1899), 469. Vestal, *Bridger,* 317–318 n6.
[34] Humfreville, *Twenty Years,* 464, 467–468.
[35] Enzler, *Bridger,* 246.
[36] Ibid, 248.
[37] E. J. Stanley, *Life of L. B. Stateler* (Nashville, TN: Publishing House of the M.E. Church, South, 1907), 178. Vestal, *Bridger,* 317–318 n6. Enzler, *Bridger,* 248.
[38] Thomas LeForge and Thomas Marquis, *Memoirs of a White Crow Indian* (New York, NY: Century Co., 1928), 8.
[39] Stanley, *Stateler,* 175–176.
[40] Ibid, 180–181.
[41] Stanley, *Stateler,* 178, 184. Enzler, *Bridger,* 250. Alter, *Bridger,* 307.
[42] John McDermott, *Red Cloud's War: The Bozeman Trail, 1866–1868* (Norman, OK: University of Oklahoma, 2010), 15.
[43] Enzler, *Bridger,* 251. Alter, *Bridger,* 309. Vestal, *Bridger,* 317–318 n6.
[44] Enzler, *Bridger,* 251. Alter, *Bridger,* 309.
[45] Bill Markley, *Geronimo and Sitting Bull: Leaders of the Legendary West* (Guilford, CT: Rowman & Littlefield Publishing, 2021), 62–68. Crutchfield, Moulton, Del Bene, eds. *Settlement,* 419–420.
[46] Robert Utley, *Frontiersmen in Blue: The United States Army and the Indian, 1848–1865* (Lincoln, NE: University of Nebraska Press, 1967), 301, 303. McChristian, *Fort Laramie,* 193. Dodge, *Bridger,* 19.
[47] Utley, *Frontiersmen,* 197, 198 n34, 223–224. McChristian, *Fort Laramie,* 193. Enzler, *Bridger,* 259.
[48] McChristian, *Fort Laramie,* 199.
[49] McChristian, *Fort Laramie,* 201, 203, 205–207. Alter, *Bridger,* 311.
[50] Utley, *Frontiersmen,* 324, 330. Enzler, *Bridger,* 255.
[51] Vestal, *Bridger,* 317–318 n6. Enzler, *Bridger,* 257.
[52] Enzler, *Bridger,* 257–258. Alter, *Bridger,* 311. Utley, *Frontiersmen,* 324.
[53] Enzler, *Bridger,* 257.
[54] Enzler, *Bridger,* 258. Utley, *Frontiersmen,* 325.
[55] Enzler, *Bridger,* 258. Spring, *Collins,* 50, 80–83, 94, 96.
[56] Utley, *Frontiersmen,* 324–325.
[57] Enzler, *Bridger,* 258, 260.
[58] Enzler, *Bridger,* 260. Dodge, *Bridger,* 19–21.
[59] Enzler, *Bridger,* 261. Utley, *Frontiersmen,* 325. Vestal, *Bridger,* 230–232.
[60] Utley, *Frontiersmen,* 326. Vestal, *Bridger,* 233, 319 n5.
[61] Enzler, *Bridger,* 262.
[62] Utley, *Frontiersmen,* 326.
[63] Utley, *Frontiersmen,* 327. Alter, *Bridger,* 315.
[64] Utley, *Frontiersmen,* 330–331.
[65] Ibid, 328–330.

[66] Utley, *Frontiersmen,* 330–331. Vestal, *Bridger,* 317–318 n6.
[67] Alter, *Bridger,* 315. Vestal, *Bridger,* 317–318 n6. Enzler, *Bridger,* 264.
[68] McChristian, *Fort Laramie,* 251. Enzler, *Bridger,* 265–266.
[69] Enzler, *Bridger,* 266. Alter, *Bridger,* 316–317.

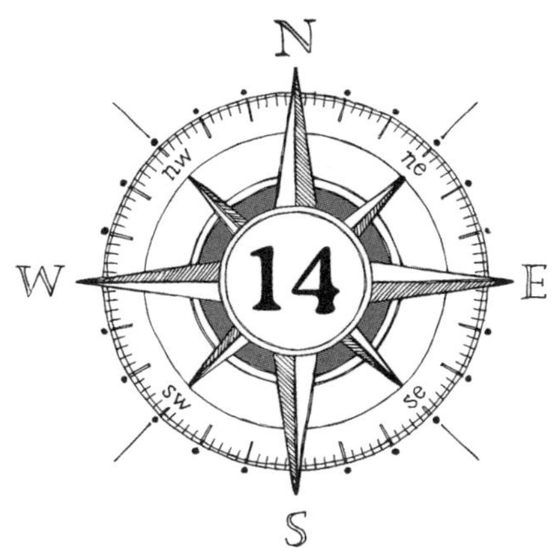

Red Cloud's War
1866–1868

As 1866 began, war parties continued raiding along the Oregon and Overland Trails and surrounded Fort Connor, renamed Fort Reno. The army began preparations to protect travelers on the Bozeman Trail, planning wagon train escorts and two additional forts. The government also planned to send a peace commission to Fort Laramie in June to encourage tribes to sign a treaty. In exchange for gifts, the government wanted them to allow travelers safe passage through the Powder River Country. The army selected Colonel Henry Carrington to lead the efforts to protect the Bozeman Trail. On January 6, 1866, he ordered officers of the Second Battalion, Eighteenth Infantry to rejoin their companies.[1]

General Grenville Dodge reinstated Jim Bridger as chief scout at $10 per day to meet with him at Fort Leavenworth from January 25 to 31 to discuss upcoming efforts in the Powder River Country. Bridger disagreed with fort building, suggesting instead a temporary camp and using mules to transport the troops' equipment and supplies. The army ignored his recommendations. Dodge insisted the army hire Bridger as a guide for the Powder River Expedition. Dodge told Carrington, "Take with you James Bridger, who is the most reliable and most competent man you can get as a guide. He has good judgement and knows that country as well as we do our A.B.C.'s." Bridger returned to Fort Laramie by March 5, where he was back on the army payroll as guide at $5 per day.[2]

On March 10, 1866, Carrington received orders to march the Second Battalion northwest into Dakota Territory to fortify the Bozeman Trail. Later that March, General William Tecumseh Sherman became commander of the Division of the Missouri. On May 1, he granted General Grenville Dodge a leave of absence to be chief engineer for the Union Pacific Railroad, which was beginning work on a transcontinental railroad.[3]

Bridger obtained the territorial license to operate ferries on the Platte, Bighorn, and Yellowstone Rivers. The army requested he build a ferry fifty-five miles west of Fort Laramie. The army provided material for the ferry operation, and Bridger allowed the army to use it free of charge. He began work on it in mid-May and hired several people to operate what would be called Bridger's Ferry.[4]

Time and again, Oglala Lakota leader Red Cloud proved himself a superior battle strategist, shrewd negotiator, and fearless advocate for his people. PHOTOGRAPH CIRCA 1880 BY CHARLES M. BELL, COURTESY OF THE BEINECKE RARE BOOK AND MANUSCRIPT LIBRARY, YALE UNIVERSITY, WA PHOTOS 7.

On May 30, government peace commissioners reached Fort Laramie as Lakota, Cheyenne, and Arapaho bands were arriving. The Oglala Lakota chief Red Cloud, one of the most influential leaders, had encouraged others to join the peace council. Several thousand Indians encamped in the fort's vicinity.[5]

The peace negotiations began on June 6. Bridger was present, but what role he played is not recorded. Certainly he was familiar with the conditions being negotiated. Red Cloud requested they wait a few days to allow more Lakota bands to arrive; the commissioners agreed. The council would resume on June 13.[6]

Henry B. Carrington served primarily as an intelligence officer during the Civil War and was then assigned as commander of the Mountain District, Department of the Missouri, in 1866. He oversaw the construction of and was stationed at Fort Phil Kearny during Red Cloud's War. PHOTOGRAPH COURTESY OF THE LIBRARY OF CONGRESS, LC-B813- 6331 B [P&P].

As the peace council reconvened, Colonel Henry Carrington leading 700 troops of the Second Battalion, Eighteenth Infantry, marched to within four miles east of Fort Laramie and encamped. Brulé Lakota Chief Standing Elk rode into Carrington's camp and met with Carrington. He asked where the soldiers were going, and Carrington replied they were headed to the Powder River Country. Standing Elk said the Oglala and Miniconjou would not allow it and would fight him.[7]

The next day, all the tribal leaders realized the purpose of Carrington's troops. The peace commissioners knew the troops were coming but had said nothing. Tribal leaders were furious. Red Cloud spoke, "I prefer to die fighting rather than by starvation. . . . Great Father sends us presents and wants new road. But White Chief goes with soldiers to steal road before Indian says yes or no!" Tribal leaders were so upset, the commissioners ended the council. The following day, Red Cloud and all the Oglala as well as the Arapaho and Cheyenne left to prepare for war.[8]

The commissioners continued negotiating with the remaining leaders. Bridger told them, ". . . the treaty would not amount to anything, but that all the Indians wanted was to receive presents and procure a supply of powder and lead, and then they would take the war path, and would plunder trains and murder emigrants going over the road." Later, on June 28, those tribes with no interest in the Powder River Country signed the agreement allowing a right-of-way through that territory, and for that, the Indian Bureau would give them supplies every six months at Fort Laramie.[9]

Colonel Carrington arrived at Fort Laramie on June 14 where he met Jim Bridger. Carrington's troops needed additional ammunition; he sent wagons to the fort to acquire 1,000 rounds, but his men were told there were none to spare. Bridger told Carrington he had seen the fort distribute kegs of gunpowder to the Indians.[10]

On June 17, Bridger led Carrington's expedition west along the Oregon Trail. On June 19, they camped where the North Platte flowed through a gorge. Two officers and ladies left camp around a bend in the gorge to hunt agates and fire pistols to hear their echoes. Bridger warned them about Indians. "They've seen ye, every day, and when ye don't see any of 'em about, is just the time to look out for their devilment." The next day, they traveled nine miles to reach Bridger's Ferry where they learned that, the previous morning, some of Red Cloud's Bad Faces band had run off livestock. Bridger opined they "were advancing directly in the face of hostilities," and the presents the government gave at Fort Laramie "were given to positive enemies or to those who had no influence at all over the warlike bands of the Big Horn and Powder River country."[11]

Bridger was always on the alert. He never slept in a tent unless it rained. He would wake during the night and quietly survey the camp. When the column was on the march, he would ride ahead but never out of sight of the troops. As he approached high ground, he rode slowly toward its base, then rode rapidly to the right or left until reaching the top.[12]

On June 24, they left the Oregon Trail, turning north at Sage Creek, heading for Fort Reno, which they reached on June 28. The following day, during broad daylight, five Sioux warriors, a woman, and a boy ran off seven horses and twenty-seven mules belonging to the sutler. Mounted infantry gave chase, but the only horse they caught was a spent Indian pony loaded with government gifts from Fort Laramie.[13]

After spending ten days improving the fort, Carrington left with four companies traveling northwest toward the Bighorn Mountains. Two companies remained behind to man Fort Reno. On July 13, Carrington's party encamped on Big Piney Creek on the Bozeman Trail with the Bighorn Mountains four miles to the west.[14]

Carrington's superiors wanted one fort built in the Big Piney area and a second at the Bighorn River. Bridger and assistant scout James Brannan recommended against a fort at Big Piney. They advised Carrington that he would find better locations farther north on Goose Creek or the Tongue River. Carrington rode out to visit those locations, not taking Bridger with him. When he returned, he disregarded Bridger and Brannan's recommendations and began building a fort on Little Piney Creek, naming it Fort Phil Kearny.[15]

Margaret Carrington, the colonel's wife, called Bridger "our sterling friend," and wrote, "Bridger had a head full of maps and trails and ideas, all of the utmost value to the objects of the expedition." When Bridger was asked why he told tall tales, he answered there was no harm in fooling people who pumped him for information and would not say *"thank ye."* To the Carringtons, he was "straightforward, truthful, and reliable."[16]

Margaret Sullivant Carrington married Henry B. Carrington in 1851 and traveled with him when the colonel led the construction of Fort Phil Kearny in 1866. Margaret later wrote *Ab-Sa-Ra-Ka, Home of the Crows* about life on the frontier. She died two weeks shy of her thirty-ninth birthday in 1870. PHOTOGRAPH COURTESY OF THE AMERICAN HERITAGE CENTER, UNIVERSITY OF WYOMING, AH002571.

On July 16, a forty-member delegation of Cheyenne leaders and their wives arrived and met with Carrington and his officers. Bridger sat on the ground off to the side and in front of them all, his elbows on his knees and chin resting in his hands. Jack Stead, the interpreter, stood beside him. They smoked pipes, said "Hows," shook hands, and then they got down to business. The Cheyenne leaders said all the tribes in the Powder River Country knew Carrington's movements. Red Cloud and his Bad Faces wanted them to join with them to make war on the Whites, but they declined. Carrington provided them a meal and gave them gifts.[17]

The next morning, Sioux raiders ran off 174 head of livestock. Captain Henry Haymond, leading twenty-six mounted infantrymen, gave chase. They recovered 104 animals before being confronted by 300 warriors. Three of Haymond's men were killed and five wounded. On their return, they came upon the plundered wagons of trader French Pete Cazeau. Nearby lay his body, those of his four employees, and that of a young woman. His Sioux wife and three children emerged from hiding and told what had happened. The Cheyenne who had visited Carrington had then stopped at Cazeau's encampment. Sioux warriors arrived. When they learned the Cheyenne had visited Carrington, they whipped them, then robbed Cazeau, and left. The next morning, they returned, killing Cazeau and the others. Continuing toward Fort Phil Kearny, the troops came upon a man with his throat cut but still alive. When they gave him water, he died.[18]

On July 20, Jim Bridger was guiding Captain Thomas Burrows and forty-six men escorting thirty-four wagons from Fort Phil Kearny back to Fort Reno for supplies. Bridger discovered marked buffalo skulls indicating a fight with White men would take place that day ahead at Crazy Woman Creek. Burrows was skeptical, wanting to camp for the night at Clear Fork, but Bridger insisted they push on. Burrows relented, ordering a forced march as Bridger rode ahead. It was after sunset, and he was two miles in advance of the troops when he topped a ridge and saw circled wagons at Crazy Woman Creek.[19]

The thirty-seven members of the wagon train were soldiers and their families headed to Fort Phil Kearny. They had been ambushed by 100 Sioux warriors who had killed one officer riding ahead of the wagons. His body was found scalped and cut to pieces.[20]

Samuel Peters, a wagon train member, wrote:

> Finally a solitary horseman was observed coming over the little ridge to our left. Before he reached the ravine he was ordered to halt. He did so and shouted back that he was a friend.

'What's your name?'

'Jim Bridger.'

And so it was. He was shown a crossing through the ravine and came on up to the corral.

'I knew there was hell to pay here today at Crazy Woman,' he said to a group of officers.[21]

Burrows' men joined them that evening, and the next morning a twenty-man detail from Fort Reno arrived. They and Burrows' men escorted the families back to Fort Reno. On July 23, Burrows began his return to Fort Phil Kearny, hauling supplies and escorting two additional wagon trains. Sioux warriors harassed them the entire way.[22]

Carrington assigned Bridger to guide Captain Nathaniel Kinney and two companies—169 men—to build a fort on the Bighorn River. Leaving on August 4, they overtook a party of 110 wagons led by Hugh Kirkendall and agreed to travel together. Reaching the Bighorn River on August 11, Kinney selected the fort site two miles below Bighorn Canyon, naming it Fort C. F. Smith. It was 91 miles northwest of Fort Phil Kearny and 281 miles from Virginia City. The ferry across the river was in poor shape, and Bridger worked to repair it.[23]

Carrington assigned Bridger and scout Henry Williams to survey the Bozeman Trail for improvements and cutoffs from Fort C. F. Smith to Virginia City. Bridger agreed to guide Kirkendall's wagon train, as well. Along the way, other wagon trains joined them. Bridger found safe passages and shortcuts.

Fort C. F. Smith consisted of a 125-square-foot stockade of wood and adobe surrounding a parade ground, with an initial garrison of about 100 troops. ILLUSTRATION COURTESY OF THE NATIONAL PARK SERVICE.

At one location where wagons had to be lowered with ropes and chains down a steep slope, Bridger found a route around it. Three men and a boy from Kirkendall's party decided to push ahead. The combined wagon trains later came upon their bodies along the Yellowstone. Three bodies were mutilated but the fourth, found in the water, was not disfigured. Bridger stated the attackers were Blackfeet since they did not touch bodies in water.[24]

Reaching Virginia City, Bridger and Williams had shortened the Bozeman Trail by twenty miles. They now had another assignment: Carrington wanted them to meet with the Crow to ensure their friendship and to request they contact Red Cloud and learn his disposition. Bridger and Williams visited White Mouth, Black Foot, and Rotten Tail's villages, numbering 500 men, at the Clark's Fork. The Crow leaders said they would remain at peace with the Whites. Red Cloud had visited, asking them to join him. The Crow leaders in turn visited Red Cloud's war party villages, which were so big, it took a half day to ride through them. Red Cloud's plan was to attack Forts Phil Kearny and C. F. Smith. The Crow leaders declined to join Red Cloud. Bridger and Williams met with other Crow leaders and heard the same answer. Bridger asked the Crow to visit Fort C. F. Smith, which they did, reporting that they'd seen a hostile, 500-lodge Sioux village on the Tongue River.[25]

On October 23, Bridger returned to Fort Phil Kearny at Colonel Carrington's request. Even within the relative safety of the fort, Bridger did not let his guard down, constantly scanning the hills for signs of Indians. Carrington viewed Bridger as honest and faithful, relying on him as his confidential guide. Bridger always seemed to know what the Indians were up to. Frances Carrington later wrote about Bridger,

Frances Courtney Grummond was a widow at twenty-one after her husband, Lieutenant George Grummond, was killed in the Fetterman battle. She later married Henry Carrington. PHOTOGRAPH COURTESY OF THE WILLIAMSON COUNTY (TENNESSEE) HISTORICAL SOCIETY.

"His devotion to the ladies and children and his willingness to cheer them the best he could were as prized as were his quaint tales. . . ."[26]

The Cheyenne chief Two Moons with several followers arrived, acting peaceful and friendly. In truth, they wanted to learn whether they could overwhelm the fort. They were invited inside and shown its defenses. Two Moons and Bridger "had quite a nice visit." Bridger warned him "the fort was impregnable." Two Moons reported to the other Cheyenne and Sioux leaders that the fort was too strong to take without great loss of life, so they decided on ambushing soldiers outside the fort.[27]

Captain William Fetterman was a veteran of Civil War battles, but he was new to the West and to the combat tactics and spirit of the Sioux and Cheyenne. PHOTOGRAPH COURTESY OF THE WYOMING STATE ARCHIVES, SUB NEG 1838.

On November 3, Captain William Fetterman arrived. Fetterman, a Civil War veteran, was impatient to fight, bragging "A single company of Regulars could whip a thousand Indians," and that "a full regiment . . . could whip the entire array of hostile tribes." In Carrington's presence, Fetterman said, "I can take eighty men and go to the Tongue River." Bridger responded, "Your men who fought down South are crazy! They don't know anything about fighting Indians."[28]

Lieutenant George Templeton, at Fort C. F. Smith, sent Carrington a message saying the Crow were contemplating joining the Sioux because the government had taken no action to attack the Sioux. Carrington sent Bridger back to Fort C. F. Smith to convince the Crow to remain peaceful. If their chiefs wanted to meet with Carrington at Fort Phil Kearny, Bridger was to accompany them and act as interpreter. Bridger arrived at Fort C. F. Smith on November 28 and found many Crow encamped around the fort who remained peaceful. At that time, Carrington received an order to discharge Bridger and other civilian guides. He returned the order, writing, *"Impossible of execution."*[29]

Facing a much larger force of Cheyenne and Lakota led by Red Cloud and other leaders, Fetterman and his eighty troops were quickly wiped out. ILLUSTRATION FROM HARPER'S WEEKLY, MARCH 23, 1867, COURTESY OF THE LIBRARY OF CONGRESS, LC-USZ62-130184.

On December 28, 1866, a party of Crow visited Fort C. F. Smith to inform the commander that the Sioux and Cheyenne had killed 97 soldiers at Fort Phil Kearny. The next day, another Crow arrived saying that 113 soldiers had been ambushed by 1,500 Sioux and Cheyenne. Bridger and the men at Fort C. F. Smith would learn that on December 21, the Sioux and Cheyenne had ambushed Captain William Fetterman and eighty men, killing them all.[30]

Margaret Carrington wrote, "This massacre proved the value and integrity of Major Bridger and his statements." And a soldier wrote:

> If Colonel Carrington and the officers had followed the advice of Bridger I do not think there would have been nearly as many of our men killed. He told the officers not to follow the Indians and to send more men on escort duty, but they thought he was old (Bridger was sixty-two at the time) and did not know anything about Indian warfare.[31]

The Crow continued to encamp around Fort C. F. Smith. The Sioux and Cheyenne wanted to attack and ordered the Crow to leave, but they stayed and would not allow an attack because they did not want Bridger endangered.[32]

On April 8, 1867, Lieutenant Colonel Innis Palmer, commander at Fort Laramie, requested Bridger along with a few Crow leaders come to Fort Laramie to report on conditions in the Powder River Country. Bridger did not make it but did have someone write a letter for him on May 5, 1867, that was published in the June 29 issue of *Army and Navy Journal.* In it, he stated the peace commissioners at Fort Laramie had signed the treaty with the wrong tribes. He corrected misinformation on the massacre at Fort Phil Kearny and stated that 2,200 lodges of Sioux, Cheyenne, and Arapaho had gathered on the Tongue River to prepare for that attack. He reported the Sioux tribes were gathering on the Powder River and were being supplied with ammunition from traders associated with the Hudson's Bay Company. He said the only way to win was to send enough troops to beat all the Sioux, Cheyenne, and Arapaho in a fight until they asked for peace; otherwise the Bozeman Trail should be abandoned.[33]

On June 11, reinforcements and supplies arrived at Fort C. F. Smith. Bridger was ordered to return to Fort Phil Kearny, and he guided the return party, pioneering a new cutoff. Reaching the fort on June 16, he met with John Kinney, a member of the Joint Indian Commission, relaying what the Crow wanted in return for keeping the peace. On July 5, John Smith took command of Fort Phil Kearny. Smith didn't want Bridger, writing, "He is not needed here, one guide for this post being enough." Soldiers continued to be attacked when away from the forts—there were attacks on haymakers at Fort C. F. Smith and on woodchoppers at Fort Phil Kearny.[34]

On September 23, 1867, Jim Bridger was discharged at Fort Phil Kearny. He returned to Fort Laramie, and it was probably during this time that Grenville Dodge met with him in the new railroad town, Cheyenne, Wyoming, to discuss routes and progress of the transcontinental railroad. The army also hired Bridger to work at nearby Fort D. A. Russell. In November, the *Kansas City Advertiser* reported that Bridger had returned from the west. In May 1868, the army hired him to guide a construction crew that was building a road from Fort Fetterman to Medicine Bow.[35]

Within decades, all that remained of Fort C. F. Smith were crumbled adobe walls. PHOTOGRAPH COURTESY OF THE ARCHIVES AND SPECIAL COLLECTIONS, MANSFIELD LIBRARY, UNIVERSITY OF MONTANA, UMT011284.

With the building of the transcontinental railroad, there were closer access points to Montana goldfields; the Bozeman Trail was no longer needed. The government signed a treaty at Fort Laramie with the Sioux, Cheyenne, Arapaho, and others to abandon the Bozeman Trail and Forts Phil Kearny and C. F. Smith. The army hired Bridger to guide the troops to dismantle the two forts and take the reusable property to Fort D. A. Russell. When the job was complete, he was discharged on July 21, 1868, permanently ending his employment with the U.S. Army.[36]

---

1 Dee Brown, *Bury My Heart at Wounded Knee: An Indian History of the American West* (New York, NY: Henry Holt and Company, 1970), 128. Crutchfield, Moulton, Del Bene, eds. *Settlement,* Vol. 2, 405. McDermott, *Red Cloud,* 30.

2 Enzler, *Bridger,* 267. Vestal, *Bridger,* 317–318 n6.

3 Stephen Ambrose, *Nothing Like It in the World* (New York, NY: Simon & Schuster, 2000), 171. McDermott, *Red Cloud,* 28–30.

4 Enzler, *Bridger,* 268–269.

[5] McChristian, *Fort Laramie,* 267–268.

[6] Margaret Irvin Carrington, *Ab-sa-ra-ka: Home of the Crows* (Philadelphia: PA: J. B. Lippincott & Co., 1869), 94. Brown, *Bury My Heart,* 128. McDermott, *Red Cloud,* 64.

[7] Brown, *Bury My Heart,* 128–129. McChristian, *Fort Laramie,* 268–269.

[8] Brown, *Bury My Heart,* 130. McChristian, *Fort Laramie,* 271.

[9] McDermott, *Red Cloud,* 64. McChristian, *Fort Laramie,* 269.

[10] McDermott, *Red Cloud,* 70–71. Carrington, *Ab-sa-ra-ka,* 75–76.

[11] Carrington, *Ab-sa-ra-ka,* 80, 83–85.

[12] McDermott, *Red Cloud,* 71–72.

[13] Carrington, *Ab-sa-ra-ka,* 85–86, 90–91, 97. McDermott, *Red Cloud,* 83–84.

[14] Carrington, *Ab-sa-ra-ka,* 97–99, 102.

[15] Carrington, *Ab-sa-ra-ka,* 103–105. Enzler, *Bridger,* 272.

[16] Carrington, *Ab-sa-ra-ka,* 92, 113–114.

[17] Ibid, 110–115.

[18] McDermott, *Red Cloud,* 94–95.

[19] Frances Carrington, *My Army Life and the Fort Phil Kearny Massacre* (Philadelphia, PA: J. B. Lippincott Company, 1910), 80–81. McDermott, *Red Cloud,* 104.

[20] McDermott, *Red Cloud,* 98–104.

[21] Carrington, *Army Life,* 80.

[22] McDermott, *Red Cloud,* 104–106.

[23] McDermott, *Red Cloud,* 122–123. Enzler, *Bridger,* 276, 278.

[24] McDermott, *Red Cloud,* 124. Enzler, *Bridger,* 278–179.

[25] Carrington, *Ab-sa-ra-ka,* 252. Alter, *Bridger,* 324–326.

[26] Carrington, *Army Life,* 80, 128. Enzler, *Bridger,* 280.

[27] Carrington, *Army Life,* 161–162.

[28] Ibid, 119, 253.

[29] Enzler, *Bridger,* 281–282. Carrington, *Army Life,* 129.

[30] McDermott, *Red Cloud,* 216, 222–228, 295.

[31] Carrington, *Ab-sa-ra-ka,* 209. Enzler, *Bridger,* 285.

[32] Enzler, *Bridger,* 286.

[33] Enzler, *Bridger,* 287. McDermott, *Red Cloud,* 361–363.

[34] McDermott, *Red Cloud,* 370. Enzler, *Bridger,* 288–290.

[35] Vestal, *Bridger,* 319 n6. Enzler, *Bridger,* 290. Alter, *Bridger,* 332.

[36] Enzler, *Bridger,* 290–291.

Jim Bridger's character, strong to begin with, was chiseled by his life on the frontier. 1866 PHOTOGRAPH COURTESY OF THE KANSAS STATE HISTORICAL SOCIETY.

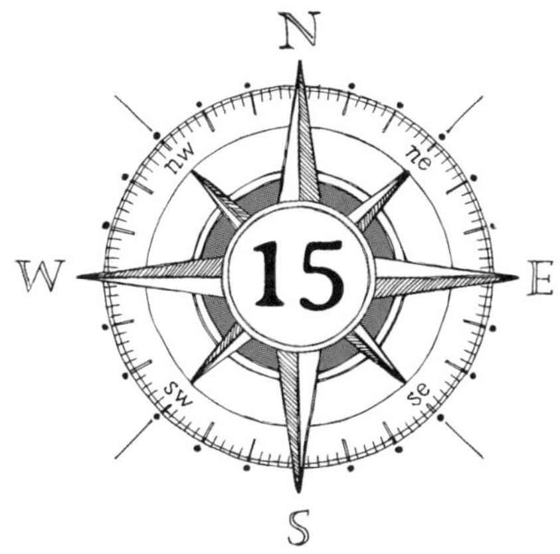

End of the Trail

1868–1881

Sixty-four-year-old Jim Bridger's eyesight was failing. He ached from an internal injury after being bucked off his mount's back in 1864.[1]

In 1868, Cheyenne, Arapaho, and Kiowa bands, disgruntled with the federal government's broken promises, were raiding in Kansas. Bridger learned that General Phil Sheridan planned a winter campaign against them. In late October, Bridger boarded a train for Fort Hays, Kansas, and met with Sheridan. He told Sheridan that a winter campaign was foolish, saying, "You can't hunt Indians on the plains in winter, for blizzards don't respect man or beast." Sheridan went ahead with his plans, marching with his troops out of Fort Hays on November 15. That night, a violent blizzard struck, blowing down tents, drenching men and animals. Cold, wet, and shivering, a miserable Sheridan sat under a wagon as "the gloomy predictions of old man Bridger and others rose up before me with greatly increased force." It was only the beginning of the army's hardships.[2]

In February 1869, Bridger applied to be the Crow Indian agent. His old friend Robert Campbell as well as many army officers supported him. General William Sherman, commander of the army, endorsed the application on March 19, submitting it to the Secretary of the Interior. Bridger's application was rejected; the Indian Department was appointing only army officers and Quakers. Bridger continued to press the federal government to pay for the ten-year lease of Fort Bridger. Years after his death, Congress authorized a $6,000

Virginia Bridger (1849–1933) married Albert Wachsman in 1864, and the couple managed her father's Westport, Missouri, farm and nearby store. 1875 PHOTOGRAPH COURTESY OF THE KANSAS CITY PUBLIC LIBRARY, MISSOURI VALLEY SPECIAL COLLECTIONS, 10011701.

payment to the Bridger family, not for the lease but for a stone wall on the property. Bridger had not built it; Mormons did.[3]

Bridger lived his remaining days at his Westport home with his son, William, and daughters Virginia and Mary and their families. He managed his properties and did a little farming. He was proud of his orchard, sending bushel baskets of apples to neighbors. When asked about his crops, he would reply, "Perfect damn failure! Perfect damn failure!" He turned the farm over to Virginia in 1872, payment being "One Dollar and love and affection I bear towards her as my daughter." William played the fiddle, and the Bridgers held dances in the front parlor every Saturday night and for other occasions. Bridger loved to sit on the veranda and talk with anyone who stopped by, especially children, telling them tales of the West.[4]

His eyesight continued to deteriorate. He used a heavy staff to feel his way when out for a walk. Virginia would saddle his horse, Ruff, and he would ride off with his dog, Sultan, running alongside. Bridger allowed Ruff to choose the route, and if they got lost, Bridger and Ruff would wait while Sultan ran home to find someone to come get them.[5]

Seventy-seven-year-old Jim Bridger died on July 17, 1881, and was buried in the nearby Watt's family cemetery. A large crowd attended the funeral. Grenville Dodge believed Bridger needed to be buried in a more prominent cemetery with a more significant memorial. In 1904, Dodge had Bridger's remains disinterred and reburied in Kansas City's Mount Washington Cemetery with a seven-foot monument.[6]

Dodge wrote, "Unquestionably, Bridger's claims to remembrance rest upon the extraordinary part he bore in the exploration of the west," and "So remarkable a man should not be lost to history and the country, and his work allowed to be forgotten."[7]

---

1 Enzler, *Bridger,* 291–292.

2 Philip Henry Sheridan, *Personal Memoirs of P. H. Sheridan,* Vol. 2 (New York, NY: Charles L. Webster & Company, 1888), 307, 311. Paul Andrew Hutton, *Phil Sheridan and His Army* (Norman, OK: University of Oklahoma Press, 1985), 42, 52–55. Enzler, *Bridger,* 292.

3 Enzler, *Bridger,* 293–294.

4 Ibid, 294–295, 297.

5 Dodge, *Bridger,* 23.

6 Alter, *Bridger,* 340–341. Enzler, *Bridger,* 298.

7 Dodge, *Bridger,* 25, 27.

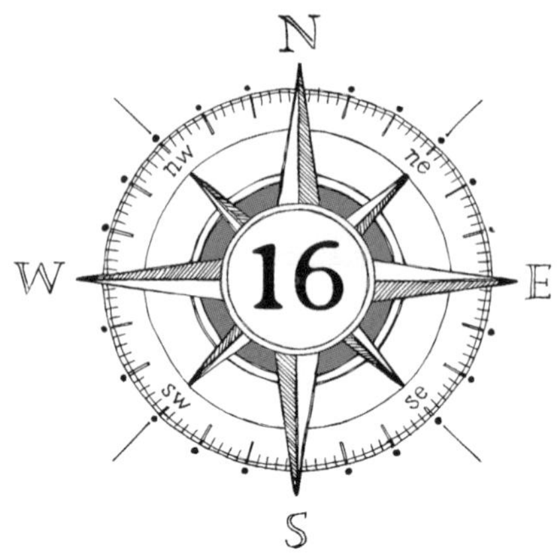

Final Thoughts

During my two-year research of Jim Bridger, my respect for him has grown. He accepted all people, no matter who they were. Only when they turned on him would he treat them as enemies. He tried to stay out of fights, but if one was unavoidable, he was in the forefront.

It's a shame—and our loss—that he didn't learn to read and write. He was intelligent, creating accurate maps from memory. He learned English, French, Spanish, a variety of Indian languages, and was proficient in sign language. After people read Shakespeare to him, he would quote passages from memory.

As to the Hugh Glass story, I believe Bridger was not the teenager who deserted Glass. Historians have pointed to Bridger because of an 1839 article that gave the young man's last name as "Bridges," and on old riverboat pilot Joseph LaBarge's recollection that tradition on the Missouri was that it was Bridger. That's it. When Alfred Jacob Miller sat around a mountaineer fire and jotted down the Hugh Glass story during the 1837 rendezvous, the first name of the person Glass confronted was Bill. If Bridger had been the young man who deserted Glass, I believe other mountaineers would have ribbed him about it.

As to Bridger selling Fort Bridger to the Mormons, I don't believe he sold it. He was an honest man, and to his dying day, he never said he sold it, continuing to attempt to collect his rental payment from the federal government.

Bridger's descriptions of the Yellowstone geothermal region to expedition leaders and scientists led to its eventual exploration in 1871 by one of those scientists, Ferdinand Hayden. The following year, Congress designated it the world's first national park.

Jim Bridger was loved by many people, from children to generals. He was well liked by many tribes. Most of his adversaries respected him. He enjoyed nothing better than to be out in nature, preferring to sleep under the stars than in a tent. It would have been great fun to sit at a campfire and listen to him tell of his exploits and tall tales. He was a man in love with the West.

Toward the end of his life, Jim Bridger said, "I wish I was back there among the mountains again—you can see so much farther in that country."[1]

---

[1] Alter, *Bridger,* 339.

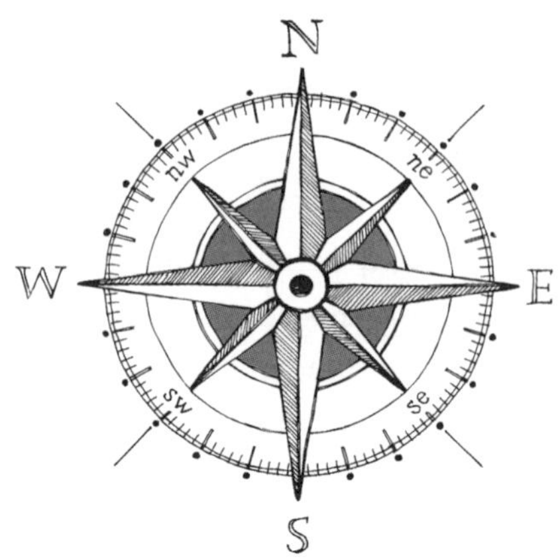

Bibliography

Books

Alter, J. Cecil. *Jim Bridger,* University of Oklahoma Press, 1950.

Ambrose, Stephen. *Nothing Like It in the World,* Simon & Schuster, 2000.

Athearn, Robert. *Forts of the Upper Missouri,* University of Nebraska Press, 1967.

Bagley, Will. *So Rugged and Mountainous: Blazing the Trails to Oregon and California, 1812–1848,* University of Oklahoma Press, 2010.

Bagley, Will. *With Golden Visions Bright Before Them: Trails to the Mining West, 1849–1852,* University of Oklahoma Press, 2012.

Barbour, Barton. *Fort Union and the Upper Missouri Fur Trade,* University of Oklahoma Press, 2001.

Berry, Don. *A Majority of Scoundrels: An Informal History of the Rocky Mountain Fur Company,* Comstock Editions, Inc., 1961.

Bigler, David, Bagley, Will. *The Mormon Rebellion: America's First Civil War, 1857–1858,* University of Oklahoma Press, 2011.

Billington, Ray Allen. *Westward Expansion: A History of the American Frontier,* The MacMillian Company, 1949.

Blevins, Winfred. *Give Your Heart to the Hawks,* Avon Books, 1973.

Bonner, Thomas, ed., Oswald, Delmont, ed. *The Life and Adventures of James P. Beckwourth,* University of Nebraska Press, 1972.

Brackett, William. "Bonneville and Bridger," *Contributions to the Montana Historical Society,* Vol. 3, State Publishing Company, 1900.

Brown, David. *Three Years in the Rocky Mountains,* Cincinnati Daily Morning Atlas, 1845.

Brown, Dee. *Bury My Heart at Wounded Knee: An Indian History of the American West,* Henry Holt and Company, 1970.

Bryant, Edwin. *What I Saw in California,* D. Appleton & Co., 1849.

Burns, Thomas W. *Initial Ithacans,* Press of the *Ithaca Journal,* 1904.

Caesar, Gene. *King of the Mountain Men: The Life of Jim Bridger,* E. P. Dutton Co., 1961.

Campbell, Robert. *A Narrative of Colonel Robert Campbell's Experiences in the Rocky Mountain Fur Trade From 1825 to 1835,* CreateSpace, 2016.

Carrington, Frances. *My Army Life and the Fort Phil Kearny Massacre,* J. B. Lippincott Company, 1910.

Carrington, Margaret Irvin. *Ab-sa-ra-ka: Home of the Crows,* J. B. Lippincott & Co., 1869.

Chittenden, Hiram Martin. *The American Fur Trade of the Far West,* Vols. 1 and 2, Academic Reprints, 1954.

Chittenden, Hiram Martin, and Richardson, Alfred Talbot. *Life, Letters and Travels of Father Pierre-Jean De Smet, S. J. 1801–1873,* Vols. 1, 3, 4, Frances P. Harper, 1905.

Cooke, Phillip St. George. *The Southern Literary Messenger,* Thos. W. White Publisher and Proprietor, 1842.

Crutchfield, James, Moulton, Candy, Del Bene, Terry, editors. *The Settlement of America: Encyclopedia of Western Expansion from Jamestown to the Closing of the Frontier,* Vols. 1 and 2, M. E. Sharp, Inc., 2011.

Dacus, J. A., and Buel, James. *St. Louis or the Inside Life of a Great City,* Western Publishing Company, 1878.

D'Azevedo, Warren, ed. *Handbook of North American Indians: Great Basin,* Vol. 11, Smithsonian Institution, 1986.

DeMallie, Raymond, volume editor. *Handbook of North American Indians, Plains,* Vol. 13, Part 1 and Part 2, Smithsonian Institution, 2001.

De Smet, Pierre-Jean. *Letters and Sketches: With a Narrative of a Year's Residence Among the Indian Tribes of the Rocky Mountains,* M. Fithian, 1843.

DeVoto, Bernard. *Across the Wide Missouri,* Houghton Mifflin Co., 1947.

DeVoto, Bernard. *The Year of Decision,* 1846, Little, Brown & Company, 1943.

Dodge, Grenville. *Biographical Sketch of James Bridger, Mountaineer, Trapper, and Guide,* Unz and Company, 1905.

Donlin, Eric Jay. *Fur, Fortune, and Empire: The Epic History of the Fur Trade in America,* W. W. Norton & Company, 2010.

Enzler, Jerry. *Jim Bridger: Trailblazer of the American West,* University of Oklahoma Press, 2021.

Ewers, John. *The Blackfeet: Raiders of the Northwestern Plains,* University of Oklahoma Press, 1958.

Ferris, Mrs. B. G. *The Mormons at Home,* Dix & Edwards, 1856.

Ferris, Warren Angus. *Life in the Rocky Mountains,* Adansonia Press, Lulu.com, 2018.

Field, Matthew, Gregg, Kate, ed., McDermott, John, ed. *Prairie and Mountain Sketches.* University of Oklahoma Press, 1957.

Frémont, John Charles. *Report of the Exploring Expedition to the Rocky Mountains in the Year 1842,* Gales and Seaton, Printers, 1845.

Frost, Donald McKay. "Notes on General Ashley, the Overland Trail, and South Pass," *The Proceedings of the American Antiquarian Society – 1944,* Vol. 54, Part 2, American Antiquarian Society, 1944.

Gowans, Fred, and Campbell, Eugene. *Fort Bridger: Island in the Wilderness,* Brigham Young University Press, 1975.

Gray, William. *A History of Oregon, 1792–1849, Drawn from Personal Observation and Authentic Information,* Harris & Holman, 1870.

Gray, William. "The Unpublished Journal of William H. Gray; from December 1836 to October 1837," *Whitman College Quarterly,* Whitman College, 1913.

Gunnison, John. *The Mormons, or the Latter Day Saints,* Lippincott, Grambo & Co., 1852.

Hafen, LeRoy., ed. *Mountain Men and Fur Traders of the Far West,* University of Nebraska Press, 1965.

Hall, James. "The Missouri Trapper," *Port Folio* Vol. XIX, Harrison Hall, 1825.

Hardee, Jim. *Pierre's Hole: The Fur Trade History of Teton Valley, Idaho,* Sublette County Historical Society, 2010.

Hasselstrom, Linda, ed. *Journal of a Mountain Man, James Clyman,* Mountain Press Publishing Company, 1998.

Hasselstrom, Linda. *Roadside History of South Dakota,* Mountain Press Publishing Company, 1994.

Hastings, Lansford. *The Emigrants' Guide to Oregon and California,* George Conklin (publisher), 1845.

Hickman, William. *Brigham's Destroying Angel: The Life, Confession, and Disclosures of Bill Hickman,* Geo. A. Crofutt, Publisher, 1872.

Humfreville, J. Lee, *Twenty Years Among Our Hostile Indians,* Hunter & Co., 1899.

Hutton, Paul Andrew. *Phil Sheridan and His Army,* University of Oklahoma Press, 1985.

Irving, Washington. *The Adventures of Captain Bonneville*, National Geographic Society, 2003.

Jeannewein, J. Leonard, and Boorman, Jane, editors. *Dakota Panorama,* Brevet Press, 1973.

Johnson, Don, ed. *The Journals of Captain Nathaniel J. Wyeth's Expeditions to the Oregon Country, 1831–1836,* Ye Galleon Press, 1997.

Johnson, Dorothy. *The Bloody Bozeman: The Perilous Trail to Montana's Gold,* Mountain Press Publishing Company, 1983.

Johnson, Kristin, ed. *"Unfortunate Emigrants": Narratives of the Donner Party,* Utah State University Press, 1996.

Johnston, William Preston. *The Life of General Albert Sidney Johnston,* D. Appleton and Co., 1878.

Jones, Landon. *William Clark and the Shaping of the West,* Farrar, Straus, and Giroux, 2004.

Larpenteur, Charles, Coues, Elliot, ed. *Forty Years A Fur Trader: The Personal Narrative of Charles Larpenteur, 1833–1872,* Ross & Haines, Inc., 1962.

LeForge, Thomas, Marquis, Thomas. *Memoirs of a White Crow Indian,* Century Co., 1928.

Marcy, Randoph. *Thirty Years of Army Life on the Border,* Harper & Brothers, Publishers, 1866.

Markley, Bill. *Geronimo and Sitting Bull: Leaders of the Legendary West,* Rowman & Littlefield Publishing, 2021.

Markley Bill, Hutton, Paul Andrew, ed., "Kenneth McKenzie, King of the Upper Missouri," *Roundup!* La Frontera Publishing, 2010.

Marsh, James. *Four Years in the Rockies, or the Adventures of Isaac P. Rose,* printed by W. B. Thomas, 1884.

McChristian, Douglas. *Fort Laramie: Military Bastion of the High Plains,* University of Oklahoma Press, 2008.

McDermott, John. *Red Cloud's War: The Bozeman Trail, 1866–1868,* Arthur H. Clark Co., University of Oklahoma Press, 2010.

McLaird, James. *Hugh Glass: Grizzly Survivor,* South Dakota Historical Society Press, 2016.

Miller, Alfred Jacob, Ross, Marvin, ed. *The West of Alfred Jacob Miller,* University of Oklahoma Press, 1968.

Moody, Ralph. *Stagecoach West,* Thomas Y. Crowell Company, 1967.

Morgan, Dale. *Jedediah Smith and the Opening of the West,* University of Nebraska Press, 1953.

Morgan, Dale, ed. *Overland in 1846: Diaries and Letters of the California-Oregon Trail,* Vols. 1 & 2, University of Nebraska Press, 1963.

Morgan, Dale, ed., and Harris, Eleanor, ed. *The Rocky Mountain Journals of William Marshall Anderson: The West in 1834,* University of Nebraska Press, 1987.

Morgan, Dale, ed. *The West of William H. Ashley,* The Old West Publishing Company, 1964.

Newell, Robert, Johansen, Dorothy, ed. *Robert Newell's Memoranda: Travels in the Territory of Missourie…,* Champoeg Press, 1959.

Newman, Peter. *Company of Adventurers: Caesars of the Wilderness,* Vol. 2. Viking, 1987.

O'Neil, Paul. *The Rivermen,* Time-Life Books, Inc., 1975.

Parker, Samuel. *Journal of an exploring tour beyond the Rocky Mountains…,* Andrus, Woodruff, & Gauntlett, 1844.

Quaife, Milo, ed. *Kit Carson's Autobiography,* R. R. Donnelley & Sons Co., 1935.

Quaife, Milo, ed. *Adventures of a Mountain Man: The Narrative of Zenas Leonard,* University of Nebraska Press, 1978.

Raynolds, William. *Report of the Exploration of the Yellowstone River,* Government Printing Office, 1868.

Robertson, R. G. *Competitive Struggle: America's Western Fur Trading Posts, 1764–1865,* Tamarack Books, Inc., 1999.

Rodenbough, Theophilus. *From Everglade to Cañon with the Second Dragoons,* D. Van Nostrand, Publisher, 1875.

Russell, Osborne, Haines, Aubrey, ed. *Journal of a Trapper,* University of Nebraska Press, 1955.

Schell, Herbert. *History of South Dakota,* University of Nebraska Press, 1968.

Schuler, Harold. *Fort Pierre Chouteau,* University of South Dakota Press, 1990.

Sides, Hampton. *Blood and Thunder: The Epic Story of Kit Carson and the Conquest of the American West,* Random House, Inc., 2006.

Sheridan, Philip Henry. *Personal Memoirs of P. H. Sheridan,* Vol. 2, Charles L. Webster & Company, 1888.

"Smallpox," *The World Book Encyclopedia,* S-Sn, Vol. 17, Field Enterprise Educational Corporation, 1976.

Smith, Page, *The Nation Comes of Age: A People's History of the Ante-Bellum Years,* McGraw-Hill Book Company, 1981.

Southesk, Earl of (James Carnegie), *Saskatchewan and the Rocky Mountains: A Diary and Narrative of Travel…,* James Campbell and Son, 1875.

Spring, Agnes Wright. *Caspar Collins: The Life and Times of an Indian Fighter of the Sixties,* Columbia University Press, 1927.

Stanley, E. J. *Life of L. B. Stateler,* Publishing House of the M.E. Church, South, 1907.

Stansbury, Howard. *Explorations of the Valley of the Great Salt Lake of Utah,* Robert Armstrong Public Printer, 1853.

Sunder, John. *Bill Sublette: Mountain Man,* University of Oklahoma Press, 1959.

Thorpe, T. B. "Remembrances of the Mississippi," *Harper's New Monthly Magazine,* No. LXVII, Vol. XII, Harper & Brothers, Publishers, December 1855.

Utley, Robert. *A Life Wild and Perilous: Mountain Men and the Paths to the Pacific,* Henry Holt and Company, 1997.

Utley, Robert. *Frontiersmen in Blue: The United States Army and the Indian, 1848–1865,* University of Nebraska Press, 1967.

Vestal, Stanley. *Jim Bridger, Mountain Man,* University of Nebraska Press, 1946.

Victor, Frances Fuller, Blevins, Winfred, ed. *The River of the West: The Mountain Years—The Adventures of Joe Meek,* Book 1, CreateSpace, 2015.

Walker, Jr., Deward, volume ed. *Handbook of North American Indians: Plateau,* Vol. 12, Smithsonian Institution, 1998.

Walton, George. *Sentinel of the Plains: Fort Leavenworth and the American West,* Prentice-Hall, Inc., 1973.

Warren, Gouverneur. *Preliminary Report of Explorations in Nebraska and Dakota in the Years 1855–'56–'57,* Government Printing Office, 1875.

Williams, Joseph. *Narrative of a Tour from the State of Indiana to the Oregon Territory in the Years 1841–2,* Edward Ebersadt, 1921.

Wislizenus, F. A. *A Journey to the Rocky Mountains in the Year 1839,* Missouri Historical Society, 1912.

Woodard, Aaron Robert. *Soft Fur and Iron Men: A History of the Fur Trade in South Dakota and the Upper Missouri,* E-Book Time, LCC, 2006.

Periodicals

Hafen, Leroy. "Etienne Provost, Mountain Man and Utah Pioneer." *Utah Historical Quarterly,* Vol. 36, No. 2, 1968.

Markley, Bill. "Fur, Defeat, and Pluck." *True West Magazine,* April 2005.

Minto, John. "Reminisces of Experiences on the Oregon Trail in 1844." *Oregon Historical Quarterly,* Vol. 2, No. 2, June 1901.

Spence, Clark. "A Celtic Nimrod in the Old West," *Montana: The Magazine of Western History* 9, No. 2, 1959.

Internet Sources

1850 US Census, Ancestry.com. Ancestry.com - 1850 United States Federal Census.

"1854 April 29 Letter to Stephen A. Douglas," The Brigham Young Center. https://brighamyoungcenter.org/s/byp/item/4668#?c=&m=&s=&cv=

1860 US Census, Ancestry.com. Ancestry.com - 1860 United States Federal Census.

1870 US Census, Ancestry.com. Ancestry.com - 1870 United States Federal Census.

1880 US Census, Ancestry.com. Ancestry.com - 1880 United States Federal Census.

"Brigham Young," Wikipedia. https://en.wikipedia.org/wiki/Brigham_Young

The Church of Jesus Christ of Latter-day Saints online Church History Biographical Database, accessed December 4, 2024. https://history.churchofjesuschrist.org/chd/individual/almerin-m-grow-1816?lang=eng

Cooke, Phillip St. George. "Scenes and Adventures in the Army," *The Southern Literary Messenger* (Richmond, VA: Thos. W. White Publisher and Proprietor, 1842). http://hughglass.org/wp-content/uploads/2015/09/Glass-story-by-Crook.pdf

Edmunds, R. David, "The Illinois River Potawatomi in the War of 1812" *Journal of the Illinois State Historical Society* (1908-1984) Vol. 62, No. 4, Champaign, IL: University of Illinois Press, Winter, 1969. https://www.jstor.org/stable/40190888?read-now=1&seq=22#page_scan_tab_contents

Enzler, Jerry. "Jim Bridger" excerpt from "Tracking Jim Bridger" originally published in *Rocky Mountain Fur Trade Journal* (Vol. 5) 2011. Museum of the Mountain Man, Sublette County Historical Society. http://hughglass.org/jim-bridger/

Flagg, Edmund. "Adventures at the Headwaters of the Missouri," *Louisville Literary News Letter* (Louisville, KY: September 7, 1839). Museum of the Mountain Man, Sublette County Historical Society. http://hughglass.org/wp-content/uploads/2015/12/FLagg.pdf

"Franklin," *Columbia Herald-Statesman* (Columbia, MO, 30 April 30, 1822), 3. Newspapers.com. https://www.newspapers.com/image/338261977/

Hall, James. "The Missouri Trapper," *Port Folio* Vol. XIX (Philadelphia, PA: Harrison Hall, 1825), 218. Museum of the Mountain Man, Sublette County Historical Society. http://hughglass.org/wp-content/uploads/2015/09/1825-Hugh-Glass-article.pdf

Landry, Clay. "Chronology of Publication of the Hugh Glass Story," Museum of the Mountain Man, Sublette County Historical Society. http://hughglass.org/sources/

"Letter From William H. Ashley to Gen. Henry Atkinson," William H. Ashley's 182 5 Rocky Mountain Papers, Library of Western Fur Trade Historical Source Documents, Mountain Men and the Fur Trade. https://user.xmission.com/~drudy/mtman/html/ashnar.html

"Letters and Journal of Mrs. Narcissa Prentiss Whitman, 1836," Library of Western Fur Trade Historical Source Documents, Mountain Men and the Fur Trade. http://user.xmission.com/~drudy/mtman/html/nwhitman.html#3

Lowe, James, "A Map of the West in his Head: Jim Bridger, Guide to Plains and Mountains," Wyohistory.org. https://www.wyohistory.org/encyclopedia/jim-bridger

"Missouri River," Wikipedia. https://en.wikipedia.org/wiki/Missouri_River

"Physical Growth of the City of Saint Louis," *St. Louis City Plan Commission-1969.* https://www.museum.state.il.us/RiverWeb/landings/Ambot/Archives/History69/index.html#boom

"St. Louis, Missouri Population History 1840 – 2021," Biggest US Cities (biggestuscities.com).

Smith, Justin. "Clearing up confusion about Fort Hall history," *Idaho State Journal,* May 14, 2021. https://www.idahostatejournal.com/freeaccess/clearing-up-confusion-about-fort-hall-history/article_7f0f387b-5187-56f7-8b64-6190e90bd3a2.html

"The Seventh Census of The United States: Utah and Slavery," *Utah Historical Society.* The Seventh Census of the United States: Utah and Slavery (Spring 2017) | Utah Historical Society

"TO Enterprising Young Men," *Missouri Gazette and Public Advertiser* (St. Louis, MO, February 13, 1822), 2, Newspapers.com. https://www.newspapers.com/image/249517987/

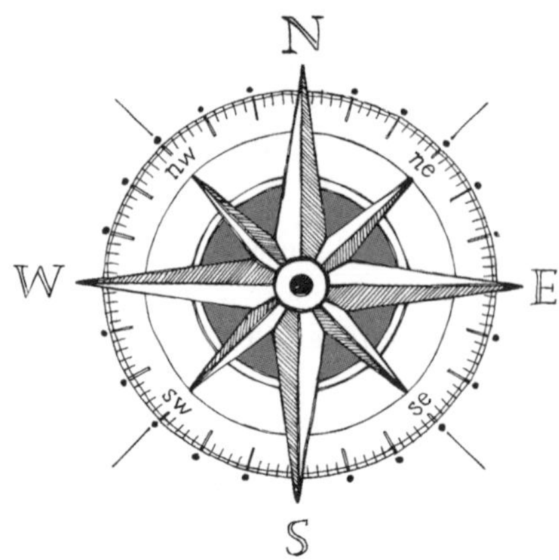

Index

Page numbers in **bold** indicate photographs, illustrations, or maps.

Index

N

O

P

R

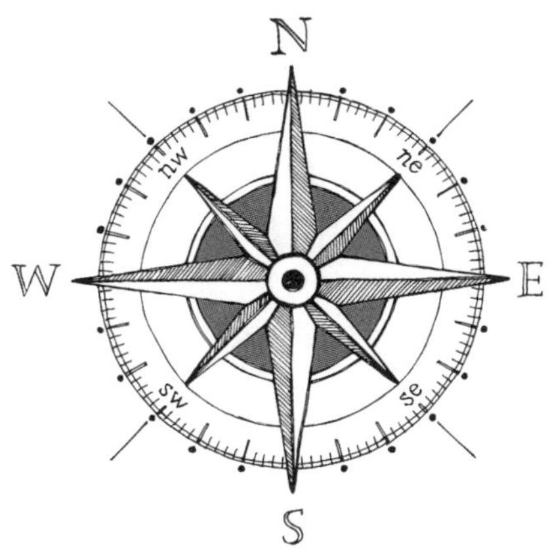

Acknowledgments

Thank you to Farcountry Press for publishing this book, with special thanks to Erin Turner, who has always believed in my projects, and Will Harmon, senior editor, who has gone to bat for me.

Thanks to everyone in the past who wrote about their experiences with Jim Bridger and their impressions of him. Thanks to Jim Bridger biographers, especially Jerry Enzler and J. Cecil Alter, for breaking the trail.

Thank you, Nancy Plain, for your in-depth review. Brad Tennant, historian and humanities scholar, thank you for your review. Rose Speirs, Elanna "Quackgrass Sally" Skorupa, Loren Leichtnam, Mike Pellerzi, Blaine Nordvold, Elliotte Littlebear, and Jon Nelson—thank you all for your reviews and insights. Dave Thompson, thanks for your writing advice. Kellen Cutsforth, thank you for your images search and support.

Special thanks to my wife, Liz, for putting up with my excessively long hours of research and writing and listening to my excitement over discovering obscure pieces of history. Thanks to all my family for all your support. Most of all, thanks to the Lord for life and the ability to use and enjoy it!

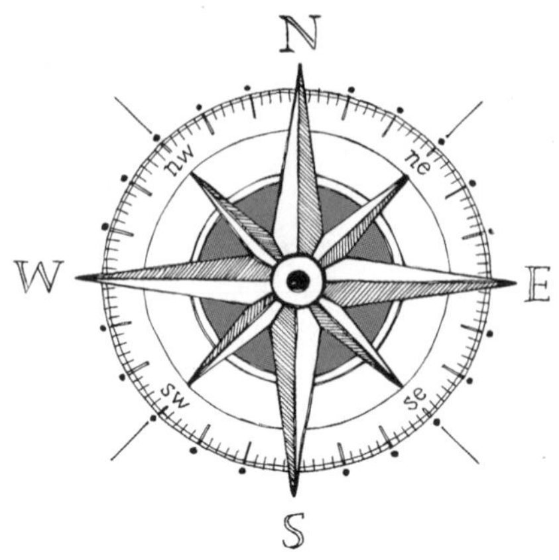

About the Author

Bill Markley, member of Western Writers of America and multiple winner of the Will Rogers Medallion award, has written eleven books, including biographies and histories of Old West characters and events. He writes for *True West* and *Wild West* magazines and is a staff writer for *Roundup* magazine.